Bee~~thoven~~

Symphony No. 2 in D Major
Op. 36

Creation, Origins and Reception History
Incorporating
Contextual Accounts of Beethoven and His Contemporaries

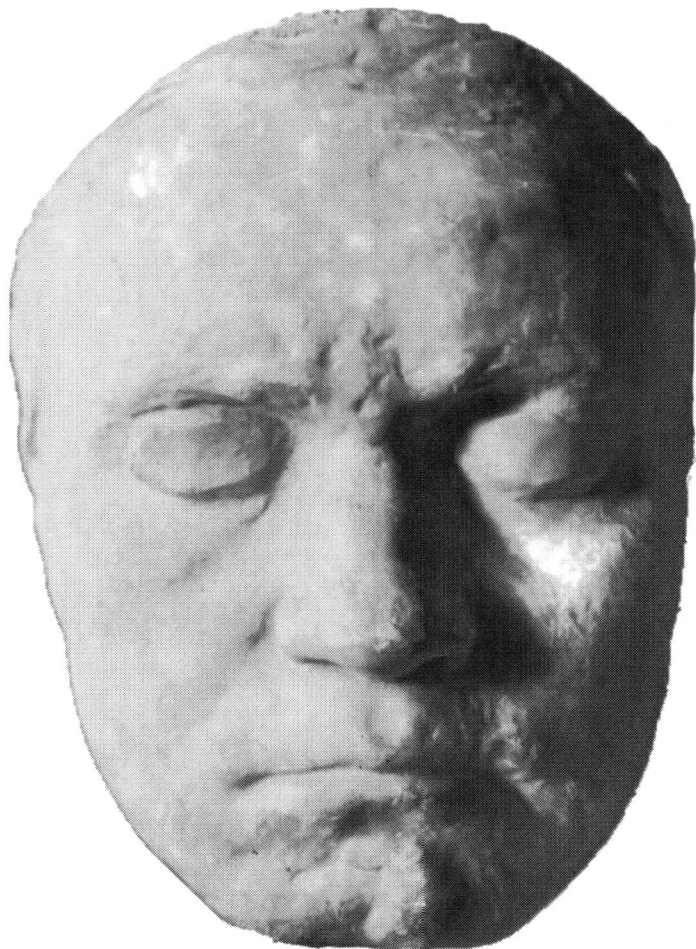

BEETHOVEN
As depicted by the life mask taken by Franz Klein in 1812
(derived from a copy in the author's possession)

BEETHOVEN

SYMPHONY NO. 2
IN D MAJOR
OP. 36

CREATION ORIGINS
AND
RECEPTION HISTORY

Incorporating contextual accounts of
Beethoven and his contemporaries

Terence M. Russell

Jelly Bean Books

The right of Terence Russell to be identified as the
Author of the Work has been asserted by him in accordance
with the Copyright, Designs and Patents Act 1988.

Copyright © Terence M. Russell 2025

Published by
Jelly Bean Books
136 Newport Road
Cardiff
CF24 1DJ

ISBN: 978-1-917022-74-3

www.candyjarbooks.co.uk

CONTENTS

AUTHOR'S NOTE   I

INTRODUCTION   IX

EDITORIAL PRINCIPLES   XVI

BEETHOVEN'S FINANCIAL TRANSACTIONS   XVIII

SYMPHONY NO. 2: CREATION ORIGINS   1

Beethoven's Orchestra   3

Vienna: Concert Venues and Music Making   8

Beethoven and Conducting   11

Accounts of Beethoven: Growing Fame   16

Heiligenstadt: Triumph over Deafness   21

Composition Origins: Sketch Sources   28

Landsberg 7 Sketchbook   32

Kessler Sketchbook   34

Sauer Sketchbook   34

Negotiations with Publishers   35

Publication in Parts   48

Tempo Indications: Metronome Marks   50
Publication in Full Score   52

SYMPHONY NO. 2 RECEPTION HISTORY   62
Reception in Beethoven's Lifetime
    Concert Performances   63
Transcriptions   86
Beethoven's Early Reception in France   90
Beethoven's Reception in England   93
Later Nineteenth-Century Reception   98
Reception in the Twentieth Century   104
Reception Nearer Our Own Time   140

BIBLIOGRAPHY   150
INDEX   185
ABOUT THE AUTHOR   191

AUTHOR'S NOTE

I have cherished the idea of making a study of the life and work of Beethoven for many years. This statement requires a few words of personal reflection. I first encountered Beethoven in my early piano lessons — Minuet in G major, WoO 10, No. 2. At the same time I became acquainted with his piano pupil Carl Czerny — *Book One, Piano Studies*. My heart sank when I discovered the rear cover advertised a further *99* books in the same series — scales, arpeggios studies for the left hand, studies for the right hand — all the way to his Op. 824! By coincidence, my *Czerny Book One* was edited by Alec Rowley — who had the same surname as my music teacher. In my childish innocence, I often wondered why *he himself* never appeared to give me a lesson!

In my teenage years I found myself drawn ever closer

to Beethoven's music in the manner that ferromagnetic materials are ineluctably held captive in the sway of a magnetic field. The impulse to which I yielded is well described in words the conductor Bruno Walter gave in one of his rare public addresses:

> 'It is my belief that young people at that age are more easily impressed by what is heroic and grandiose; that they more easily understand works of art in which passionate feelings are violently uttered in raised accents, and that the lighter sounds of cheerfulness are less impressive to them.'

I do indeed recall the stirring effect made on me on first hearing the Overture *Egmont*, the unfolding drama of the Fifth Symphony and the declamatory opening chords of the *Emperor* Piano Concerto.

I resolved to read everything I could about Beethoven, starting with Marion Scott's pioneering English-language study of the composer in *The Master Musicians series*. My father took out a subscription for me for *The Gramophone* magazine, enabling me to read reviews of the new 'LP' recordings — none of which though I could afford! The LP was then — 1950s — beginning to supplant the 78 rpm shellac records, stacks of which could be purchased for as little as six pence each in 'old' money. I listed to the radio to hear Anthony Hopkins 'Talking about music' and to other musicological luminaries including Howard Fergusson, Hans Keller, Paul Hamburger, Denis Matthews, and Peter Stadlen.

At this same time, I had the privilege of hearing Beethoven's music performed by the *Hallé Orchestra* under the baton of Sir John Barbirolli, and experienced the *Carl*

II

Rosa Opera Company perform the composer's only opera *Fidelio*, I borrowed the piano-reduction score from the City Library to become better acquainted with this moving work — only to find the score's fists full of notes were well beyond my capabilities. Nonetheless, since then *Fidelio's* every note has been woven into my DNA. I also recall the period when the *London Promenade Concerts* were designated 'Friday night is Beethoven night'.

Through these influences I resolved to visit Vienna to see where Beethoven had lived and worked. But how? The support for such travel was beyond the means of my family. Fortunately, in my final year at school (1959), an opportunity presented itself. I saw a poster that stated *WUS — World University Service* — required volunteers to work in the Austrian town of Linz to help relocate refugees who were living there in improvised wooden shacks — displaced and dispossessed victims of the Second World War. To those participating all expenses would be paid together with free accommodation — in one of the crumbling wooden shacks! From Linz, I planned to make my way to Vienna.

I applied to *WUS* and, despite being a mere school-leaver, I was accepted. The *WUS* authorities doubtless reasoned the building-trade skills I had acquired during my secondary education in the building department of a technical school would be useful. This proved to be the case. At the refugee camp I dug trenches and was allowed to assist as a bricklayer. All about me were wide-eyed children eager to help but mostly getting in the way. I recall one afternoon when a reporter from *The Observer* newspaper paid a visit to our construction site to gather material for an article he was writing on European post-war recovery — he generously admired my trenches and brickwork!

Of lasting significance was another visit, this time from a Belgian priest. He took a group of us to the nearby

Mauthausen Concentration Camp, recently opened as a silent and solemn memorial to those who had perished there. It was a deeply moving experience. Years later I learned of the views of the ardent Beethovenian Sir Michael Tippet. After the horrors of the *Holocaust*, he posed the question for mankind: 'What price Beethoven now?' He posited: 'Could we any longer find solace in Beethoven's setting of Schiller's *Ode to Joy* and its utopian vision — "Be embraced you Millions"?'

My refugee contribution duly came to end and Vienna beckoned. On arrival there I found scenes reminiscent of *The Third Man* and *Harry Lime*. I recall, for example, encountering cobblestones piled high in the streets waiting to be replaced after having been disturbed by the heavy armoured vehicles that had so recently passed over them. But Vienna was welcoming. I visited the houses where Beethoven had lived and worked and paused outside others associated with him that were identified by a commemorative plaque and the Austrian flag. A particularly memorable occasion was attending a recital in the great salon within the palace of Beethoven's noble patron Prince Lobkowitz — the very one where the *Eroica* Symphony had been premiered. Ultimately, my steps led me to the composer's first resting place in the *Währinger Ortsfriedhof.* I paid silent homage to the great man and, as I did so, discovered nearby the resting place of Franz Schubert to whom Beethoven was an endless source of admiration and inspiration.

I felt a youthful impulse to discover yet more about Beethoven and his music. But absorption in musicology would have to take second place. My chosen career beckoned in the guise of architecture — 'the mother of the arts' and 'the handmaid of society'. There was room though for Beethoven's music and from that time on it has been my constant companion through attendance at recitals, in concerts and music-making in the home. And at home a reproduction of Franz Kline's 1812 study of the composer has greeted me each day for more than half a century.

On my retirement from a career in architectural practice, research and university teaching, the opportunity finally presented itself for me to devote time to researching Beethoven musicology. Having attained my eightieth year also emboldened me to make progress with my good intentions!

With these autobiographical remarks outlined I will say a few remarks about my working method— see also the comments made in *Editorial Principles*.

As a member of staff of The University of Edinburgh, I had the good fortune to have access to the *Reid Music Library*, formed from a nucleus of books bequeathed by General John Reid and augmented over the years by such custodians as Sir Donald Francis Tovey, sometime *Reid Professor of Music* and renowned Beethoven scholar. Over a period of three years, I made a survey of the many works in the Reid collection. I consulted each item in turn making records on paper slips — many hundreds — that I deemed to be relevant for my researches. I confined my searches to book-publications, as reflected in my accompanying bibliography. All of this was quite some years ago, the cut-off date for my researches being 2007. Beyond this date I have not surveyed any further works. I am mindful though that Beethoven musicology and related publication continue to be a major field of endeavour in the manner of the proverbial 'ever rolling stream'.

In the intervening years since completing my archival researches, personal tribulations associated with family illness and bereavement slowed my progress in giving expression to my projected intentions. Latterly, however, with renewed energy, and more time at my disposal, I have been able to make progress. My studies take the form of a set of monographs. The first set of these, trace the creation origins and reception history of each of Beethoven's piano sonatas and string quartets. The resulting texts also incorporate contextual accounts of Beethoven and his contemporaries. Also included in my musicological surveys are two related Beethoven anthologies. The set of monographs in question, identified by short title, are:

> *Beethoven: An anthology of selected writings.*
> *Beethoven: The piano sonatas: An anthology of selected writings.*

The Piano Sonatas:
Op. 2—Op. 28
Op. 31—Op. 81a
Op. 90—Op. 111

The String Quartets:
Op. 18, Nos. 1—6
Op. 59, Nos. 1—3 (Razumovsky); Op. 74 (The Harp);
    Op. 95 (Quartetto serioso)
Op. 127, Op. 132 and Op. 130 (Galitzin)
Op. 131, Op. 135; Grosse Fuge, Op. 133 and Op. 134
    (*Fugue transcription*)

I provide further information about these studies in the introduction to each individual monograph. Suffice it for me to state here the basic premise upon which my work is founded. I believe it is rewarding, concerning the life of a great artist, to find connections between who he *was* and what he *did*; in Martin Cooper's words 'between his personality, as expressed on the one hand in human relationships, and on the other in artistic creation'. (*Beethoven, The Last*

Decade) That is not to say I consider it essential to the enjoyment of Beethoven's music to know this or that fact about it. His music can be enjoyed, as millions do, with — in Robert Simpson's apt phrase —'an innocent ear', for what it is and how it reaches out to us in purely musical terms without any prejudging of its merits based upon extra-musicological facts. Maynard Solomon expresses similar thoughts:

> 'It is doubtless true that we need have no knowledge whatever of a composer's biography, or knowledge of any other motivating factor of any kind, to appreciate the artwork on some fundamental level.' (*Beethoven Essays*, 1988, p. 116)

I must make a further point. I am mindful that a scholar who ventures into a field of study that is not rightly his may be regarded with some suspicion. In this regard I can but ask the reader to place his or her trust in me in the following way. I have attempted to bring to my work the care which publishers and their desk editors have required of me in my book writings relating to architecture — listed elsewhere.

As inferred, it is now more than sixty years since I paid homage to Beethoven in Vienna's *Währinger Ortsfriedhof* and my warmth of feeling towards the composer and his music have grown with the passing of the years. My studies are not intended to be propaedeutic — that would be pretentious. However, if in sharing with others what I have to say contributes to their knowledge and understanding of the composer, and thereby increases their own feelings towards him and his works, my own pleasure in bringing my work to completion will be all the more enhanced.

When Beethoven arrived in Vienna, he was unknown. He was armed though with a note of encouragement from his youthful friend and benefactor Count Ferdinand Wald-stein. It contained the often-quoted words: 'Receive Mozart's spirit from Haydn's hands.' Some forty years later Beethoven passed away in the House of the black-robed Spaniards at 200 *Alservorstädter*, the *Glacis* where he had lived since the autumn of 1825. Soldiers had to be called to secure the doors to the inner courtyard of the house from the pressure of onlookers. His body was blessed in the *Alservorsttädt Parish Church*, schools were closed and perhaps as many as 10,000 people formed a funeral procession — an honour ordinarily reserved for monarchs. The *Marcia Funebre* from the composer's Op. 26 Piano Sonata was performed at the funeral ceremony. Franz Grillparzer read the funeral oration. Franz Schubert, who, as remarked in life so admired Beethoven, was one of the pallbearers. The composer's mortal remains were lowered into a simple vault. Beethoven now belonged to history.

Dr Terence M. Russell
Edinburgh 2020

To the foregoing I am pleased to add the following works:

The Piano Concertos
The Symphonies: An Anthology of Selected Writings
Symphony No. 1 In C Major, Op. 21
Symphony No. 2 in D Major, Op. 36
Symphony No. 3 in E-flat Major, Op. 55
Symphony No. 4 in B-flat Major, Op. 60

TMR
2024

INTRODUCTION

The American musicologist Louise Elvira Cuyler writes about Beethoven the symphonist in a manner that make a fitting opening to our introduction to Beethoven's Symphony No. 2 in D major, Op. 36:

> 'Beethoven was born, it would seem, to write symphonies ... Beethoven's nine symphonies have stood for more than a century and a half as ideals for others to emulate. There is neither an uncertain composition nor a genre of work among the nine. Each is a confident, individual statement from an artist for whom music was the supremely expressive language. Beethoven restored music to the proud pinnacle it had occupied in earlier times when, along with arithmetic, geometry, and astronomy, it was included

in the quadrivium of liberal arts. He proclaimed himself a *Tondichter* (tone poet). In so doing, he set himself apart from his craftsmen-forebears of the eighteenth century, and he placed his art on a par with literature, philosophy, and religion, as a means to uplift, instruct, and heal mankind.'[1]

In 1802, the period of gestation of the Second Symphony, Beethoven was a young composer of thirty-two with a developing career and a growing reputation. He had secured the patronage of several of Vienna's aristocracy, notably Prince Karl Lichnowsky who provided him with financial support. It was in Lichnowsky's music salon, and those of others of Vienna's nobility, that Beethoven demonstrated his unrivalled capacity for improvisation at the keyboard. At the height of his powers, he could vanquish such would-be rivals as Daniel Steibelt in pianistic duels — contests in which each participant would vie one against the other in displays of pianistic bravura. Beethoven had his equals, in technical virtuosity and finger dexterity, but all who heard him improvise — such as his piano pupil Ferdinand Ries — affirm Beethoven was without equal.

As a composer for the piano, Beethoven was reaching a wider audience with such noteworthy compositions as the Piano Sonata, Op. 13 (*Pathétique*) — dedicated to Karl Lichnowsky — and the Piano Sonata, Op. 27, No. 2 (*Moonlight*) — dedicated to Countess Giulietta Guicciardi, another piano pupil and one of the many young women for whom Beethoven developed a deep affection. He had also made his mark in the genre of chamber music with such compositions as his three Sonatas for Piano and Violin, Op. 12 — dedicated to his teacher Antonio Salieri — and his six String Quartets, Op. 18 — dedicated to Prince Franz von Lobkowitz, another of his patrons. Beethoven had showcased his pianistic and compositional skills with his Piano Concerto in B-flat major, Op. 19 and his following one in C major, Op. 15 (their opus numbers being in reverse order) and he was well on the way to completing his more dramatic Piano Concerto in C minor, Op. 37. His Oratorio *Christus am Ölberge* placed him alongside his teacher Haydn — the acknowledged master of the genre — and his soon-to-be completed music for the Ballet *Die Geschöpfe des Prometheus*, Op. 43 would establish him as a composer of music for the theatre.

Armed with this body of attainments — and with his C major Symphony, Op. 21 already before the public — Beethoven was well equipped to venture forth along his 'new path' and to turn his attention to the composition of his Second Symphony.[2]

The Second Symphony was composed largely between 1801 and 1802 and Beethoven had every reason to contemplate his future with confidence. Publishers not only vied for his works but were prepared to pay the high prices he demanded for them. His equanimity was, however, shaken to its very foundations with the realization that his hearing was failing. In October 1802, he gave expression to his innermost feelings in the so-called *Heiligenstadt Testament* that movingly conveys his despair at this time. It was amidst this inner turmoil that Beethoven completed the Second Symphony, a work not only imbued with self-confidence but, moreover, one that portends even greater things to come.

In their study *The music of Man*, Yehudi Menuhin and Curtis Davis assign to Beethoven's symphonic achievement 'that universality of utterance which partakes alike of the rigours of a mathematical equation and the emotions of human experience'. They elaborate:

'It was Beethoven who gave to the symphony orchestra the final basic shape we know today. While he inherited the orchestra of Haydn and Mozart, he extended its range and variety, added the trombones which were more commonly reserved for the opera, and experimented with the piccolo and the contra-bassoon.'

With reference to the upheavals brought about in Europe by the armies of Napoleon Bonaparte, and the latter's assertive, self-willed, single-mindedness, they find a parallel in Beethoven's own personality and suggest: 'That spirit of rebellious resistance is already felt in the Second Symphony.'[3]

In the May 1824 issue of the *Berliner Allgemeine musika-lische Zeitung*, the German music theorist and musicologist Adolf Bernhard Marx reflected on Beethoven's achievement in the symphonic repertoire. He accepted the composer's earliest work in the genre, the First Symphony, Op. 21, was essentially Mozartian in character. Concerning the Second Symphony, however, he maintained that although it was written in a similar spirit, he acknowledged Beethoven had greatly expanded the compass of the music 'beyond [that of] Mozartian symphonies.'[4]

The composition is greater in scope than the symphonies of both Haydn and Mozart. Its introduction has unprecedented length and overall it has a performing time of more than half an hour. Beethoven's musical innovations were, however, too revolutionary for some and for these reasons the reaction of contemporary music critics was mixed. For example, a Leipzig critic went so far as to describe the finale of the Second Symphony as 'a repulsive monster, a wounded tail-lashing serpent, dealing wild and furious blows as it stiffens into its death agony' — taken to be a reference to

Beethoven's deliberately capricious false endings and reprises.

Reservations about the D major Symphony were quickly set aside as the work's merits became better understood and appreciated. Beethoven's eminent biographer Alexander Wheelock Thayer, writing in the mid-nineteenth century, enthused about the composition in the following terms:

> '[It is] a work whose grand style and imposing introduction – a brilliant *allegro*, a *larghetto* – "so lovely, so pure and amiably conceived" [qv Epistle to Philippians 4: 8], written in the scenes [countryside] which gave inspiration to the *Pastoral* [Symphony] of which its serene tranquillity seems a precursor; a *scherzo* as merry, wayward, skipping and charming as anything possible; ... and a finale, the very intoxication of spirit intoxicated with fire.'[5]

Writing half a century later, the former doyen of Beethovenians, Professor Sir Donald Francis Tovey, wrote in a similarly fulsome manner: '[Beethoven's] Second Symphony was [no less than] the most brilliant and triumphant piece that had ever been written up to that time.'

Tovey writes of the work's 'easy breadth and power' and how it represents 'an amply sufficient advance on anything of its kind'.[6]

Our study of Beethoven's Symphony in D major, Op. 36 is in two parts:

First, we consider the work's creation origins. Consistent with our aim to include contextual accounts of Beethoven and his contemporaries, we incorporate into our discussion the following considerations: the composition of

Beethoven's orchestra; music-making in Vienna's concert venues; accounts of Beethoven and his growing fame; his sojourn in Heiligenstadt and resolve to triumph over deafness; the composition origins of the Second Symphony — as evident in the surviving sketch sources, notably the Landsberg 7, Kessler, and Sauer Sketchbooks; Beethoven's negotiations with publishers; the eventual publication of the composition, first in parts — as was the custom at the period in question — and, finally, the publication in full score as we know the music today.

Second, we proceed to consider the reception history of the Second Symphony under the following headings: the work's reception in Beethoven's lifetime — as expressed by music critics following concert performances; the wider dissemination of the music through transcriptions; early reception in France — Paris; early reception in England, notably through the concerts of the London Philharmonic Society; later nineteenth-century reception; reception in the twentieth century; and reception nearer our own time.

Regarding the latter, Beethoven's 250th Birth Anniversary celebrations, held during 2020, have served to remind us of the continuing admiration of Beethoven and the enthusiasm for his music.

TMR
2024

[1] Louise Elvira Cuyler, *The Symphony*, New York, Harcourt Brace Jovanovich, 1973, pp. 49–50.
[2] At the period under consideration, Beethoven expressed dissatisfaction with his compositions to date and had resolved 'to take a new path'.
[3] Yehudi Menuhin and Curtis W. Davis, *The Music of Man*, London, Macdonald and Jane's, 1979, pp. 148–49.
[4] As quoted in: Wayne M. Senner, Robin Wallace and William Meredith editors, *The Critical Reception of Beethoven's Compositions by his German Contemporaries*, Lincoln: University of Nebraska Press, in association with the American Beethoven Society and the Ira F. Brilliant Center for

Beethoven Studies, San José State University, 1999, Vol. 1 p. 64.

[5] Elliot Forbes editor, *Thayer's Life of Beethoven*, Princeton, New Jersey: Princeton University Press, 1967, p. 306.

[6] Michael Tilmouth editor, *Donald Francis Tovey: The Classics of Music: Talks, Essays, and other Writings Previously Uncollected*, Oxford, Oxford University Press, 2001, p. 330.

EDITORIAL
PRINCIPLES

By its very nature a study of this kind draws extensively on the work of others. Every effort has been made to acknowledge this in the text by indicating words quoted or adapted with single quotation marks. Wherever possible, for the sake of consistency, I have retained the orthography of quoted texts making only occasional silent changes of spelling and capitalization. Deleted words are identified by means of three ellipsis points ... and interpolations are encompassed within square brackets [ ]. Quoted words, phrases and longer cited passages of text remain the intellectual property of their copyright holders.

I address the reader in the second person notwithstanding that the work is my own — produced without the benefit of a desk editor. It follows that I must bear the responsibility for any errors of misunderstanding or misinterpretation for which I ask the reader's forbearance. A collaboration I must acknowledge is the help I received from the librarians of the *Reid Music Library* at the University of Edinburgh. Over the three-year period it took me to compile my reference sources, they served me with unfailing courtesy, often supplying me with twenty or more books at a time. In converting my manuscript into book-format, I wish to thank my editorial coordinator, William Rees, for his support and painstaking care. I would also like to thank Shaun Russell (no relation) for his work designing the covers for each of the volumes.

My admiration for Beethoven provided the initial impulse to commence this undertaking and has sustained me over the several years it has taken to bring my enterprise to completion. That said I am no Beethoven idolater. I am mindful of the danger that awaits one who ventures to chronicle the work of a great artist. I believe it was Sigmund Freud who suggested that biographers may become so disposed to their subject, and their emotional involvement with their hero, that their work becomes an exercise in idealisation. In response to such a putative charge let me say. First, I am no biographer. I do however make occasional reference to Beethoven's personal life and his relationships with his contemporaries. Second, I acknowledge Beethoven has his detractors. Accordingly, I have not shrunk from allowing dissentient voices critical of Beethoven and his work to be heard. These, however, are few and are silenced amidst the adulation that awaits the reader in support of the endeavours of one of humanity's great creators and one who courageously showed the way in overcoming personal adversity.

TMR

BEETHOVEN'S
FINANCIAL
TRANSACTIONS

B eethoven's negotiations with his music publishers make
many references to his compositions. Today they are
recognised for what they are — enduring works of art — but
referred to in his business correspondence they appear
almost as though they were mere everyday commodities —
for which he required an appropriate remuneration.
Beethoven resented the time he had to devote to the
business-side of his affairs. He believed an agency should
exist, for fellow artists such as himself, from which a
reasonable sum could be paid for the work (composition)
submitted, leaving more time for creative enterprises. In the
event Beethoven, like Mozart before him, had to deal with
publishers largely on his own. Beethoven, though, did
benefit in his business dealings from the help he received

from his younger brother Kasper Karl (Caspar Carl). From 1800, Carl worked as a clerk in Vienna's Department of Finance in which capacity he found time to correspond with publishers to offer his brother's works for sale and — importantly — to secure the best prices he could. In April 1802 Beethoven wrote to the Leipzig publishers Breitkopf & Härtel: '[You] can rely entirely on my brother who, in general, attends to my affairs.' Whilst Carl promoted Beethoven's interests with determination, he appears to have lacked tact and made enemies. For example, Beethoven's piano pupil Ferdinand Ries — who for a while also helped the composer with his business negotiations — is on record as describing Carl as being 'the biggest skinflint in the world'.

The currencies most referred to in Beethoven's correspondence are as follows:

Silver gulden and florin: these were interchangeable and had a value of about two English shillings.

Ducat: 4 1/2 gulden / florins: valued at about nine shillings.

Louis d'or: This gold coin was adopted during the Napoleonic wars and the French occupation of Vienna and Austria more widely. It had a value of about two ducats or approximately twenty shillings or one-pound sterling.

Beethoven was never poor — in the romantic sense of 'an artist starving in a garret'. On arriving in Vienna in 1792, he was fortunate to receive financial support from his patron Prince Karl Lichnowsky who conferred on him an annuity of 600 florins — that he maintained for several years. Between the months of February and July of 1796, Beethoven undertook a concert tour taking in Prague, Dresden, Leipzig and Berlin. He was well-received and wrote to his other younger brother Nikolaus Johann: 'My art is winning me friends and what more do I want? ... I shall make a good deal of money.' Later on, in 1809, Napoleon Bonaparte's youngest brother Jérôme Bonaparte offered Beethoven an appointment at his Court with the promise of an income of 4,000 florins. Alarmed at the prospect of losing Beethoven — now the most celebrated composer in Europe — three of Vienna's most notable citizens, namely, the Archduke Rudolph (Beethoven's only composition pupil), Prince Kinsky and Prince Lobkowitz settled on the composer the same sum of 4,000 florins. Inflation, however, brought about by the Napoleonic wars, soon eroded its value; personal misfortune to Lobkowitz and Kinsky also took its toll.

Beethoven undoubtedly had to work hard to secure a reasonable standard of living. Notwithstanding, despite his occasional straitened circumstances, he contributed generously to the needs of others. For example, he allowed his works to be performed at charitable concerts without seeking any benefit to himself; in 1815 his philanthropy earned for him the honour of Bürgerrecht — 'freedom of the City'.

Beethoven earned a great deal of money when his music was performed, to considerable acclaim, at several concerts held in association with the Congress of Vienna (1814–15). He did not, though, benefit from it personally; he invested it on behalf of his nephew Karl. It is one of the misfortunes of Beethoven's life that in money-matters he was in somewhat culpably improvident. This is poignantly evident in a letter he wrote on 18 March 1827 to the Philharmonic Society of London — just one week before his death; the Society had made him a gift of £100. He sent the Society 'his most heartfelt thanks for their particular sympathy and support'.

'Beethoven produced his greatest compositions, including piano sonatas of epic scope and monumental symphonies which defined what symphonies would become in future years. Yet of all those works, none is more truly heroic than the Second Symphony, which though completed during this traumatic year [the year of the Heiligenstadt Testament], shows none of the creator's torment. Rather, it is filled with sunshine and high-spirits, as if it had been written by a man without a care in the world. Only a composer of single-minded devotion to art, who could set aside his own most pressing concerns in favour of artistic goals, could have produced such a symphony at such a time. In that aspect, this charming composition is the essence of heroism.'

Elisabeth Schwarm Glesner, *Classical Music Pages, Ludwig van Beethoven, Symphony No. 2, Op. 36.* Website text.

CREATION
ORIGINS

The year of the Second Symphony, 1802, was the beginning of a period of unparalleled creativity for Beethoven that has been described as his *Heroic Period*. On 29 June 1801, possessed of this awareness, he wrote to his close friend and confident Franz Wegeler:

'My compositions bring me in a good deal; and I may say that I am offered more commissions than it is possible for me to carry out. Moreover, for every composition I can count on six or seven publishers, and even more, if I want them ... I live entirely in my music; hardly have I completed one composition when I have already begun another. At my present rate of composing, I often produce three or four works at the same time.'

1

This is one of the composer's longest letters, and it is one of his most poignant. Beethoven's letter to Wegeler had a more sombre import. He confided to his friend the realization his hearing was deteriorating. He informed him:

> '[That] jealous demon, my wretched health, has put a nasty spoke in my wheel; and it amounts to this, that for the last three years my hearing has become weaker and weaker ... and sometimes I gave way to despair ... For almost two years I have ceased to attend any social functions, just because I find it impossible to say to people: I am deaf. If I had any other profession I might be able to cope with my infirmity; but in my profession it is a terrible handicap ... I can hear sounds, it is true, but cannot make out the words ... Heaven alone knows what is to become of me ... Oh, how happy should I be now if I had perfect hearing.'[1]

It is amidst these circumstances that the Second Symphony in D major, Op. 36 came into being. Notwithstanding Beethoven's despair, the work is one of his most musically witty and jovial and betrays no hint of the inner turmoil that had accompanied its gestation.

In our study of the composer's First Symphony in C major, Op. 21, we discussed Beethoven's move from his native Bonn to take up residence in Vienna, of his earning a reputation as one of the foremost virtuoso pianists of his day, and the startling originality of his compositions. In our discussion of the creation origins of the Second Symphony, we continue this narrative in a similar spirit by tracing the evolution of the composition and the circumstances bearing upon it.

BEETHOVEN'S ORCHESTRA

Beethoven's orchestra of the period typically consisted of strings with two each of flutes, oboes, clarinets, bassoons, trumpets, horns, and timpani. In Beethoven's hands, however, it was not a static entity. Consider, for example, the following:

Symphony No. 1, the *Andante* is without a second flute;

Symphony No. 2, the *Larghetto* is without a trumpet;

Symphony No. 3, a third horn is added;

Symphony No. 4 has one flute;

Symphony No 5, introduces three trombones (the first use of in a symphony), piccolo, and double bassoon;

Symphony No. 6 uses trombones and piccolo in the *Storm* and solo cellos in the *Andante*;

Battle Symphony combines piccolo, triangle, cymbals, bass drum, three trombones and — 'off stage' — two great drums, two rattles, four trumpets, and military drums;

Symphony No. 7 shows a reversion to the more standard orchestra;

Symphony No. 8, the second movement is without timpani and trumpets;

Symphony No. 9, makes use of three trombones, double bassoon, piccolo, triangle, cymbals, bass drum, with the innovatory four solo voices and chorus.[2]

For the subscription concerts of the winter of 1807–08, to which we make reference later, Beethoven employed 13 first violins,12 second violins, 7 violas, 6 cellos, 4 double basses, and a single compliment of woodwind. For these

3

concerts, orchestral works by Beethoven included his first four symphonies for which he drew on the resources of a combination of professional musicians and dilettantes.[3]

Vienna's theatres (see later) provided not only a venue for concerts but also a retinue of orchestral players. In 1808, the orchestra in the Theater an der Wien consisted of 12 violins, 4 violas, 3 cellos, 3 bases, 2 each of flutes, oboes, clarinets, horns, trumpets and timpani and, by 1815, the Redoutensaal could provide an orchestra of 36 violins, 14 violas, 12 cellos and 17 double bases. Larger orchestras progressively became the norm. In 1817, the *Tonkünstler-Societät* performed Beethoven's *Christus am Oelberg* with 20, 20, 8, 7, 6, 4, of the above combinations, and in 1824 the Ninth Symphony was performed with 24 violins, 14 violas, 12 cellos and 12 bases.[4]

The British violinist-musicologist Clive Brown has made a special study of 18th- and 19th-century performance-practice and draws attention to the extent to which Beethoven's orchestra, and resulting sound, differed from that of today. He remarks:

'This is strikingly true of the sounds of the individual instruments and their effects in combi-nation: brass instruments were valveless, wood-wind had fewer keys and were more sharply differentiated from one another in tone and quality than their modern counterparts, while the skin-covered timpani made a particularly distinct sound. Members of the violin family ... continued to be strung with gut until the end of eighteenth century, giving a clearer articulation and brighter sound. The bow too was in a transitional stage ... The balance of the orchestra was weighted much more in favour of the wind instruments. Instead

4

of the usual eight to ten desks of first violins [as in] a modern symphony orchestra, most early nineteenth-century German orchestras had only three or four desks, and where string numbers were substantially increased (as for festive performances, and in the case of the premiere of the Eighth Symphony in 1814), it was usual to double the wind instruments.'[5]

We also need to bear in mind that orchestral pitch was about a semitone lower than today. Attitudes to vibrato were also different. It was little used on wind instruments and on strings it was adopted more-or-less as an ornament; vibrato was essentially the preserve of the soloist. How would Beethoven's orchestra have sounded? Musicologist Anne-Louise Coldicott suggests:

'The sound and balance of the orchestra were different from today. Overall the wind were louder and more piercing than the strings; oboes were louder and more penetrative, bassoons produced a more vital sound, and only the flutes, made of wood, were softer than present-day instruments. The strings were softer due to their gut strings and their different manner of articulation dictated by contemporary bows.'[6]

The English conductor Sir Roger Norrington is known and respected for his historically informed performances and writes:

'Every single instrument was subtly different from today's equivalent, and each was perfectly adapted to the world of Classical music. The strings cleaner but more plaintive, articulate easily and expressively. The woodwind each has an individual colour, creating character and clarity of ensemble within the section. The horns' hand-stopped notes giving a vivid, dramatic variety to their playing, while the tympani, small and beaten with hard sticks, sound as if they have come straight from the field of Waterloo. This sheer variety of sound is essential to Beethoven, who was using a full orchestra that had recently matured under the hands of Haydn and Mozart.'[7]

Donald Francis Tovey writes in characteristically trenchant terms about Beethoven's orchestration and our response towards it:

'Beethoven enlarged the range of orchestral thought more than any other composer between Gluck and Wagner. The circumstances of his deafness made him the victim of some miscalculations: and pedantic views of orchestration lead many critics to exaggerate these ... Two things must be learnt by everybody who wishes to understand Beethoven: first, that errors of calculation are not the same things as errors of imagination; secondly, that a symphony is not an opera. Beethoven's errors of calculation are no greater than those of any composer who has not been able to hear a rehearsal of his work ... Errors of imagination do not exist in Beethoven's art ... Compared with Mozart's, Beethoven's scoring is rough, redundant, and capricious. But Beethoven's ideas are not

Mozart's and can be expressed neither in
Mozart's scoring nor in Wagner's scoring.'[8]

At the heart of Tovey's remarks lies the proposition, how
faithful should we be to observing Beethoven's text? The
following offers one answer. Between June and July 1990,
Nikolaus Harnoncourt recorded Beethoven's Second and
Fifth Symphonies. Mindful of Harnoncourt's reputation for
'historic performance-practice', he was asked about his
approach to the interpretation of the composer's orchestral
music by professor Hartmut Krones — Head of the Department of Musical Studies and Performing Practice at the
Vienna College of Fine Arts. Krones asked Harnoncourt if
he ever did any 'retouching' of Beethoven's scores? Harnoncourt responded:

> 'I ... do not do any retouching whatsoever as a
> matter of principle, neither octaving nor realloca-
> tion of certain notes/passages to other instru-
> ments. If Beethoven had not possessed
> instruments that were capable of more, or of
> playing differently, then he surely would not just
> have distributed certain notes differently — this
> would have changed the whole instrumentation
> significantly. And that's why I think it is always a
> mistake to change individual notes or registers. I
> believe in the correctness of the composer's
> instrumentation and the correctness of the overall
> linguistic character, both with regard to individual
> notes, and as regards the overall sound.[9]

We give further consideration to Beethoven's use of the
orchestra in our discussion of the reception history of the
Second Symphony.

VIENNA:
CONCERT VENUES AND MUSIC MAKING

When Beethoven arrived in Vienna, in November 1792, he was fortunate to discover a musically-minded city that was provided with several concert venues and a number of flourishing music societies.

The most important public concerts in Vienna were those given by the *Tonkünstler-Societät* — the Society of Musicians. This was a benevolent society that sought to aid elderly Viennese musicians — sometimes described as 'decayed' — and their dependents. The Society held two, so-called, benefit concerts at Easter and Christmas for which purposes the musicians adopted Vienna's Burgtheater. This venue could accommodate a large orchestra. For example, when Mozart gave his first concert there, in April 1781, the Society was able to provide him with an orchestra consisting of 40 violins, 8 violas, 9 cellos, 11 double-basses, 2 flutes, 7 oboes, 6 bassoons, 2 English horns, 4 French horns, 2 trumpets, and a timpanist. Haydn and his music were popular. In the concert season 1799–1800, when Beethoven was his pupil, his *The Creation* was performed to much acclaim. At the 23 December 1797 concert, Beethoven's Variations *Là ci darem la mano* from Mozart's Opera Don Giovani were performed. The following year, on 1 April 1798, Beethoven shared the programme with his teacher Haydn when he took the piano part in his Quintet for Piano and Winds, Op. 16. Regarding the performance of Beethoven's compositions, a gap then appears in the Society's records until 1817; by this time, Beethoven was recognised as Vienna's most celebrated composer. On 30 and 31 March 1817, his immensely popular Seventh Symphony received a performance alongside his Oratorio *Christus am Ölberge*.

Masked balls played a prominent part in Viennese musical

life, their venue being the *Redoutensäle*. This provided dance and concert halls — one large and the other small — that had been converted from an opera house under the instigation of the Empress Maria Theresia. To accompany musical occasions, the '*Great Redoutensaal*' could accommodate some forty orchestral plyers and the smaller hall about half this number. In the last years of his life, Mozart had written music for these festive events as did Haydn in 1792 with twelve German Dances and Minuets. Three years later Beethoven, again as Haydn's pupil, made his début as a composer of orchestral music with his own dance music. In 1814 his Eighth Symphony received its premiere in the large *Redoutensaal* and two years later it became the chosen venue for the Society Concerts of the *Gesellschaft der Musikfreunde*.[10]

The Kärntnertortheater was known as the *Kaiserliches und Königliches Hoftheater zu Wien* (Imperial and Royal Court Theatre of Vienna). Mozart's Piano Concerto K. 503 received its premier there in 1787, as did Beethoven's *Fidelio* — in its present-day form — in 1814, and his Ninth Symphony in 1824. The Kärntnertortheater was a small theatre. It had only three galleries with seats, its upper two floors being provided with benches and space for standing. When full to capacity it may have housed an audience of about a thousand. For their services, string and wind players received a mere annual 125 florins.[11]

On 13 June 1801 the Theater an der Wien opened. The *Allgemeine musikalische Zeitung* described it as being 'The most comfortable and satisfactory in the whole of Germany'. It came about through the entrepreneurial zeal and artistic success of the impresario Emmanuel Schikaneder, remembered today as the librettist of Mozart's *The Magic Flute*. It soon became regarded as the premiere theatre in Vienna and provided a venue for serious and comic opera and ballets. Three major concerts were given in Lent at the

Theater an der Wien and presented Beethoven with the opportunity to hold concerts there of his music; he actually lived in the premises during 1803–04 and did some of his composing there.

The Second Symphony received its first performance at the Theater an der Wien on 5 April 1803, together with his Third Piano Concerto and the Oratorio *Christ on the Mount of Olives*. The Third Symphony, *Eroica*, was heard on 7 April 1805; the Violin Concerto on 20 November 1806; and, perhaps most memorably, on 22 December 1808 the Theater an der Wien was the scene of Beethoven's gigantic concert that included the Fifth and Sixth Symphonies, the *Choral Fantasia*, and the Fourth Piano Concerto.[12]

During the summer, concerts were performed in rooms at the Augarten, an attractive landscaped garden by the suburb of Vienna called Leopoldstadt. As early as 1782, Mozart had conducted so-called *Morgenkonzerte* in the Garden Hall of the Palais Augarten. There were typically twelve concerts there each summer that commenced early in the morning — before Vienna's summer heat had become too oppressive. In 1795, the management of the concerts was transferred to the custody of the famous violinist Ignaz Schuppanzigh, with whom Beethoven established a close friendship and working relationship. Schuppanzigh premiered a number of Beethoven's string quartets, in particular the compositions of his final years. The music correspondent to the *Allgemeine musikalische Zeitung* relates: 'The Augarten orchestra consisted mostly of amateurs, except for the wind instruments and the double basses.' According to a contemporary account: 'Even ladies of the highest nobility were to be heard. The auditorium was very brilliant, and everything went off with order and with decorum.' Of the standard of performance, however, the author of the account had reservations:

'The concertos are seldom well accompanied,
but the symphonies go better ... the room is very
good, but the orchestra is badly placed ... without
being raised up.'[13]

Beethoven played at the Augarten on 24 May 1803. He
accompanied the violinist George Polgreen Bridgetower in
the premiere of the *Kreutzer* Sonata, Op. 47; originally
composed for Bridgetower, Beethoven later dedicated it to
Rudolphe Kreutzer —as a consequence of Beethoven falling
out with Bridgetower. The next year Beethoven conducted
a concert at the Augarten that included his Second Symphony and the Piano Concerto in C minor, Op. 37. The
solo part was played by the composer's pupil, Ferdinand
Ries. Ries himself records:

'Beethoven had given me his beautiful Concerto
in C minor, Op. 37 in manuscript so that I might
make my first public appearance *as his pupil* with
it [Ries's italics].'

With a touch of pride he adds: 'I am the only one who ever
appeared as such while Beethoven was alive.'[14]

BEETHOVEN AND CONDUCTING

When Beethoven arrived in Vienna it was still the custom
for the orchestra to be directed by the leader of the first
violins or, in the case of concertos, from the keyboard.
Commenting on this, Clive Brown observes:

'One consequence of directing an orchestra from
the first violin or keyboard was that performances
must almost entirely have lacked the wider variety

of nuance and tempo-modifications which were later to be considered the hallmarks of a conductor's interpretation: the old system inevitably necessitated a constant pulse in the music.'[15]

The conductor directing the orchestra with a baton was beginning to appear in response to the growing complexity of the symphony as manifest, for example, in the later symphonies of Mozart and, in particular, those of Beethoven.

Beethoven himself was not a natural conductor. It was to his further disadvantage that he had few opportunities to learn the craft since he never held the appointment of *kapellmeister* either at Bonn or in Vienna. He occasionally conducted performances of his works — whilst he still retained some hearing — but, in the modern-day sense, he had no qualifications as a conductor and had no routine experience as such. Moreover, he never travelled far afield to benefit from hearing orchestras outside of Vienna. He did have some experience of conducting, though, as Anton Schindler explains:

'At the time when his hearing was yet perfect, he had not often occasion to come in contact with the orchestra, and especially to acquire practice in the conducting department at the theatre, which is the best school for that purpose.'[16]

In his Autobiography *Mémoires de Hector Berlioz* — published in 1879 (the year after his death) Berlioz expressed his opinions on composers conducting their own works — with an aside to Beethoven:

'It is generally supposed that every composer is a born conductor, that is to say that he knows the art of conducting without having to learn it.

12

Beethoven was an illustrious example of the fallacy of this opinion, and one might name a host of other masters whose compositions are held in general esteem, but who, the moment they take up the baton, neither mark time nor nuance, and would indeed literally bring the musicians to grief if the latter did not quickly perceive the inexperience of their leader and make up their minds to pay no attention to his whirling arms.[17]

Descriptions of Beethoven conducting, that accord with Berlioz's remarks, have been commented on in similar terms by several of Beethoven's musician-contemporaries. These are found, for example, in the recollections of Carl Czerny, Ignaz Moscheles, Johann Friedrich Reichardt, Ferdinand Ries, Ignaz von Seyfried, and Louis Spohr. They describe Beethoven standing before the orchestra in animated fashion, making gestures with his arms and body by way of conveying the dynamics of the music. He would crouch low down to indicate *pianissimo* and leap into the air to denote *fortissimo*.

Ignaz von Seyfried was particularly well qualified to express an opinion on Beethoven's conducting. He was a composer, teacher and conductor at the Theater an der Wien, had studied piano with Mozart and, like Beethoven, studied composition with Johann Albrechtsberger. Under Beethoven's direction, he rehearsed the Second, Fifth, and Sixth Symphonies. Commenting on the years between 1800 and 1805, before Beethoven's hearing had begun to fail, von Seyfried describes Beethoven's manner when conducting in the following terms:

'Our Beethoven was not one of those fastidious composers whom no orchestra could please;

sometimes he was too lenient, and would not even repeat passages which went badly at the rehearsal; "It will go better next time", he would say. But he was most particular about expression, the small *nuances*, the numerous alterations of light and shade, and the frequent passages in *tempi rubato*, all of which he was, however, quite ready to discuss with anyone. When he saw that the performers entered into his ideas, played together with increasing spirit, and captivated by the magic of his music were carried away by enthusiasm, then his face would grow bright, and with pleasure beaming from every feature, and an agreeable smile, he rewarded the successful achievement with a thundering "Bravi tutti".'[18]

As Beethoven's hearing progressively worsened, his bodily gestures when conducting became ever more exaggerated. Louis Spohr recalls the occasion in December 1813 when he took part, as violinist, in a performance of the Seventh Symphony. Being unfamiliar with Beethoven's conducting style he relates how he was 'surprised in the highest degree' — although he had been told beforehand of what he now saw with his own eyes. He continues:

'Beethoven had accustomed himself to indicate expression to the orchestra by all manner of singular bodily movements. So often as a *sforzando* occurred, he tore his arms, which he had previously crossed upon his breast, with great vehemence asunder. At *piano* he crouched down lower and lower as he desired the degree of softness. If a *crescendo* then entered he gradually rose again at the entrance of the *forte* ... it was obvious that the poor man could no longer hear the *piano* of his music.'[19]

For a final observation on Beethoven conducting — perhaps we should say *attempting* to conduct — we draw on the recollections of Wilhelmine Schröder-Devrient. She was a young opera singer who, by all accounts, had a phenomenal voice — Beethoven once described it as being 'as big as the side of a house'! In 1821 she established her reputation in Vienna as a highly acclaimed dramatic artist in the role of Pamina in Mozart's *Die Zauberflöte*; remarkably she was just seventeen at the time. The following year she appeared to considerable acclaim as Agathe in Weber's *Der Freis-chütz* — earning warm praise from the composer himself. Later that year she took on the challenging role of Leonora in Beethoven's revised opera *Fidelio* that had not been performed for several years. Beethoven himself insisted on directing the dress rehearsal from which occasion Wilhelmine left the following moving account:

'Beethoven sat in the orchestra and waved his baton above the heads of us all, and I never had seen the man before. At that time the Master's physical ear already was deaf to all tone. With confusion written on his face, with more than earthly enthusiasm in his eye, swinging his baton to and fro with violent motions, he stood in the midst of the playing musicians and did not hear a single note.'

She further describes how Beethoven's best efforts served merely to throw singers and orchestra into confusion and to put them entirely off beat, Beethoven, all the while being unaware of the ensuing circumstances, was apparently content with the rehearsal, 'for he laid down his baton with a happy smile'. Schröder-Devrient further recalls

> 'It fell to the lot of the violinist-conductor Michael Umlauf to tactfully suggest he should take charge of the actual performances. This he subsequently did, Beethoven apparently being consigned to having to sit behind Umlauf — lost in profound meditation.'[20]

ACCOUNTS OF BEETHOVEN:
GROWING FAME

By the time Beethoven had completed his First Symphony and was starting work on the Second, he had already achieved a considerable reputation in the salons of the nobility as a virtuoso pianist; his powers of improvisation were universally held to be without equal — often to the dismay of his would-be rivals. More widely, with each succeeding composition he enlarged the scope of its musical genre and started to lay claim to be the most original and adventurous composer of the day. The American musicologist Maynard Solomon has placed Beethoven's compositional achievements, as a symphonic composer, within their wider context. He summates these in the following terms:

> 'One senses during these years, and especially in the years 1798 to 1802, Beethoven's determination to achieve mastery of the Viennese high-Classic style within each of its major instrumental genres. The challenge of the piano trio was met earliest with Op 1 in 1795; the string trio with Op. 9 in 1798; the string quartet with Op. 18 in 1799

and 1800; the string quintet with Op. 29 in 1801; the classic piano concerto with the Third Concerto inn 1800; the duo sonata with Opp. 23, 24, and 30 in 1801–02; and the symphony with the D major Symphony in 1802.'

Solomon concludes his evaluation of Beethoven's achievements to date saying:

'Beethoven was now well launched upon his "new path" — a qualitative change in his style which would become a turning point in the history of music itself.'

Solomon's reference to Beethoven's 'new path' requires a word of explanation. According to his piano pupil Carl Czerny, it was soon after the completion of his Piano Sonata, Op. 28 that Beethoven remarked to his friend, the mandolin player Wenzel Krumpholz: 'I am only a little satisfied with my previous works. From today on I will take a new path.' [21]

Although preoccupied with his compositions, Beethoven found time to give instruction to several piano pupils. Perhaps the most gifted of these was the child prodigy Carl Czerny who, by the age of ten, could play most of Mozart's piano compositions — including the concertos. His other, and older contemporary piano pupil of distinction, was Ferdinand Ries. Ries was the son of Beethoven's violin teacher Franz Ries, from his youthful days in Bonn; this familial relationship may have contributed to Beethoven's close attachment to Ferdinand when he went to Vienna in October 1801 to receive piano lessons from the composer. Ries is regarded as a reliable observer and chronicler of Beethoven and later recorded his impressions of his teacher jointly with Gerhard Wegeler, in their *Biographie Notizen über ... Beethoven* (1838).

Ries confided his appreciation of the care Beethoven took with his piano lessons in a letter he wrote on 6 May 1803 to the Bonn music publisher Nicholas Simrock:

> 'Beethoven takes more trouble with me than I could have believed. Each week I receive three lessons, usually from 10 o'clock to 2.30. I can almost play his Sonata *Pathétique*, which might give you pleasure, because the precision that he demands is hard to imagine.'

Ries closes this part of this letter with an observation characteristic of that expressed by other of his pianist contemporaries: 'To hear him improvise, however, may not be imagined at all — I have already had this pleasure five times.'[22]

The development of the piano remained a subject of great interest to Beethoven; it is not exaggerating to say that no other instrument underwent such radical transformation in the course of his lifetime. Given his pre-eminence as a virtuoso of the keyboard, Beethoven's opinion was often sought concerning the suitability of a particular instrument. One such occasion arose in 1803 when the Leipzig-based publisher Breitkopf and Härtel requested such advice. On 23 November the composer's brother Carl (Kaspar Karl) replied on Beethoven's behalf. He was by then assisting Beethoven with his business negotiations with publishers and had undertaken to act as an intermediary for the purchase of suitable pianos. Beethoven was typically asked to give advice about their construction and reliability. On this occasion Beethoven recommended the Bohemian fortepiano manufacturer Johann Bohacck. He was known for his five-octave, knee-lever action instrument that was similar to the Walter pianoforte owned by Mozart. Haydn also owed one of Bohacck's instruments. His finest instrument, with a case made from imported mahogany, cost 80 ducats, whilst a cheaper model, made from cherry wood, could be had for 50 ducats. Although Beethoven recognised the sturdy construction of Bohacck's pianos, he considered they were becoming out of date and expressed the hope 'in time he shall make instruments equal, or even superior, to those of other manufacturers'.[23]

Such was Beethoven's reputation, that manufacturers were prepared to sell him one of their instruments at a reduced price. Later, such eminent manufacturers as Érard of Paris and Broadwood of London were only too willing to make Beethoven a gift of one of their finest instruments — rather as celebrities today are presented with some trophy-item from a sponsor eager to derive benefit from the prestige of being associated with a person of distinction in a particular sport.

A measure of Beethoven's growing fame at this period is further indicated by the circumstance of him being persuaded to have his portrait painted — no easy matter considering his impatient and irascible demeanour. The artist who undertook the commission was Joseph Mähler. Being a personal friend of the composer was perhaps the reason for Beethoven relenting to submit to the ordeal, as he regarded it, of sitting still for a long period. Mähler portrayed Beethoven in an Arcadian setting striking a lyre, in the background is a temple of Apollo — one of the Olympian classical deities. Although this portrait situates the composer in a somewhat idealised pastoral setting, Beethoven's contemporaries considered the artist had not sacrificed his appearance in striving for romantic effect. Beethoven clearly approved of Mähler's likeness of him since the portrait remained in his possession until his death. [24]

The portrait in question became the source of an amusing

incident. Sometime in 1804, Beethoven wrote to Mähler for the return of his portrait — it was apparently still in his studio. The reason for Beethoven's request was that a lady visitor-admirer (unnamed) had requested the loan of the portrait to hang in her room during her stay in Vienna. Regarding the request for the loan of the portrait, Beethoven remarked to Mähler: 'Who can resist such *charming advances?*'[25]

Beethoven never owned his own house, he chose instead to live in rented accommodation — in part through financial necessity. Throughout his time in Vienna he changed apartments on numerous occasions. We close this part of our account of Beethoven by considering where he was living at the period of composition of the Second Symphony.

We learn something of Beethoven's domestic circumstances from a letter he wrote on 14 July 1804 to Ferdinand Ries. From April 1803 Beethoven was provided with an apartment at the Theater an der Wien by Emmanuel Schikaneder, who, from 1801, was the manager of the property. Beethoven's accommodation was modest and he eventually found it unsatisfactory. He explained to his pupil:

'If you, dear Ries, know where to find better rooms, I shall be very glad indeed ... I should very much like to have rooms in a large quiet square or on the Bastei.'[26]

The latter is a reference to the Mölkerbastei, an imposing residence located in central Vienna. The property was inherited by Baron Pasqualati, from whom the expression Pasqualati House is derived. Baron Johann von Pasqualati, a close contemporary of Beethoven (1777-1830) was a *Hofagent*, a court official who assisted Beethoven in financial, professional and judicial matters. Moreover, he was a music lover, an accomplished pianist and a founder

20

member of the *Gesellschaft der Musikfreunde*. He was generous to Beethoven and retained his apartment for him during the composer's occasional departures. Beethoven reciprocated this friendship in 1814 by composing the *Elegischer Gesang*, Op. 118 to commemorate the anniversary of the death of Pasqualati's wife. In Beethoven's time Pasqualati house stood on what was then Vienna's city boundary; from his apartment's fourth floor he could look across the leafy surroundings to the *Wienerwald* — Vienna Woods.[27]

HEILIGENSTANDT:
TRIUMPH OVER DEAFNESS

According to his own account, Beethoven began to experience difficulties with his hearing from about 1798, initially in the form of disturbing and intrusive sounds known as tinnitus. A few years later his malady was so evident it disposed Ferdinand Ries to comment: '[Beethoven] was so sensitive to the onset of his deafness that one had to be very careful not to make him feel the disability by talking loudly.' Ries describes his awareness of the extent of Beethoven's loss of hearing from an occasion in 1802 when he was out walking with him in the countryside:

> 'I called his attention to a shepherd in the forest who was playing most pleasantly on a flute cut from lilac wood. For half an hour Beethoven could not hear anything at all and became extremely quiet and gloomy, even though I repeatedly assured him that I did not hear anything longer either (which was however, not the case).'[28]

In due course, other of Beethoven's close acquaintances

became aware of his failing hearing and how it was torment-
ing him. On 13 November 1804, Stephan von Breuning
wrote to Franz Gerhard Wegeler to confide his worries
about their mutual friend: 'You cannot conceive, my dear
Wegeler, what an indescribable, I might say *fearful* effect
the loss of hearing has had upon him.' Breuning goes on to
express his concern this was having on the composer's
already 'violent temperament' and the manner in which he
was beginning to show mistrust 'often towards his best
friends'.[29]

For some time Beethoven had been receiving medical
advice from the physician Dr. Gerhard von Vering — a
senior, and distinguished, army medical officer. He had
treated the composer with some success for abdominal
pains but had made no progress in alleviating his hearing
condition. Consequently, Beethoven became dissatisfied
and, in November 1801, he wrote to Wegeler seeking his
advice. In particular he wanted his opinion concerning Dr.
Johann Schmidt, a physician of considerable repute, a
professor of anatomy and, congenial to Beethoven, an
accomplished violinist.[30] In the winter of 1801–02
Beethoven placed himself under Schmidt's care. Schmidt
appears to have considered a period of peace and tranquillity would be of benefit to the composer; he suggested
residing somewhere in the countryside away from Vienna's
bustle and activity. Sometime later, Beethoven showed his
appreciation for the care and attention Schmidt bestowed
upon him by dedicating to him his own arrangement of his
celebrated Septet, Op. 20, for piano, clarinet, or violin,
and 'cello, Op. 38.

In April 1802, Beethoven acted upon Dr. Schmidt's
advice and departed Vienna to take up residence in a
modest property in Heiligenstadt, then a secluded village
some two miles north of the city. Beethoven's rooms

offered the composer sight of the Danube, the fields round about and the more distant panorama of the Carpathian Mountains. Something of the enchantment of this location is conveyed in a watercolour study of the village and its surroundings that is preserved today in Vienna's Kunsthistorisches Museum.[31]

Of related interest is the illustrator of the watercolour, known to art historians as Johann Peter Lyser (real name Ludwig August Burmeister), created a sketch-impression of Beethoven as he may have appeared when walking the highways and byways of the countryside. Although created largely from his imagination — Lyser probably never met Beethoven — it effectively captures his profile and determined gaze.[32] Beethoven looks distinctly unshaven and windswept. As Carl Dalhaus observes (his study being one of several sources reproducing the image), the significance of the portrait lies in that, 'It represents the romantic image of Beethoven: the image of the revolutionary, the genius unconcerned with externals.'[33]

Returning only occasionally to Vienna, Beethoven's social sacrifice was considerable. It isolated him from his brother, his closest friends, and contact with the circle of distinguished families to whose various lady-members he was giving piano lessons. Moreover, as Beethoven's biographer Alexander Thayer remarks, such isolation was probably not good for the composer: 'It gave him too many lonely hours in which to brood over his calamity ... and the benefit to his hearing proved to be small or none.'[34]

Beethoven gave expression to his despondency in the so-called *Heiligenstadt Testament*. This document, in effect a letter to his brothers Carl and Johann, recounts his despair over his worsening deafness. Given the poignancy that pervades the document, a parallel is to be found in the lines of John Keats whose awareness of his impending mortality disposed him to write, 'I have fears that I may cease to be / Before my pen has gleaned my teaming brain'.[35] Significantly, towards the close of his text, Beethoven affirms his resolve to overcome his misfortune in order to complete his artistic destiny.

His *Testament* may, in the Aristotelian sense, have helped him to purge his emotions and, through his art, find renewal and restoration — what Barry Cooper has described as 'a kind of ceremonial burial'.[36] Beethoven eventually passed through his 'dark night of the soul', emboldened by his indomitability of spirit and self-belief and with the realization that his 'inner ear' — his precious compositional faculty — was still intact. Saint John of the cross speaks of 'darkness' representing the hardships and difficulties encountered in life. We take the generic meaning of his words to signify Beethoven's triumph over his feelings of depression and the isolation he felt imposed by his encroaching deafness.

The Austrian physician and musicologist Dr. Anton Neumayr has made a detailed study of Beethoven's many illnesses and the bearing they may have had not only on his physical wellbeing but also on his possible state of mind. He refers to the *Heiligenstadt Testament* as Beethoven 'putting his wounded heart's cries of pain on paper' and how, in his opinion,

> 'the act of writing out his thoughts was essentially a conscious acknowledgement, an act of self-therapy by which he sought to free himself from the depression racking his soul'.

Then, mindful of the composer's subsequent creative achievements, he adds:

'The mental resilience that enabled him to overcome his depression also freed enormous impulses that led to the development of a new style in his compositional art.'[37]

In Electra Yourke's memorable phrase: 'The gate of music is the ear.' As she elucidates, our faculties of musical perception, and the ability to perform music, depend upon 'the perfection of our auditory apparatus'. She suggests Beethoven protected his creative imagination in the form of 'a dome of sound' such that his *inner ear* remained intact; '[Beethoven] no longer needed external stimuli to organize ... sounds into melodies or harmonies'.[38]

At the end of the summer Beethoven returned to Vienna, not with his hearing restored but, to quote Cooper once more, 'with his spirit revived and ready to break new ground in the development of his art'.[39]

As to Beethoven the pianist, he last performed in public at the keyboard in the 1814 premier of the so-called *Archduke* Trio, Op. 97: this was to the mortification of his friends and admirers as he either jangled the strings excessively in the *fortissimos* or played inaudibly in the *pianissimos*. References to the effect the loss of hearing meant for Beethoven occur throughout his later correspondence. For instance, in the summer of 1815 he wrote to Johann Xaver Brauchle, a minor composer who was then employed as the tutor to the children of the Countess Anna Maria Erdödy — an accomplished pianist and one of Beethoven's many aristocratic, women-friend admirers. He confides:

'I am not well ... Peevish about many things, more sensitive than all other mortals, and tormented by my poor hearing I often feel only *pain* in the society of others [Beethoven's italics].'[40]

At the close of 1817, Beethoven appears to have come to terms with his impaired hearing; he realized it would not improve. He became ever more reliant upon the ear trumpets devised for him by the pioneer of the metronome, Johann Mälzel (Maelzel) who provided the composer with a variety of designs The first was a conical-shaped device made from copper; another was a piped-shaped trumpet with a perforated cover — to keep insects out!; and two others were of similar design but supplied with a headpiece to help bear their weight. They are thought to have been of little use but Beethoven continued to place his trust in them and future innovations from which he did not live to benefit.[41] In his later years, Beethoven had to make recourse to notebooks — *conversation books* — so that instead of having to yell at him, friends and visitors could write down their thoughts.

Returning to Beethoven's period of anguish in the summer of 1802, Thayer quotes the following text from the *Heiligenstadt Testament*:

'[Thus] I bid farewell — and indeed sadly — yes, that fond hope — which I brought here with me to be cured to a degree at least — this I must now wholly abandon ... Oh Providence — grant me at last but one day *of pure joy* — it is so long since real joy echoed in my heart ...'.

Thayer concludes his quotation *De profundis clemavit* — 'from the depths!'. He then remarks:

'And yet in that retirement [Heiligenstadt]

whence came a paper of such profound sadness was wrought out the Symphony in D; a work whose grand and imposing introduction — brilliant *allegro*, [and] a *larghetto* so lovely, "so pure and amiably conceived", written in the scenes which gave inspiration to the divine *Pastorale* of which its serene tranquillity seems the precursor; a *scherzo* "as merry, wayward, skipping and charming as anything possible" ... and a finale, the very intoxication of a spirit "intoxicated with fire" — made it, like the Quartets, an era both in the inner life of its author and in the history of instrumental music.'[42]

The words in double quotation marks are derived from Thayer's reading of the Russian author Alexander Oulibishev's *Beethoven, ses critiques et ses glossateurs* (1857).

Notwithstanding the moving sentiment of Thayer's text, Cooper cautions against taking the passage too literally:

'Thayer's assertion has been repeated many times since and even today visitors to Beethoven's memorial house [Heiligenstadt] are told this is where [Beethoven] wrote his Second Symphony. Yet, in truth, the sketches for the Symphony were more-or-less completed a month before he began his sojourn there and any work on it at Heiligenstadt would therefore have been mere finishing touches, hardly likely to affect its overall mood of cheerfulness.'[43]

It is to the sketch origins of the Second Symphony, therefore, that we now direct our attention.

COMPOSITION ORIGINS:
SKETCH SOURCES

Donald Tovey remarks:

> 'No artist has left more authoritative documentary
> evidence as to the steps of his [creative] develop-
> ment than Beethoven. His sketches and compo-
> sitional drafts cover the so-called "three-periods"
> of his career, and give insights into the origins of
> many of his most important works; throughout,
> the same level of rigorous self-criticism, integrity
> and tireless search for "perfection" is evident.'

Tovey further remarks:

> 'The number and triviality of Beethoven's prelim-
> inary sketches should not ... be taken as evidence
> of a timid and vacillating spirit. But if we regard
> his sketches as a diary, their significance becomes
> inestimable.'[44]

Beethoven set down ideas for a new piece starting on a fresh
page, frequently noting ideas for different movements
alongside each other. As his powers of invention took hold
he would insert further thoughts cramming them into any
available space or even going back to make use of pages
previously left blank. As a consequence, sketches for
different compositions co-exist side-by-side, many to be
discarded but others to be fully worked into the compositions we know and cherish today. In his lecture *Questions
about Music* Roger Sessions, in his role as Charles Eliot
Norton Professor, remarked:

'Beethoven could have made a great deal out of any one of the earlier versions [of his sketches] ... Obviously it would have been a different piece, and since that piece is not in existence, we can never know what it would have been like.'[45]

Gustav Nottebohm, a pioneer in the study and decipherment of Beethoven's sketchbooks, has this to say:

'[In] spite of this unsystematic procedure it is evident that as a rule Beethoven was clear about his objectives from the start; he remained true to his original conceptions, and once an idea was grasped, he carried it through to the end ... We may seek [in the sketchbooks] the artist himself, in the unity of his whole character and spirit, and in the harmony of his inner powers.'[46]

In his scholarly commentary to Beethoven's sketchbooks, Alan Tyson suggests they may have 'performed a special function for him in maintaining his morale as well as in facilitating his creative processes'. They did indeed become indispensable to him and at times, when his working method came up in conversation, he was given to quoting from Schiller's *Joan of Arc*: 'Without my banner I dare not come'.[47]

Before proceeding to a discussion of Beethoven's work on the Second Symphony, we pause for a moment to further consider his outlook, regarding his compositions thus far, and his determination 'to take a new path'. Despite his achievements, he resolved to do better.

Shortly after completing his D major Piano Sonata Op. 28 (published in 1801), Beethoven expressed dissatisfaction, in particular, over his piano writing to date. He confided this to his close friend, the mandolin and violin player Wenzel Krumpholz; he was an accomplished performer and a member of Prince Nikolaus Esterhazy's orchestra. We learn of Beethoven's feelings concerning his piano music through an interesting chain of events that are as follows. Krumpholz conveyed Beethoven's expression of dissatisfaction with his work to Carl Czerny — who was also an intimate friend of Krumpholz. Years later (1842) Czerny left an account of Beethoven's remarks in a short autobiography he made of his life that was later deposited in the archives of the *Gesellschaft der Musikfreunde* at Vienna. Czerny's account only came to light in 1870 when the keeper of the archives published it in his *Annual Report* to coincide with the celebrations planned for that year — Beethoven's Birth Centenary.

In 1880, Czerny's account of Beethoven's conversation with Krumpholz was eventually published by the musicologist Ludwig Nohl — to whom, amongst other things, posterity owes a debt for discovering the lost autograph of one of Beethoven's most cherished miniature compositions, his bagatelle *Für Elise.* Back in 1803, Beethoven had apparently exclaimed to Krumpholz: 'God knows why my piano music still makes the worst impression on me.' But, with characteristic resolution — and relevant to our discussion of the Second Symphony — he confided to his sketchbook how he 'intended to make a fresh start' — his first steps along his 'new path'.[48]

A characteristically fulsome expression of enthusiasm from Alexander Thayer redirects us to the Second Symphony:

> '[What] wonderful capacity for labour does it show, that, before the close of the year [1802], in spite of ill health and periods of the deepest despondency, and of all the interruptions caused by his ordinary vocations after his return to town

[from Heiligenstadt to Vienna], he had also completed the [Piano] Sonatas, Op. 31, the two extensive sets of Variations, Op. 34 and 35, and the noble Second Symphony! — all of them witnesses that he had really entered upon his "new path", neither of them more so than the Symphony so amazingly superior to its predecessor in grandeur and originality. This was, in fact, the grand labour of the summer.'[49]

Sketches for the Second Symphony originate from mid 1800. Beethoven did not work on the composition continuously, however, he set it aside to give his attention to other works. For example, drafts for the first movement occur alongside sketches for the Piano and Violin Sonatas, Op. 23 and Op. 24, the Piano Sonatas Op. 26 and Op. 27, No. 1, and, notably, ideas for the Ballet *Die Geschöpfe des Prometheus — The Creatures of Prometheus,* Op. 43. Given the significance of *Prometheus* for the development of Beethoven as an orchestral composer, the composition is deserving of additional remarks.

Beethoven had some prior experience of composing ballet music. In 1791 he had collaborated with his friend Count Ferdinand Waldstein in the festivities for the carnival season in Bonn. He wrote music for the ballet-play *Ritterballet* — 'Knights' Ballet' — a form of fancy-dress ball. *Prometheus*, though, was altogether grander and inherently more serious. It was probably composed in response to a commission and was doubtless attractive to Beethoven since it offered him the prospect of presenting himself in public as an accomplished stage-composer. The ballet master in charge of the choreography was Salvatore Viganò who had arrived in Vienna a few years earlier and had already achieved success there. The première of *Prometheus* eventually took place in the Burgtheater. It was Beethoven's most substantial orchestral score to date, consisting of over two-thousand bars in full score. The German musicologist Martin Geck suggests Beethoven's music for Salvatore Viganò has been underestimated in terms of its contemporary importance and its place in the history of ideas. He states:

> 'The myth of Prometheus, punished by Zeus for stealing fire from the gods was extremely topical [at the period under consideration]. As the bringer of light and benefactor of humanity, Prometheus was an icon of Enlightenment idealism.'

Geck adds:

> 'There is no doubt that the many performances of this ballet, at the Hofburg, brought Beethoven more into the public eye than any one of the one-off performances of any of his symphonies.'[50]

Prometheus became the subject of an amusing anecdote. It is on record, from the recollections of the collector of printed music Alois Fuchs, that Haydn chanced to meet Beethoven one day in the street and remarked how much he had enjoyed *Prometheus*. Beethoven is alleged to have responded — in his characteristically punning style — 'But it is far from being "a *Creation*!".' The latter, of course, being a reference to Haydn's Oratorio, *The Creation*, that had been composed just a few years earlier.

LANDSBERG 7 SKETCHBOOK
The so-called Landsberg 7 Sketchbook Is one of eight of Beethoven's sketchbooks that were purchased by the Berlin Royal Library in 1862 from the estate of the

collector of manuscripts Ludwig Landsberg. It had been previously owned by the music publisher Artaria and Co. who obtained it from the sale of the composer possessions following his death in 1827. It is now in the possession of the Staatsbibliothek Preussischer Kulturbesitz, West Berlin where it may be consulted on microfilm. An edition of the manuscript was published in 1927 by K. L. Mikulicz of Leipzig.

Beethoven used the sketchbook from the summer of 1800 until March 1801. In its present-day state it consists of 93 leaves. Alongside sketches for the Second Symphony, Op. 36, sketches for other works include: Piano Sonata, Op. 13 (*Pathétique*); String Quartet, Op. 18, No.1; Violin Sonatas, Op. 23, No. 4 and Op. 24, No. 5 (*Spring*); Piano Sonatas Op. 26 and Op. 27, No. 1; and music for the Ballet *The Creatures of Prometheus*, Op. 43.

Sketches for the first movement of the Second Symphony start at the beginning of the book and continue through to about page 59. As remarked, Beethoven is known to have set aside work on the Symphony in order to concentrate on the commission he had received for the Ballet. He resumed work on the Symphony in the Kessler sketchbook — see below.[51]

Writing of Beethoven's work on the Second Symphony, the Irish musicologist and academic Basil Deane suggests:

'In some respects, the Second Symphony Op. 36 represents an important advance in Beethoven's conception. The sketches of the work that have survived, and in particular those of the first movement, throw a revealing light on the composer's method and attitudes. In this case, Beethoven does not follow his general practice of hammering his themes before sketching the entire movement. Instead he conceives the expansion as a whole from start to finish, and refines his ideas in successive versions.'[52]

KESSLER SKETCHBOOK

The Kessler Sketchbook takes its name from the composer and pianist Joseph Christoph Kessler (1800–72) to whom it was given by Carl Andreas Stein, a member of the family of piano manufacturers, and was subsequently acquired by the Vienna *Gesellschaft der Musikfreunde* – where it may be consulted today on microfilm. This sketchbook is almost unique in having survived with its 96 leaves (192 pages) intact. Evidence indicates it being used by Beethoven between December 1801 and July 1802. Thayer writes:

'For nearly all the works completed in 1802, studies are to be found in the Kessler Sketchbook ... which covers the period from the fall [autumn] of 1801 to the spring of 1802.'[53]

This source was first studied and described by the pioneering Beethovenian Gustav Nottebohm in *Ein Skizzenbuch von Beethoven* (Leipzig, Breitkopf und Härtel, 1865). Pages 33–44 reveal uninterrupted sketches for the final movement of the Second Symphony alongside studies for the Piano Sonata Op. 31, No. 1, the Violin Sonatas Op. 30, and the Piano Variations in E-flat major, Op. 35.[54]

SAUER SKETCHBOOK

Between the spring and autumn of 1801 Beethoven used the Sauer Sketchbook. This sketchbook was purchased on 5 November 1827 at the auction of Beethoven's estate by the Viennese art and music dealer Ignaz Sauer. Like the

Landsberg 7 Sketchbook it may originally have consisted of 96 leaves but today it exists only in dismembered form. It may have contained sketches for the Second Symphony.[55] Sketches for the *Larghetto* and Scherzo of the composition are now lost, and it is tempting to conjecture they may once have formed part of the Sauer miscellaneous leaves.

The Second Symphony was all but completed between February and April 1802.[56] An incentive to make progress with the composition was to have the work performed at an *akademie* — benefit concert. In the event this had to be postponed since Beethoven was not able to rent the theatre he wanted for the occasion — see later.

In his recollections of Beethoven, Ferdinand Ries states, Beethoven gave him the Autograph Score of the Second Symphony 'out of pure friendship'.[57] It was a typically generous act on Beethoven's behalf since, once a composition was completed and with the publisher, his manuscripts held little further interest for him. Unfortunately, for posterity, Ries lent the Autograph to a friend who failed to return it. As a consequence, it is now considered to be lost — although musicologists entertain the hope it may one day be rediscovered.

NEGOTIATIONS WITH PUBLISHERS

Beethoven's correspondence with publishers is extensive and bears testimony to the circumstance that having his compositions published — for the fees he demanded — was, for the most part, a protracted undertaking. Fortunately, in his business dealings with publishers, he received assistance from his younger brother Carl (Kaspar Karl) and, for the duration he was resident in Vienna, from his pupil Ferdinand Ries. The time Beethoven spent correcting copyists' errors — incurred by them endeavoring to decipher his manuscripts — was a frequent cause for delays in publication, as were Beethoven's parallel transactions with rival publishers; Beethoven was not averse to setting one off against the other.

We discern how tiresome Beethoven found the business-side of composition to be from a letter he wrote on 15 January 1801 to the Leipzig-based publisher Franz Anton Hoffmeister; he had expressed an interest in publishing some of the composer's works. Regarding the negotiations involved, Beethoven lamented: 'Well that tiresome business has now been settled.' He calls it tiresome because, as he remarks, 'He should like such matters to be differently ordered in this world'. He goes on to say:

> 'There ought to be in the world *a market for art* [Beethoven's italics] where the artist would only have to bring his works and take as much money as he needed.'

He further laments how he has to be both an artist and 'to be to a certain extent a business man as well, and how can he manage to be that — Good Heavens!'[58]

Whilst he had possession of some hearing, there is evidence Beethoven made modifications to his text following a performance. For example, he wrote to Breitkopf and Härtel on 4 March 1809 stating:

> 'Tomorrow you will receive a notice about some small corrections which I made during the performance of the [Fifth and Sixth] Symphonies. When I gave these works to you, I had not yet heard either of them performed — and one should not want to be so like a god as not to have to correct something here and there in one's created works.'[59]

It is with the publisher Breitkopf & Härtel that we now trace Beethoven's somewhat protracted negotiations bearing on the publication of the Second Symphony.

1802

The head of the Leipzig publishing firm was Gottfried Christoph Härtel — to whom we shall refer simply as Härtel. On 27 November 1801, Härtel wrote to Beethoven expressing the interest his firm had in publishing certain of the composer's works.[60] On 28 March the following year, Beethoven's brother Carl replied to Härtel. He apologised for the long delay in making a reply and explained he was now helping Beethoven with his business affairs. He stated it was 'his pleasure for us to be able to serve you with a grand Quintet [Op. 29],' for which he requested 38 ducats in Viennese currency. He added: 'Beyond this, in three to four weeks, we shall have a grand Symphony [Op. 36] and a Concerto for the Piano [Op. 37]'.[61]

On 22 April, Carl wrote once more to Härtel. He explained his brother would have written himself but that he was preoccupied with negotiations with Baron von Braun; Beethoven was anxious to secure a venue in which to hold his *akademie* concert. Braun played a prominent role in Vienna's cultural life. He was a pianist of some ability, a recognised composer and held the post of Court Banker. More significantly, he controlled the management of Vienna's two Court Theatres — the Kärntnertor Theater and Burgtheater — and his proprietorship of the Theater an der Wien. Thereby, Braun made enemies — including Beethoven — over his strict control over theatrical, opera, and concert performances.

Carl explained how Beethoven was vexed with Braun, calling him 'a stupid and crude fellow', for not granting him access to the theatre he required for the performance of his new orchestral compositions. Regarding the Second Symphony, Carl asked Härtel 'to wait a bit longer' with the expectation it would be performed at a forthcoming concert. Beethoven appears, eventually, to have restored amicable relations with Braun since it was at the Theater an der Wien that he later premiered the *Eroica* Symphony, the Third Piano Concerto, the Oratorio *Christus am Ölberge*, the Violin Concerto, and the ill-fated Opera *Fidelio*. Braun may, by then, have been more warmly disposed to Beethoven through him having dedicated to his wife Josephine the Piano Sonatas, Op. 14, the transcription of Piano Sonata Op. 14, No. 1 as a String Quartet, and the Violin Sonatas Op. 31.[62]

We learn of progress with the Second Symphony from a letter Beethoven wrote on 9 April to Ferdinand Ries; he was now acting as his assistant, alongside Carl van Beethoven and remained so until the summer of 1805. Beethoven asked Ries to proofread some orchestral string parts — thought to refer to the Second Symphony.'[63]

On 10 June, Härtell responded to the letters of 28 March and 22 April in somewhat cautious terms. He explained how the problems of piracy were bearing down on his firm: '[In] Germany the profit from the publication of a significantly new original work benefits many publishers but not the rightful one.' He explained how the rightful publisher could not sell his work as cheaply as the pirate printer, since he had to bear the cost of the composer's fees.

To illustrate the problem Härtell had to confront, he cited what happened following the publication of Beethoven's Piano Trios Op. 1 by the Viennese firm Artaria. Shortly after their publication, he stated, Simrock in Bonn and some half-a-dozen Parisian publishers brought out their own unauthorised editions. Two years later this challenge to publishers was still clearly manifest as is evident from a further exchange of letters between Beethoven and Härtell. On 26 August 1804, Beethoven wrote to Härtel offering him for publication his recently composed *Eroica* Symphony Op. 55, the, Triple Concerto, the three Piano Sonatas, Opp. 53, 54, and 57, and the Oratorio *Christ on the Mount of Olives*, Op. 85. For these compositions he requested 2000 gulden. Given the scale and artistic merit of these compositions, it is not surprising Beethoven should ask such a high price, prompting him to remark:

> 'I assure you on my honour that in the case of some individual works, such as, for instance, sonatas, I am really the loser, seeing that people [other publishers] give me up to 60 ducats for a single sonata for pianoforte solo. I beg you not to think that I am bragging.'[64]

Notwithstanding Beethoven's entreaties Härtel declined, giving the reason that once more his sales in Germany had been greatly diminished by pirate printings. He gave the following illustration:

> 'We have had this experience with Mozart's *Requiem* and *Don Giovanni*, Handel's *Messiah*, Haydn's *Masses* and similar works which caused us too great a loss.'[65]

Härtell felt obliged to inform Beethoven how these circumstances constrained his publishing house from being able to remunerate him as they would wish. He explained they were prepared to purchase the Symphony, Op. 36 and the Concerto Op. 37 but only for a smaller fee than Carl was endeavouring to secure on his brother's behalf. Härtell concluded by expressing the hope that his firm would in future be able to offer Beethoven more favourable terms depending upon the 'mercantile success' of his works.[66]

It is a measure of Beethoven's growing fame that at the close of the year he was approached by another music publisher. In November 1802 Beethoven received a letter from Johann Anton André, a composer and founder-member of a publishing firm based at Offenbach. André is recognised in musicology for his negotiations with Constanza Mozart for the publication of many of the compositions left after Wolfgang's death. These included the scores of *The Marriage of Figaro*, *The Magic Flute* and *Eine Kleine Nachtmusik*. Doubtless, being aware of Beethoven's standing in music — now spreading beyond the confines of Vienna — André was eager to approach the composer in the hope of publishing some of his works.

On 23 November 1802, Carl van Beethoven responded once more on his brother's behalf. He offered André the Second Symphony, Op. 36 and the C minor Piano Concert, Op. 37. He requested 300 florins for each composition together with eight printed copies of the engravings. Beethoven frequently made such a request of his music publishers so that he could give a copy of his most recent work to close friends and fellow musicians. It is indicative of Beethoven's productivity that Carl also offered André the two *Romances* for Violin and Orchestra, Op. 40 and Op. 50 and the Piano Sonatas, Op. 49. Carl's prices for his brother's compositions appear, though, to have been too high for André since no further negotiations appear to have taken place between the two parties.[67]

1803

The following year Carl resumed the care of Beethoven's business affairs. On 22 January 1803 he offered Breitkopf

& Härtel several works including the Second Symphony, Op. 36 and the Third Piano Concerto, Op. 37 for a total sum of 600 florins; he requested these works should be published by the end of May. For good measure, Carl also offered the Overture and numbers 8, 10, and 16 from the Ballet *Die Geschöpfe des Prometheus*, Op. 43. For each of the four numbers, which Carl said the publishing house could publish singly, he requested 60 ducats. Carl further asked Härtel if he would be prepared to take over the publication of three piano sonatas for which he wanted to invite subscribers. Nothing, however, appears to have come of this proposal.[68]

Härtel, the business man, responded to Carl on 28 January — once more rather cautiously. He was ever mindful of the challenges facing music publication, at the period in question, with the realization of the keen competition from rival publishing houses and the ever-present threat from rogue pirate publishers. Notwithstanding Härtel's recognition of Beethoven's growing fame as a composer, and the artistic merit of his works, he explained he could not yet judge their mercantile value. For this reason, he proposed a fee of only 500 florins for the Second Symphony and the Third Piano Concerto upon immediate delivery of the manuscripts.[69]

Not having received a response to his letter of 28 January, Härtel wrote once again to Carl on 3 March asking if his offer of 500 florins for the Second Symphony and the Third Piano Concerto was acceptable. He was eager to receive the manuscripts in order to commence work on the required engravings so that they could be made available for sale at the Leipzig *Messe* — 'Easter Fair'.[70]

Carl responded on 15 March, although somewhat indirectly. He was unwell with rheumatic fever and had to dictate his letter to Beethoven's other brother Johann who

41

signed it on Carl's behalf. Of greater interest, and indicative of the competition that existed between rival publishers, is that Carl informed Härtel he had now sold both the Symphony and Concerto for 700 florins to another Viennese publisher, namely. the Kunst- und Industrie-Comptoir (*Bureau des Arts et d'Industrie).* As a gesture of goodwill, Carl intimated he was prepared to offer 'further works' — taken to be a reference to the three Piano Sonatas, Op 31 — 'in the coming weeks'.[71]

In due course Beethoven's chosen publisher for the C minor Concerto was the Kunst- und Industrie-Comptoir. They were a firm of music publishers and dealers in maps and prints. Founded in 1801, Beethoven was among their earliest composer-clients and they remained his principal publisher from 1802 to 1808. Major works of his published by the consortium include:

CONCERTOS: Third and Fourth Piano Concertos, Triple Concerto, Violin Concerto, and Beethoven's arrangement of it for Piano Concerto

ORCHESTRAL WORKS: Second and Third Symphonies, *Coriolan* Overture

PIANO AND CHAMBER WORKS: Piano Sonata, Op. 28, *Waldstein* Piano Sonata, String Quartet arrangement of Piano Sonata Op. 14 — Beethoven's only example, and the *Razumovsky* String Quartets.[72]

Later in the year it was Ferdinand Ries who acted on Beethoven's behalf. On 16 May he wrote to the publisher Nikolas Simrock in Bonn offering him the three Piano Sonatas, Op. 31 — further evidence of the intrigue that took place between Beethoven and his publishers. Worthy of note is that Ries did not hold Carl in high esteem. This is apparent in what he had to say about him:

> 'Charl [sic] Beethoven is the biggest skinflint in the world — for a single ducat he would take back 50 words of promise, and his good brother makes the greatest enemies because of him. For every note that Beethoven plays there is a corresponding base element in his brother's soul.'[73]

Despite Carl having turned down Härtel's offer to purchase the right to publish the Second Symphony, he wrote once more to the publisher on 21 May 'about a new symphony' on which he requested his opinion. This may be taken as a reference to the D major Symphony, Op. 36 that Beethoven had by now probably revised following his 5 April concert (see later). Of passing interest is Carl's offer to Härtel to publish transcriptions of several of Beethoven's piano works for quartet and some instrumental pieces for piano. These had been undertaken by the Austrian composer Xavier Kleinheinz, according to Carl 'under my brother's direction'.[74]

A few days later, on 25 May, we find Carl writing once more on his brother's behalf to the publisher Nikolaus Simrock, resident, we recall, in the composer's hometown Bonn. It illustrates Beethoven was not averse to offering the same works for simultaneous publication, albeit in different cities. On this occasion he offered the Second Symphony for 400 florins. This was a high price since we, recall, he had requested 500 florins from Härtel for *both* the Symphony and Third Piano Concerto — also illustrative of Carl's propensity for striking a hard bargain.[75]

Härtel responded on 2 June to Carl's letter of 25 May:

'We highly esteem your kind offer concerning the Overture and the Symphony [No. 2] as proof of the regard you have for us.' At the same time, however, He expressed a note of caution. As fervently as he wished to publish the composer's works, he was reluctant to bring out single or occasional pieces. He much preferred to publish the compositions of a composer in a single, uniform edition. He maintained music lovers — especially of piano pieces — preferred this to works that appeared from different publishers in varying formats and styles of engraving.[76] At the close of the month, on 30 June, Härtel wrote once more to Beethoven with what appears to be an expression of regret:

> 'It would have been very agreeable to us if your brother, who wrote to us about a new symphony of yours [Op. 36] and had indicated your intentions'.[77]

We learn of the compositional progress Beethoven was making with the Second Symphony from a letter Ferdinand Ries wrote on 6 August to Nikolaus Simrock. He remarks: 'Beethoven is now writing two symphonies, one of which is now practically finished'. The symphony in progress can be taken to be a reference to the *Eroica* Symphony, Op. 55 and that 'practically finished' is clearly a reference to Beethoven making revisions to the Second Symphony — following its performance on 5 April 1802. Of further interest is Ries's remark:

> 'Beethoven will now remain here [in Vienna] at most another year and a half. Then he is going to Paris, which I am extremely sorry about. Even though I told him, in jest, that he would have to take me along as his pupil and treasurer.'

44

Ries's suggestion that Beethoven was considering relocating to Paris has some foundation. Beethoven, notwithstanding his indomitability of spirit, was still a young composer and was not immune to the attacks on his music by certain music critics as, for example, when a Leipzig critic went so far as to describe the finale of the Second Symphony, shortly after its first performance, as 'a repulsive monster, a wounded tail-lashing serpent, dealing wild and furious blows as it stiffens into its death agony'. In the event, Beethoven did not leave for Paris. Indeed, it is difficult to imagine him prospering there with only a limited knowledge of the French language and without the support of his brother Carl to assist with his many transactions with publishers.[78]

Beethoven's feelings towards his critics is conveyed in a letter he wrote on 15 January 1801 to Franz Hoffmeister. He refers to the reviews of his works by the Leipzig critics of the *Allgemeine musikalische Zeitung*. He states he does not take them seriously, but they had clearly annoyed him. He protested: 'Just let them talk, they will never be immortal nor would they be able to take immortality away from anyone upon whom Apollo had bestowed it.' Beethoven clearly considered himself to be one so favoured by the gods.[79]

Beethoven's uncertainty about remaining in Vienna is further made evident in a letter he wrote on 6 July 1804. Beethoven felt obliged to respond to a letter that he had received from the organist, conductor and composer Gottlob Wiedebein. He was himself considering taking up residence in Vienna and sought the composer's advice. Beethoven's reply is illuminating:

'I am sorry not to be able to offer you my help [encouragement] unreservedly. You imagine that it would be easy to make your way here. But that

would be very difficult, for Vienna is swarming
with teachers who try to make a living by giving
lessons.'

The next part of Beethoven's reply reveals he was still
considering leaving Europe's music capital:

'If it were certain, however, that I were going to
remain in Vienna for good, I would let you
[encourage you] come here and try your luck.
But I shall probably leave here next winter, I
could then do nothing more for you myself.'

Wiedebein appears to have taken Beethoven's advice to
remain where he was although, in 1810, he did spend three
months in Vienna where he eventually made Beethoven's
acquaintance.[80]

On 14 October, Carl wrote to Härtel regarding the
publisher's continuing interest in receiving a concerto or a
symphony: 'You can have one or two symphonies, or a
symphony and a concerto for piano, cello and violin with
full orchestra'. For the latter two works he requested 700
florins — provided they appeared before Easter of 1804. At
the period under consideration, the performance of theatrical and operatic music was forbidden in Vienna during Lent.
Beethoven, thereby, sought to take advantage of this by
holding an *akademi* concert before the Easter celebrations.
The symphonies to which Carl refers are the Second (in the
process of revision} and Third — the *Eroica* (in sketch draft).

The concerto for three soloists mentioned in the letter
can be assumed to be the so-called Triple Concerto, Op.
56 that was subsequently published by Breitkopf & Härtel
in 1804. In this letter, Carl took up the cudgels on his
brother's behalf to take a swipe at the music critic writing

in the 5 July 1803 issue of the *Allgemeine musikalische Zeitung* that, as it so happened, was published by Breitkopf & Härtel. The journal's music correspondent had made pejorative remarks about the Oratorio *Christus am Ölberge*, inducing Carl to rebuke the unfortunate Härtel: '[I] find it very remarkable that you accept such *crap* [italics added] in your Zeitung.' (The German *mist* may be translated more politely as *dung* or *manure* but the inference is much the same.)[81]

On 22 October Ries, assisted Beethoven once again, this time by writing to Nikolaus Simrock to invite him to accept the publication of the *Eroica* Symphony. He requested the price of 100 gulden on the grounds: 'In his own [Beethoven's] opinion it is the greatest work that he has yet written.' Later in the letter Ries remarks, 'Symphony No. 2 is not yet ready', which suggest Beethoven was still putting the final touches to the revisions of the score prior to its intended publication.[82]

In November, Härtel responded to Carl's letter of 14 October with an offer to publish the Second and Third Symphonies for 500 florins — not the 700 as requested. Carl replied on 23 November stating he could not accept the offer, adding, with a touch of irony: 'I am sorry about this, but you may also regret it in the future, because these symphonies are either the worst my brother has written or the best.'[83]

The exchange of correspondence between Beethoven and his publishers for the year 1803 closed on 11 December with Ries writing to reassure Nikolaus Simrock that Beethoven had not yet sold the Second Symphony and was, apparently, reserving it for a concert tour. If this was the case it did not materialise. Ries also stated his teacher was 'composing a new one' — the *Eroica*.[84]

PUBLICATION IN PARTS

At the close of the eighteenth century it was customary to publish orchestral music in parts. Instrumental pieces were typically played under the direction of the violin-leader who was guided solely by the first violin-part before him. The well-established structure and orchestration of late eighteenth-century works enabled the music to be faithfully interpreted in this way without recourse to a full score. However, with the advent of the later symphonies of, for example, Haydn and Mozart, and, more notably, those of Beethoven, the need for the players to be directed by a conductor became more evident. Notwithstanding, the first six of Beethoven's symphonies were still published, after the manner of the old-style, in parts.[85]

The original edition of the Second Symphony was published in parts by the Bureau des Arts et d'Industrie, Vienna in March 1804. Based on his study of the surviving original sources, the Beethoven scholar Jonathan del Mar suggests a date of publication 'at least by 10 March'. He adds:

> '[The] putative set of manuscript parts is now lost, but from which the work would have been played at its first [public] performance on 5 April 1803. It seems also likely that this set also served as the *Stichverlage* [engraver's copy].'

Mar further remarks that since the Autograph and manuscript parts are now lost,

> 'the 1804 edition is the sole surviving authentic source from which every other source and edition has always been derived and on which ... any new urtext edition has entirely to base itself'.[86]

A few fragments of the original orchestral parts have in fact survived; these include the second horn part published by the Bureau des Arts et d'Industrie.[87]

The German musicologist Armin Rabb observes:

> 'The instrumental parts in the original edition were prepared by a single engraver, and Beethoven must certainly would have had the opportunity to read the proofs. Nonetheless, the decision to publish the work in parts automatically occasioned numerous inconsistencies which have necessitated a number of [subsequent] editorial alterations in the musical text.'[88] [We discuss some of these later]

The Title Page to the first edition reads:

> 'GRANDE SINFONIE /: pour / deux Violons, Alto, deux Flûtes, deux Hautbois, / deux Clarinettes, deux Bassons, deux Cors, deux / Trompettes, Timballes, Violoncelle et Basse, / Composée et dediée / à son Altesse Monseigneur le Prince / CHARLES DE LICHNOWSKY / par / Louis van Beethoven. / Op. 36. / à Vienne, au Bureau d'Arts et d'Industrie.'[89]

The dedicatee Prince Karl von Lichnowsky gained Beethoven's affection and gratitude, and his wife, although only five years older than Beethoven, became a 'second mother' to him. The prince and princess earned the unusual right to suggest changes and improvements to his compositions — notably his Opera *Fidelio*. Lichnowsky was an early admirer of Beethoven following his arrival in Vienna. He was himself musical and had lessons from Mozart. He provided accommodation for Beethoven in his own residence from 1793 to 1795. In addition, he gave Beethoven financial support of 600 florins annually until he had secured a regular income. He also presented Beethoven with a gift of a set of fine string instruments that are preserved today in Beethoven House, Bonn.[90]

In return for his patronage, in addition to receiving the dedication to the Second Symphony, Lichnowsky also received the dedications of other of the composer's early major works including: the Trios, Op. 1; the Piano Sonatas Op. 13, *Pathétique*, and Op. 26. Lichnowsky's wife was hardly less honoured and received the dedication to the Ballet Score, *The Creatures of Prometheus*, Op. 43. Moreover, Beethoven dedicated his Rondo in G, Op. 51, No. 2, to the Prince's sister, Countess Henriette and the Variations and Fugue, Op 35 and the Piano Sonata Op. 90 to the Prince's brother Count Moritz Lichnowsky.

TEMPO INDICATIONS:
METRONOME MARKS

With the advent of Johann Nepomuk Maelzel's new metronome instrument (1816—17), Beethoven seized upon its potential as a means of securing reliable tempi for the performance of his works. A report in the *Wiener Vaterländische Blätter* (*Vienna Patriotic Periodical*) stated:

> 'Herr Beethoven looks upon this invention as a welcome means with which to secure the performance of his brilliant compositions in all places in the tempos conceived by him, which to his regret have so often been misunderstood.'

To this end, Beethoven had a pamphlet printed by the publisher Sigmund Anton Steiner that gave his suggested metronome markings for the string quartets he had composed to date, namely, Opp. 18, 59, 74 and 95; he also included markings for his first eight symphonies.[91] In addition, on 17 December 1817, the *Leipziger Allgemeine musikalische Zeitung* published a list of 'tempos for every movement of the symphonies of Herr L. v. Beethoven as determined by the composer using Maelzel's metronome'.[92]

Further indication of Beethoven's wish to have his orchestral works performed, at what he considered to be the 'correct' tempi, is evident in a letter he wrote to the Mainz publisher Bernhard Schotts in December 1826, regarding his *Choral* Symphony:

'The metronome markings will be sent to you very soon. Do wait for them ... [I] have received letters from Berlin informing me that the first performance of the Symphony was received with enthusiastic applause which I ascribe to the metronome markings.'

He closes with a typical Beethovenian epithet: 'We can scarcely have *tempi ordinari* any longer, since one must fall into line with the ideas of unfettered genius.'[93]

Beethoven's metronome markings are today considered by some authorities to be too fast. It has been suggested the reason for this is that Beethoven, in his later years, was confined by deafness to an inner world of *imagined* sound and ascribed quicker markings to his music than he would have if he had the benefit of experiencing his music *in performance*. However, the English conductor Sir Roger Norrington — respected for his historically-informed performances of Baroque and Classical music — cautions against dismissing Beethoven's tempo indications too readily:

'Beethoven inherited a whole series of traditional speeds, including an *allegro* which was not very fast and an *andante* which was by no means slow. He [was] most insistent on the importance of using a metronome (partly, no doubt, because his deafness prevented him from directing performances). In virtually every case his metronome marks tally with an eighteenth-century understanding of tempo indications.'[94]

PUBLICATION IN FULL SCORE

We have remarked, Beethoven's orchestral music was initially published in the form of instrumental parts without a full score. However, there were exceptions and some of the composer's works appeared in full score early in the nineteenth century. The score to *Christus am Oelberg* appeared in 1811and was followed by the Mass in C during the following year— both brought out by Breitkopf and Härtel at Leipzig. We*llington's Victory* Symphony was published as a lithograph score, in 1816, by Sigmund Steiner of Vienna. The *Choral* Symphony appeared in print (score and vocal parts) in 1826 followed by the great Mass in D in 1827 — both by Bernhard Schott's of Mainz.[95]

Concerning the first six symphonies of Beethoven, publication in full score would have to wait several years after the compositions had appeared in instrumental parts:

First Symphony, parts in 1801 and score in 1809;
Second Symphony, parts in 1804 and score in 1808;
Third Symphony, parts in 1806, and score in 1809;
Fourth Symphony, parts in 1808 and score in 1823;
Fifth Symphony, parts in 1809 and score in 1826;
and Sixth Symphony, parts in 1809 and score in 1826.

The first editions of Symphonies Seven, Eight, and Nine were published concurrently in parts and full score. Prior to their publication in score, the first six symphonies were conducted either from manuscript copies of the full score — on loan from the archives of such publishers as Breitkopf & Härtel in Leipzig — or were directed from the first violin parts alone.[96]

On 13 May 1822, Nikolaus Simrock in Bonn wrote to Beethoven urging him to make progress with the completion of the *Missa Solemnis* — then his major preoccupation — for which he had paid 100 Louis d'or. In the course of his letter Simrock adds: 'For the present I have undertaken to publish your six Symphonies [i.e. Nos. 1—6] in full score.' He gave the reason:

> '[I] wanted to dedicate to my worthy old friend a worthy monument, and I hope you will be satisfied with the edition since I have done my utmost for it!'[97]

The scores of the First and Second Symphonies appeared in 1822 followed by that of the *Eroica* Symphony a few months later and that of the Fourth Symphony in 1823. In the event, notwithstanding his expressed intentions, Simrock never published the scores of the Fifth and Sixth Symphonies. They were published by Breitkopf & Härtel in 1826. Simrock's editions are significant insofar as they are the first German editions, of the works in question, to appear in full score and, moreover, include the composer's metronome marks together with such editorial interventions as slurs and staccato markings. Beethoven duly received his copy of Simrock's scores but it is not thought he was personally responsible for editing their texts. [98]

In England, the London-based publishers Cianchettini

& Sperati were some years ahead of their German counterparts in bringing out full-score editions of Beethoven's symphonies — and those of other celebrated composers. In May 1807, under the patronage of the Prince of Wales, they invited subscriptions for 'A compleat collection of Haydn, Mozart and Beethoven symphonies in score'. Two numbers appeared in the months of November and December until the enterprise ceased publication in 1809. These editions incorporated Beethoven's first three symphonies.

The Cianchettini & Sperati Beethoven full-scores were derived from the editions that had been published, as we have seen, in Vienna a few years earlier. They were, therefore, in essence, pirate editions that were issued entirely without Beethoven's knowledge or approval.[99] That said, Jonathan del Mar considers the early London edition of the Second Symphony is of interest insofar as

> 'it contains many alterations to the text which may be regarded as editorial, often resolving inconstancies and problems posed by other apparently doubtful readings of the [instrumental parts] used in the 1803 performance'.[100]

The London editions appeared under the imprint:

> 'A / Compleat Collection / OF / HAYDN, MOZART, / and / BEETHOVEN'S / Symphonies, / IN SCORE, / Most respectfully Dedicated, by Permission, to / H. R. H. / THE / Prince of Wales, — LONDON: Printed by Cianchettini & Sperati Importers of Classical Music. / No XXV. Princes Street Cavendish Square.'[101]

Commencing in 1862, Breitkopf & Härtel published a complete edition (*Gesamtausgabe*) of Beethoven's works. Its full title was:

'Ludwig van Beethovens Werke: vollständige kritisch durchgesehene überall berechtigte Ausgabe' ['*Ludwig van Beethoven's Works: complete, critical, thoroughly revised, authorized edition*'].'

Publication continued though to 1865, by which time some 263 works had been incorporated. A supplementary volume appeared in 1888. Beethoven had cherished such an undertaking in his lifetime, perhaps being influenced by his awareness of such an edition of Handel's music — with which he had become familiar late in life and which he so greatly admired. He even envisaged adding new compositions in a complete edition of his works to fill gaps in his output. For their edition of the score of the Second Symphony, Breitkopf & Härtel made use of Simrock's 1822 edition — the only source available to them. Of the *Gesamtausgabe* edition, Jonathan del Mar appraised its value in the following terms:

'The text was tidied up removing ambiguities and inconsistencies wherever possible ... so that under the editorial guidance of the distinguished conductor Julius Rietz a sensible and workable text was produced which, with few emendations in later printings, has served the musical world well for the past 130 years.' (del Mar was writing in the 1990s).[102]

A new complete edition of Beethoven's music began publication in 1961, under the auspices of the Beethoven

House in Bonn. When complete it will consist of some fifty-six volumes. We can only imagine the pleasure such an enterprise would have given Beethoven if anything approaching its proportions had appeared in his lifetime.

1   Emily Anderson editor and translator, 1961, Vol. 1, Letter No. 51, pp. 57—65.
2   Adapted from Paul Mies, *Beethoven's Orchestral Works* in: *The Age of Beethoven, The New Oxford History of Music, Vol. VIII,* Gerald Abraham, editor, 1988, pp. 122—23.
3   Otto Biba, *Concert Life in Beethoven's Vienna,* in: Robert Winter, editor, *Beethoven, Performers, and Critics: The International Beethoven Congress, Detroit, 1977,* 1980, p. 88.
4   Anne-Louise Coldicott *Performance Practice in Beethoven's Day* in: Barry Cooper, *The Beethoven Compendium: A Guide to Beethoven's Life and Music,* 1991, pp. 283—84.
5   Clive Brown, Liner notes to, *Ludwig van Beethoven, Beethoven: Symphony No. 1 and 2,* The Academy of Ancient Music conducted by Christopher Hogwood.
6   Anne-Louise Coldicott *Performance Practice in Beethoven's Day* in: Barry Cooper, *The Beethoven Compendium: A Guide to Beethoven's Life and Music,* 1991, pp. 283—84.
7   Roger Norrington, Liner notes to *Beethoven, Symphonies 1 & 6*, The London Classical Players, EMI CDC 7497462, 1988.
8   Donald Francis Tovey *The Forms of Music:* Musical Articles, originally Published in *The Encyclopaedia Britannica,* Oxford University Press, 1944, pp. 79—80.
9   Introductory notes to the recording of Beethoven's Symphony No. 2 by the Chamber Orchestra of Europe, conducted by Nikolaus Harnoncourt, June—July, 1990.
10 For the wider context of Beethoven and his relationship with Haydn, and his early years as his pupil, see: H. C. Robbins Landon, *Haydn: The Years of 'The Creation',* 1977., pp. 33—34.
11 Mary Sue Morrow, *Concert Life in Haydn's Vienna: Aspects of a Developing Musical and Social Institution,* 1989, pp. 71—81, and pp. 113—14, and p. 115. Morrow's account of Vienna's principal theatres includes seating plans and contemporary engravings of both their exteriors and interiors.
12 Musicologist David Wyn Jones, gives an account of Beethoven and his relationship with the Theater an der Wien, see his: *The Life of Beethoven,* Cambridge University Press, 1998, pp. 69—72.
13 H. C. Robbins Landon, *Haydn: The Years of 'The creation', 1796—800,* 1977, pp. 33—34. For a comprehensive study of concert life in Beethoven's Vienna see Anne-Louise Coldicott, *Beethoven's Musical Environment* in: Barry Cooper, 1991, pp. 87—91.
14 Elliot Forbes editor, *Thayer's Life of Beethoven,* 1967 p. 355. Thayer remarks: 'It is not clear here whether Ries is making explicit reference to a perfor-
15 Clive Brown, Liner notes to, *Ludwig van Beethoven, Beethoven: Symphony*

mance of the C minor Concerto. The point being that Beethoven's other piano pupil, Carl Czerny, rendered a similar service to that by Ries when he performed the *Emperor* Piano Concerto on 12 April 1818 — Beethoven being too deaf by then to play the work himself.

No. 1 and 2, The Academy of Ancient Music conducted by Christopher Hogwood.

16 Quoted from Ignaz Moscheles' translation of *Schindler's Life of Beethoven*. Vol.1, p. 112, derived from: Adam von Carse, *The Orchestra from Beethoven to Berlioz: A History of the Orchestra in the First half of the 19th Century, and of the Development of Orchestral Baton-Conducting*, W. Heffer, 1948, pp. 365–66.

17 Sam Morgenstern editor, *Composers on Music: An Anthology of Composers' Writings*, 1956, pp. 117–18.

18 Ignaz von Seyfried, as recounted in: Ludwig Nohl, *Beethoven Depicted by his Contemporaries*, 1880, pp. 49–56 and Oscar George Theodore Sonneck, *Beethoven: Impressions of Contemporaries*, 1927, pp. 35–46. See also Elliot Forbes editor, *Thayer's Life of Beethoven*, 1967 p. 371.

19 Elliot Forbes editor, *Thayer's Life of Beethoven*, 1967 pp. 565–66.

20 Derived from Oscar George Theodore Sonneck, *Beethoven: Impressions of Contemporaries*, Oxford University Press 1927, pp. 129–30. See also: Peter Clive, 2001, pp. 325–6 and p. 374.

21 Maynard Solomon, *Beethoven*, 1977, p. 106. The words attributed to Wenzel Krumpholz are derived from Oscar George Theodore Sonneck, *Beethoven: Impressions of Contemporaries*, Oxford University Press, 1927, pp. 156–57.

22 Theodore Albrecht editor and translator, 1996, Vol. 1, Letter No. 58, pp. 100–03.

23 *Ibid*, Letter No. 74, pp. 123–24.

24 The portrait in question is reproduced in many publications and can be viewed by accessing the Beethoven House Digital Archives, *Beethoven Gallery* and Library Document B 2388. See also: H. C. Robbins Landon, 1992, plate 6.

25 Emily Anderson, editor and translator, 1961, Vol.1, Letter No. 107, p. 105.

26 *Ibid*, Vol. 1, Letter No. 92, p. 111.

27 For a comprehensive survey and discussion of the many houses Beethoven occupied at various periods, see: *Beethoven's Residences*, in Hans Conrad Fischer and Erich Kock, *Ludwig van Beethoven: A Study in Text and Pictures*, St. Martin's Press, 1972. pp. 113–120.

28 Franz Wegeler *Remembering Beethoven: The Biographical Notes of Franz Wegeler and Ferdinand Ries (1833, 1845)*, Andre Deutsch, 1988 (reprint), pp. 86–87.

29 Theodore Albrecht, 1996, Vol. 1, Letter No. 90, pp. 148–9. A facsimile reproduction of this letter can be seen in the Beethoven House Digital Archives, Library Document Sammlung Wegeler, W 126. Note, it gives the date 13 October 1804.

30 Emily Anderson editor and translator, 1961, Vol. 1, Letter No. 54, pp. 66–9.

31 For a reproduction of the watercolour see: Leon Plantinga, *Beethoven's Concertos: History, Style, Performance*, Norton, 1999, Plate 4.

32 See: Beethoven House, Digital Archives, Library Document B 888.

33 Carl Dahlhaus, *Ludwig van Beethoven: Approaches to his Music*, 1991 (the text accompanying plate 14).

34 Elliot Forbes editor, *Thayer's Life of Beethoven*, 1967 pp. 303–6.

[35] John Keats, '*When I have fears that I may cease to be*'. Keats wrote his lines, in part, prompted by the deaths of members of his family, but also in recognition of the malign influence of the consumption that gripped him and sent him to the grave at the tragically early age of twenty-five.

[36] Barry Cooper, *Beethoven: The master Musicians Series*, Oxford University Press, 2000, p. 121.

[37] Anton Neumayr, *Music and Medicine*, Medi-Ed Press, 1994–1997, p. 249.

[38] Electra Slonimsky Yourke editor, Nicolas Slonimsky: Writings on Music, Vol.4, p. 150.

[39] Barry Cooper, *Beethoven: The Master Musicians Series*, 2000, p. 121.

[40] Emily Anderson, editor and translator, 1961, Vol. 2, Letter No. 550, pp. 519–20.

[41] Beethoven's hearing aids are illustrated on the Beethoven House, Digital Archives, Library Document, R 2. See also: Denis Arnold and Nigel Fortune editors, *The Beethoven Companion*, 1973, plate 8.

[42] Elliot Forbes editor, *Thayer's Life of Beethoven*, 1967 p. 306.

[43] Barry Cooper, *The Beethoven Compendium: A Guide to Beethoven's Life and Music*, 1991, p. 171.

[44] Donald Francis Tovey, *Ludwig van Beethoven* in: *The Classics of Music*, Michael Tilmouth editor, 2001, pp. 333–4.

[45] Edward T. Cone editor, *Roger Sessions on Music: Collected Essays*, 1979, p. 45.

[46] Gustav Nottebohm, *Two Beethoven Sketchbooks: A Description with Musical Extracts* (1887), Gollancz, 1979 (reprint).

[47] Alan Tyson, *Sketches and Autographs*, in: Denis Arnold, and Nigel Fortune, editors, *The Beethoven Companion*, Faber and Faber, 1973, pp. 443– 58. The artist Donna Dralle has created an imaginary study in pencil and watercolour titled *Beethoven Stitching a Notebook*:See: http//www.graphixnow.com/fine_art/images/fine_art_pgs/lvbsew.jpg

[48] See: Ludwig Nohl, *Beethoven Depicted by his Contemporaries*, Reeves, 1880, p. 48 and Denis Matthews, *Beethoven Piano Sonatas*, British Broadcasting Corporation, 1967, p. 2.

[49] Elliot Forbes editor, *Thayer's Life of Beethoven*, 1967 p. 317. Thayer's listing of Beethoven's compositions for the period in question may be more fully describds as follows: Three Sonatas for Piano and Violin, Op. 30; Three Piano Sonatas, Op. 31; Bagatelles for Piano, Op. 33; Six Variations for Piano, Op. 34; Variation for Piano, Op. 35 (on a theme from the Contradance No. 7, WoO 8) and *Prometheus*, Op. 43 – originally numbered Op. 24.

[50] Martin Geck, *Beethoven*, Haus, 2003, p. 28.

[51] For a discussion of the Landsberg 7 Sketchbook, see: Douglas Porter Johnson editor, *The Beethoven Sketchbooks: History, Reconstruction, Inventory*, Clarendon Press, 1985, p. 72 and pp. 101–12; Barry Cooper, *The Beethoven Compendium: A Guide to Beethoven's Life and Music*, 1991, p. 185; and Joseph Kerman, *Beethoven's Early Sketches* in: Paul Henry Lang, *The Creative World of Beethoven*, 1971, p. 35.

[52] Basil Deane, *The Symphonies and Overtures* in: Denis Arnold and Nigel Fortune editors, *The Beethoven Companion*, 1973, pp. 285–86.

[53] Elliot Forbes editor, *Thayer's Life of Beethoven*, 1967 p. 317.

54 A reprint of the Kessler Sketchbook is available as: Gustav Nottebohm, *Two Beethoven Sketchbooks: A Description with Musical Extracts*, Gollancz, 1979. For a discussion of the Kessler Sketchbook see the sources listed in endnote 31.

55 Beethoven House, Digital Archives: *Sinfonie Nr. 2 (D-Dur), Op. 36*.

56 Beethoven House, Digital Archives: *Sinfonie Nr. 2 (D-Dur), Op. 36* and Barry Cooper, *Beethoven: The Master Musicians Series*, 2000, p. 112.

57 Franz Gerhard Wegeler and Ferdinand Ries, *Biographische Notizen über Ludwig van Beethoven* (*Biographical Notes on Ludwig van Beethoven*) Koblenz, 1838, p. 77.

58 Emily Anderson, editor and translator 1961, Vol. 1, Letter No. 44, pp. 47-8. For a facsimile reproduction of this letter see: Beethoven House, Digital Archives, Library Document, NE 160.

59 Emily Anderson editor and translator, 1961, Vol. 1, Letter No. 199, pp. 217–18.

60 Theodore Albrecht editor and translator, 1996, Vol. 1, Letter No. 35, pp. 64–65.

61 *Ibid*, Vol. 1, Letter No. 37, pp. 68–69. For a facsimile reproduction of this letter, in Karl van Beethoven's hand, combined with a transcription of his text see: Beethoven House, Digital Archives, Library Document, HCB Br 294.

62 Theodore Albrecht editor and translator, 1996, Vol. 1, Letter No. 38, pp. 70–71.

63 *Ibid*, Vol.1, Letter No. 77, pp. 129–30. For a facsimile reproduction of this letter, in Beethoven's hand, combined with a transcription of his text, see: Beethoven House, Digital Archives, Library Document, HCB Br 188.

64 Emily Anderson editor and translator, 1961, Vol. 1, Letter No. 96, pp. 115–17.

65 Theodore Albrecht editor and translator, 1996, Vol. 1, Letter No. 83, pp. 140–41.

66 *Ibid*, Vol. 1, Letter No. 42, pp. 74–76.

67 *Ibid*, Vol. 1, Letter No. 49, pp. 84–85. This letter is the only surviving proof of Beethoven's negotiations with André's publishing house. See also: Beethoven House, Digital Archives, Library Document, BH 147.

68 *Ibid*, Vol. 1, Letter No. 52, pp. 90–91. For a facsimile reproduction of this letter, in Beethoven's hand, combined with a transcription of his text, see: Beethoven House, Digital Archives, Library Document, HCB Br 301.

69 Theodore Albrecht editor and translator, 1996, Vol. 1, Letter No. 53, pp. 92–94.

70 *Ibid*, Vol. 1, Letter No. 56, p. 98.

71 *Ibid*, Vol. 1, Letter No. 57, pp. 99–100. For a facsimile reproduction of this letter in Beethoven's hand, combined with a transcription of his text, see: Beethoven House, Digital Archives, Library Document, HCB Br 303.

72 For other evaluations of Beethoven's creative output, bearing on the period under consideration as expressed in relation to his negotiations with various publishers, see: Elliot Forbes, 1967, p. 362; Peter Clive, 2001, pp. 200–01; Barry Cooper, 1991, p. 193, and Barry Cooper 1991, p. 193.

73 Theodore Albrecht editor and translator, 1996, Vol. 1, Letter No. 58, pp. 100–03.

74 *Ibid*, Vol. 1, Letter No. 57, pp. 102–03.

[75] *Ibid*, Vol. 1, Letter No. 60, pp. 103–04.

[76] *Ibid*, Vol. 1, Letter No. 61, pp. 104–05.

[77] *Ibid*, Vol. 1, Letter No. 63, pp. 107–08.

[78] *Ibid*, Vol. 1, Letter No. 65, pp. 110–13.

[79] Emily Anderson, editor and translator 1961, Vol. 1, Letter No. 44, pp. 47-8. For a facsimile reproduction of this letter see: Beethoven House, Digital Archives, Library Document, NE 160.

[80] Emily Anderson, editor and translator 1961, Vol. 1, Letter No. 90, pp. 109–10.

[81] Theodore Albrecht editor and translator, 1996, Vol. 1, Letter No. 70, pp. 118–19.

[82] *Ibid*, Vol. 1, Letter No. 71, pp. 119–22.

[83] *Ibid*, Vol. 1, Letter No. 74, pp. 123–25.

[84] *Ibid*, Vol. 1, Letter No. 75, pp. 125–27.

[85] Quoted, with adaptations, from Adam von Ahnen Carse, *The Orchestra from Beethoven to Berlioz: A History of the Orchestra in the First Half of the 19th century, and of the Development of Orchestral Baton-Conducting*, 1948, pp. 430–31.

[86] Jonathan del Mar, *Critical Commentary to Symphonie Nr. 2 in D-dur*, Bärenreiter Kassel, Basel, undated.

[87] For a facsimile reproduction of the second horn part of the Second Symphony, published by the *Bureau des arts et d'Industrie*, see: Beethoven House Digital Archives, Document HCB C Md 1, C 36/51.

[88] Armin Raab, Preface to: *Beethoven, Symphonie, Nr.* 2, G. Henle G. Henle, Verllag, München, *Gesamtausgabe*, 1994.

[89] For a facsimile reproduction of the Title Page of the Bureau des Arts et d'Industrie score edition of the Second Symphony, see: Beethoven House Digital Archives, Library Document HCB C Md 1 C 36/51.

[90] For a facsimile reproduction of a portrait of Karl Lichnowsky, see: Beethoven House Digital Archives, Library Document B 2423.

[91] Anne-Louise Coldicott, *Performance Practice in Beethoven's Day* in: Barry Cooper, *The Beethoven Compendium: A Guide to Beethoven's Life and Music*, 1991, pp. 280–09.

[92] Quoted by Armin Raab, Preface to: *Beethoven, Symphonie, Nr.* 2, G. Henle, Verllag, München, *Gesamtausgabe*, 1994.

[93] Emily Anderson editor and translator, 1961, Vol. 3, Letter No. 1545, p. 1325.

[94] Roger Norrington, Liner notes *Beethoven, Symphonies 1 & 6*, The London Classical Players, EMI CDC 7497462, 1988.

[95] Adam von Ahn Carse, W. Heffer, 1948, pp. 426–27, and pp. 430–31.

[96] Quoted, with adaptations, from Jonathan del Mar, *Critical Commentary to Symphonie Nr. 2 in D-dur*, Bärenreiter Kassel, Basel, undated.

[97] Theodore Albrecht editor and translator, 1996, Vol. 2, Letter No. 285, pp. 203–04.

[98] Jonathan del Mar, *Critical Commentary to Symphonie Nr. 2 in D-dur*, Bärenreiter Kassel, Basel, undated. See also: Elliot Forbes editor, *Thayer's Life of Beethoven*, 1967 p. 817.ß

[99] Pamela J. Willetts, *Beethoven and England: An Account of Sources in the British Museum*, British Museum, 1970., pp. 26–27.

[100] Jonathan del Mar, *Critical Commentary to Symphonie Nr. 2 in D-dur*, Bärenreiter Kassel, Basel, undated.

[101] For a facsimile reproduction of the Cianchettini & Sperati's Score edition of

the Second Symphony, see: Beethoven House Digital Archives, Library Document HCB C Md 120.

[102] Jonathan del Mar, *Critical Commentary to Symphonie Nr. 2 in D-dur*, Bärenreiter Kassel, Basel, undated.

RECEPTION
HISTORY

Beethoven enjoyed the benefit of having early performances of his orchestral music performed before
receptive musicians and music connoisseurs. These took
place at informal gatherings in the great salons of his
patrons Prince Lichnowsky and Prince Lobkowitz. Over
time, with public performances of the symphonies taking
place in Vienna and further afar in Leipzig and Berlin,
reviews of the composer's music were published in such
journals as the *Allgemeine musikalische Zeitung*. With
the benefit of repeated hearings, Beethoven's orchestral
music became more favourably assimilated and understood. For example, in 1818 the English musician
Cipriani Potter visited Vienna, became acquainted with
Beethoven, and wrote of his meeting with the composer
and of the reception of his music: '[It] is now listened to

with an attention and delight that his real friends and admirers could scarcely have anticipated.' Potter's testimony was later published in 1861 as *Recollections of Beethoven, with Remarks on his Style*, in issue 226 of the London *The Musical Times*. And in 1821, fellow Englishman John Russell (not to be confused with the diplomat Lord John Russell) recorded his impressions of music-making on the continent in his *A Tour of Germany and some of the Provinces* in which he records: 'Beethoven is the most celebrated of living composer's in Vienna, and in certain departments, the foremost of his day.'[1]

In our discussion of the reception history of Beethoven's Second Symphony in D major, Op. 36, we first consider the response to the music following its performance in concerts held during Beethoven's lifetime. We then proceed to cite its reception through the medium of transcriptions for the piano and small instrumental ensembles. Our survey then considers reception in the nineteenth century, including early reception in France (Paris) and England, notably through the concerts promoted by the fledgling Philharmonic Society of London. We conclude by making reference to later nineteen-century reception and that expressed nearer to own time.

RECEPTION IN BEETHOVEN'S LIFETIME:
CONCERT PERFORMANCES
1803

We learn of Beethoven's preparations for a performance of the Second Symphony from a note he sent to Ferdinand Ries in March. Ries was then acting as Beethoven's copyist and he asked him to check through the score for errors — and 'to be careful'. This is the score that, as we have noted, he later gave to Ries but which was subsequently lost.[2] The recorded performance of the Second Symphony took place on 5 April 1803, but some authorities believe it may have had an earlier run through at a private performance held at Prince Lichnowsky's Vienna's apartments or in the house of some other nobleman.[3]

Beethoven's forthcoming public concert was announced in the *Wiener Zeitung* of 26 March and 30 March: 'On the 4 April, Herr Ludwig van Beethoven will produce a new Oratorio, set to music by him, *Christus am Ölberge* in the Theater an der Wien.' This calls for a number of remarks. First, in their enthusiasm to announce the concert the journal got the date wrong — the concert took place on 5 April 1803. Second, under the auspices of Emmanuel Schikaneder — impresario and owner of the Theater an der Wien — Beethoven, then living on the premises, was in effect the house composer. Third, and of greater significance, is that the announcement gave prominence to Beethoven's new choral work — with no mention of the other works to be performed, namely, the First and Second Symphonies and the Third Piano Concerto. The event was nothing less than an 'all Beethoven' concert. It is not surprising that the Oratorio should feature prominently in the concert announcement. Here was the young Beethoven daring to compete with his teacher Haydn — revered and the acknowledged master of the oratorio genre.

This was Beethoven's first public appearance as a dramatic vocal composer and he was determined to make a favourable impression by having the concert acknowledged as a significant event in Vienna's musical calendar. With this in mind, the *Allgemeine musikalische Zeitung* made it known that ticket prices would be raised — as they had been done at the Burgtheater for the Tonkünstler-Societät performances of Haydn's oratorios. For Beethoven's concert, seats at the front of the house were doubled, those for reserved seats were tripled, and boxes were charged at twelve florins instead of the usual two florins.[4]

The rehearsal for the concert did not go well — at least initially. We learn this from an account left by Ries who called on Beethoven at five o'clock in the morning of the concert only to find him in bed — not asleep but writing on sheets of manuscript paper. Reis relates:

'To my question as to "What it was?" he answered — "trombones". The trombones [were] also played from *these* sheets at the concert ... The rehearsal began at eight o'clock in the morning ... It was a terrible rehearsal, and at half past two everybody was exhausted and more or less dissatisfied. Prince Karl Lichnowsky, who attended the rehearsal from the beginning, had sent for bread and butter, cold meat and wine, in large baskets. He pleasantly asked all to help themselves, and this was done with both hands, the result being that good nature was restored again. Then the Prince requested that the Oratorio be rehearsed once more from the beginning, so that it might go well in the evening and Beethoven's first work in this genre be worthily presented. And so the rehearsal began again.'[5]

When Ries finally heard the Second Symphony performed, the second movement in particular moved him, disposing him to remark:

'There was something most striking about the *Larghetto quasi andante* of the Symphony in D ... The *Larghetto* is so beautifully, so purely and

happily conceived and the melodic line so natural
that one can hardly imagine anything in it was ever
changed.'[6]

Despite the high seat prices — that may have deterred some
— the concert was a financial success for Beethoven. He made
a profit of 1800 florins — about the equivalent that a bachelor
resident in Vienna required to live by — albeit, modestly.[7]
Contemporary notices of Beethoven's music were, however,
somewhat muted in their praise. The music critic for the
journal *Der Freymüthige* — who was probably the distinguished dramatist August von Kotzebue — reported:

'True, the two symphonies and single passages in
the Oratorio were voted very beautiful, but the
[Oratorio] in its entirety was too long, too artificial
in structure and lacking expressiveness especially
in the vocal parts.'

He elaborated:

'Even the valiant Beethofen [sic] ... was not quite
happy and was not able, despite the efforts of
numerous admirers, to obtain much applause.
Both the symphonies and parts of the Oratorio
were received with approval but the whole was
too drawn out, too contrived in construction and
lacking in expressive relevance, especially in the
vocal writing.'[8]

More supportively, Andreas Streicher, the celebrated piano-
maker and friend of Beethoven, writing in the *Allgemeine
musikalische Zeitung* generously stated

'It confirms my long-held opinion that Beethoven can, in time, effect just such a revolution in music as did Mozart. He hastens to his goal with great strides.'

Streicher was not impressed, though, by *Christus am Ölberge*, considering it 'needed more characterisation and a better thought-out plan'.[9]

A review appeared in the Journal *Zeitung für die elegante Welt* on 7 April 1803 describing 'public concerts in Vienna'. The main work mentioned was once more the Oratorio *Christus am Ölberge*, the libretto to which was criticised, but prompted the reviewer to comment: 'Herr van Beethoven showed that a composer of genius is capable of making something great from the worst material'. The reviewer considered the First Symphony to be more worthy than the Second because it was performed 'with unforced ease', but conceded in the Second Symphony 'a striving for novel and striking effects is more visible'.[10]

1804
Writing of the year 1804, Thayer remarks:

> 'The First Symphony had hardly left Hoffmeister's press when it was added to the repertory of the Gewandhaus Concerts at Leipzig, and during the three following years was repeatedly performed at Berlin, Breslau, Brunswick, Dresden, Frankfurt-am-Main, and Munich.'

The Gewandhaus Orchestra performed the Second Symphony in 1804 and remained a staunch supporter of the composer's orchestral music, performing the *Eroica*

Symphony in 1807 and in 1809 the *Pastoral* Symphony was heard together with the C minor Symphony. The Gewandhaus Orchestra also featured the *Choral* Symphony in its 1826 concert season. Reflecting on Beethoven's achievements for the year 1804 disposed Thayer to enthuse:

> 'Beethoven, then, although almost unknown personally beyond the limits of a few Austrian cities — unaided by apostles to preach his gospel, owing nothing to journalist or pamphleteer ... had, in the short space of eight years, by the simple force of his genius as manifested in his published works, placed himself at the head of all writers for the pianoforte, and in public estimation had risen to the level of the two greatest of orchestral composers. The unknown student that entered Vienna in 1792, was now in 1804 a recognised member of the great triumvirate, Haydn, Mozart and Beethoven.[11]

The D major Symphony was performed on 27 March in a performance that was later reviewed on 9 May in the *Allgemeine musikalische Zeitung.*[12] The music correspondent opened his account in a manner that conveys the respect Beethoven was now receiving as an orchestral composer:

> 'It cannot be a matter of indifference to any society of musicians and friends of art that at last a second symphony by Beethoven has just now appeared (engraved in Vienna by the Kunst- und Industrie-Comptoir).'

The unprecedented scale of the composition was clearly uppermost in the correspondent's mind as he enthused:

> 'It is a colossal work, of a depth power, and artistic knowledge like *very few*. [*AmZ*'s italics] It has a level of difficulty, both from the point of view of the composer and in regard to its performance by a large orchestra (which it certainly demands), quite certainly unlike *any* symphony that has ever been made known. It demands to be played again and yet again by even the most accomplished orchestra, until the astonishing number of original and sometimes very strangely arranged ideas become closely enough connected, rounded out, and emerge like a great unity, just as the composer had in mind. It must also be heard again and again before the listener, even a knowledgeable one, is in a position to follow the details in the entire piece and the entire piece in the details to enjoy it with enthusiasm in the necessary sense.'[13]

Anton Schindler refers to a concert held in the summer of 1804 at the Augarten in which the Second Symphony was performed together with the C minor Piano Concerto. Of the Symphony his writes:

> 'An interval of four years had elapsed between the first performance of the C major Symphony and this new one, enough time for the creative and ambitious artist to free himself entirely from Mozart's style and to evolve his own. This new work is proof of Beethoven's vigorous independ-

ence, yet this emancipation had already exhibited itself in Beethoven's previous chamber music.'

In support of his latter assertion Schindler cites

'the pronounced personal style in melody and phrase stricture in the Piano Sonatas Op. 2, Op. 7, and Op. 10 not to mention the *Pathétique* and the six String Quartets, Op. 18'.[14]

On 15 August the music correspondent of the *Allgemeine musikalische Zeitung* referred to the Augarten concert in an article titled 'News from Vienna'. On this occasion he was somewhat less fulsome in his praise:

'The concert began with Beethoven's Grand Symphony in D major, a work full of new, original ideas, of great power, effective instrumentation and learned development, which, however, would benefit from shortening of some passages and by sacrifice of many modulations that are far too strange.'

At the same concert Ferdinand Ries performed the composer's C minor Piano Concerto, Op. 37 that the music critic found closer to his taste, disposing him to remark: 'This Concerto belongs incontestably among Beethoven's most beautiful compositions.' Of interest is that Beethoven allowed Ries to include a cadenza of his own composition. This included some brilliant and difficult passage-work that Ries brought off so successfully it induced Beethoven, on its successful execution, to loudly exclaim "Bravo". Ries records: 'This electrified the entire audience and at once gave me a standing among the artists.'[15]

Later in the year, on 28 November, the music critic of the *Allgemeine musikalische Zeitung* reported 'Details of Concert Music in Berlin'. The Second Symphony was played once more which the critic in question believed to be 'the most difficult problem that can be posed for an orchestra', particularly 'for an orchestra that has not constantly practised together'. That said, the critic considered the players confronted the challenges Beethoven had set them 'famously'. He praised: the violins for their 'uniformity, precision and fire'; the violas and bases 'for being prompt'; the 'distinguished playing' of the flute and horns — but he considered the bassoon to be 'too strong'. With regard to the composition as a whole, he concluded — with a sting in the tale: '[There] is much originality, richness, and often a surplus of harmony and occasionally, however, bizarrerie'.

Of the music itself, the critic commented discerningly:

> 'The Symphony begins impressively with a short largo, alternating with cantabile solo phrases by the winds, and then proceeds to a modulating allegro. The *Andante quasi allegro* in A flat has a very pleasant melody and a broad working-out. The minuet with trio is entirely new and even small features such as the short horn solo, which enters in the middle, have a special effect. The last presto occasionally becomes wild, but it is worked out exquisitely.'

As for the audience's reaction he states:

> 'The applause by the connoisseurs expressed gratitude to the musicians for surmounting the difficulties well and for performing them for nearly three-quarters of an hour.'[16]

We opened our account of the year 1804 with remarks made by Beethoven's biographer Alexander Thayer. We enter into the same spirit with further of his observations. At the close of the year Beethoven could reflect on having secured the support of several music publishers in bringing forth several major compositions, namely: the Symphony No. 2 in D major, Op. 36, by Kunst- und Industrie-Comptoir (Bureau des Arts et d'Industrie) in Vienna; the Overture to the Ballet *Die Geschöpfe des Prometheus*, Op. 13 and the Variations for Piano, Violin and Cello, Op. 44, by Hoffmeister and Kühnel in Leipzig; and the Piano Sonata, Op. 31, No. 3, by Nägeli in Zurich.

1805

The *Allgemeine musikalische Zeitung* opened the New Year 1805 with its 2 January issue that contained an article titled 'Music in Leipzig, Christmas 1804'. The Journal's music critic reflected that two recent performances of Beethoven's Second Symphony had enabled the audience to enjoy the work *completely* (*AmZ's* italics) 'despite its great difficulties'. He elaborated on what he considered to be the work's defects, but closed with words that have proved to be prophetic:

> 'As has been observed in Vienna and Berlin, we also find the entire piece too long and some details overworked. We would also like to add that the all too frequent use of all the wind instruments impedes the effect of many beautiful passages, and the finale strikes, even now after closer acquaintance, as all too bizarre, wild and shrill. But all of this is far outweighed by the powerful spirit that breathes in this colossal work,

by the breadth of new ideas and their almost totally original treatment, as well as by the depth of artistic knowledge, that one can cast the work's horoscope and find that it will remain and be heard with ever new satisfaction when a thousand currently celebrated fashionable pieces have long since been dead and buried.'[17]

On 26 April an article appeared the *AmZ's* sister journal *Der Freimüthige*. Published in Berlin, it was a journal dedicated to a survey of the arts in general for 'serious and impartial readers'. The journal's music correspondent had recently heard a performance of the *Eroica* Symphony. Although this work is outside of our present discussion, what he had to say sheds light on the disposition of audiences at this time for and against Beethoven's orchestral music.

ADVOCATES:
'One party, Beethoven's most special friends, contend that this particular Symphony [No. 3, *Eroica*] is a masterpiece, that this is exactly the true style for music of the highest type and that if it does not please now it is because the public is not sufficiently cultivated in the arts to comprehend these higher spheres of beauty; but after a couple of hundred years its effect will not be lessened.'

OPPOSITION:
'The other party absolutely denies any artistic merit in the work. They claim it reveals symptoms of an evidently unbridled attempt at distinction and peculiarity, but that neither beauty, true

sublimity nor power have anywhere been achieved either by means of unusual modulations, by violent transitions or by the juxtaposition of the most heterogenous elements.'

THIRD PARTY:
'The third, very small party, stand in the middle. They concede that there are many beautiful things in the Symphony, but admit that the continuity often appears to be completely confused and that the endless duration of this longest and perhaps most difficult of all symphonies is tiring even for the expert; for a mere amateur it is unbearable.'

The reviewer chastised Beethoven for using three horns, regarding this as an undesirable trick, and asserted that the creation of something beautiful and sublime was the true expression of genius and not 'something merely unusual and fantastic'. The contributor acknowledged Beethoven himself, in his own early works, had demonstrated this but he complained:

'One wishes that H[err] v[an] B[eethoven] would use his recognised great talent to present us with works similar to his first two Symphonies in C and D, to his spirited Septet in E flat ... and other of his early compositions which will assure B. a place among the foremost instrumental composers.'

The reviewer also recognised Beethoven's independence of mind:

'One fears, however, that if Beethoven continues along this road, he and the public will make a bad journey ... Overwhelmed by a mass of disconnected ideas and by a continuing tumult of all the instruments, the listener would leave the concert hall with only an unpleasant feeling of exhaustion.'[18]

1806

On 1 April, Beethoven wrote to the opera singer Freidrich Mayer. He asked Meyer if he would ask Ignaz von Seyfried if he would conduct a performance of his Opera *Fidelio* on his behalf. What Beethoven also had to say suggests the standard of orchestral playing left much to be desired. He resolved to keep his distance from the orchestra so that his patience would not then 'be so severely tried, as it would be if I were near the orchestra and had to listen to the murdering of my music'; clearly, Beethoven still had sufficient hearing in order to be able to comprehend a full orchestra. He continued:

'I shall not say anything about the wind instruments but — that all the *pianissimos* and *crescendos*, all the *decrescendos* and all the *fortes* and *fortissimos* should have been deleted from my opera!'

Beethoven concluded by demanding a further rehearsal warning: 'If not, things will be worse every day!' Beethoven had cause to feel let down in view of the care he took with the presentation of his scores. Emily Anderson, from whom we have just quoted, remarks: '[Beethoven's] superb attention to detail, with all kinds of signs to indicate dynamics, tempi, and attacks, is obvious in all of his scores.'[19]

In May 1805 the Bureau des Arts et d'Industrie published an arrangement of the Second Symphony for piano violin and cello that was reviewed in the 1 October 1806 issue of the *Allgemeine musikalische* Zeitung. The reviewer first acknowledged the D major Symphony was 'rightly celebrated' and intimated who might benefit from the piano-trio arrangement. He suggested, in this form it would help the better understanding of what he described as 'this very difficult work' and help those hearing or performing it 'to repeat the pleasure of the complete performance'. For these reasons, he encouraged the reduction to three instruments should 'in many respects be received with thanks'. He had reservations though. He considered the *Andante* lost 'the *opposition* of string and wind instruments' and 'the charm and distinctive characteristics of specific instruments'. The reviewer also considered the last movement's 'tumultuous, wild adventurousness' could not be arranged satisfactorily. That said, his final verdict was to acknowledge

'one would hardly have believed that, in regard to the major points, [an arrangement] so satisfactory and yet so well suited to all three instruments could be made'.[20]

According to the Title Page, the Trio had been prepared 'by the composer himself'. Regarding this, Carl Czerny recalls the trio version of the Second Symphony was the work of Ferdinand Ries and that he himself made a number of arrangements that were corrected by Beethoven and then sold by his brother Carl. The inference being that the music was allowed to pass as though it had been arranged by the composer himself.[21] We consider other arrangements of the Second Symphony in due course.

Following a bitter quarrel with his patron Prince Lichnowsky — Beethoven refused Lichnowsky's request to perform for a group of visiting French Soldiers — he stayed for a period in Silesia, at the Castle of Count Franz von Oppersdorff, a keen lover of music who maintained an accomplished orchestra. Whilst staying with Oppersdorff the Count had his musicians perform the Second Symphony; some authorities suggest he may also have heard the work played through when Beethoven was staying with Prince Lichnowsky at his summer residence near Troppau. In any event, such was the outcome that Oppersdorff commissioned a further symphony from the composer — the Fourth in B-flat major— for which, after the customary payment (in this case of 500 florins), he received the dedication.

1808

A series of concerts was established in Vienna for the 1807—08 concert season, known as the *Liebhaber-Concerte* — 'Music-Lover's Concert'. These were promoted by Johann von Häring, a banker who was recognised for being one of Vienna's foremost amateur violinists; he had the distinction of performing chamber music with Mozart. A measure of his standing is that he possessed instruments by Amati, Guarneri, and Stradivarius. Häring made a significant contribution to Viennese musical life and was elected director (leader) of the orchestra when the *Liebhaber-Concerte* commenced.

Häring had an excellent command of English and assisted Beethoven in his negotiations with publishers such as George Thomson, of Scotland (Edinburgh) and influential musical figures in England such as Sir George Smart — a founder member of the Philharmonic Society of London. It was Häring who wrote a long letter to Smart on Beethoven's behalf, sometime between 16—19 March 1815, offering for sale in England several of

Beethoven's recently composed works. These included: the then immensely popular *Battle Symphony* or *Battle of Vittoria*, in full score for 70 guineas, or as arranged for piano for 30 guineas; and the equally popular Seventh Symphony, also offered for 70 guineas in full score, or as arranged for piano for 30 guineas. For some reason he offered the *Pastoral* Symphony for the reduced price of 40 guineas in full score and 20 guineas as arranged for piano.[22]

A number of the *Liebhaber-Concerte* were directed by the celebrated violinist Franz Clement, known to Beethovenians for premiering his Violin Concerto. In the opening concert season 1807–08, Clement directed performances of Beethoven's First, Second, and Fourth Symphonies as well as his First Piano Concerto.[23]

From Thayer we learn:

'The audiences were composed exclusively of the nobility of the town and foreigners of note, and among these classes the preference was given to the cognoscenti and amateurs ... [In] twenty meetings, symphonies, overtures, concertos, and vocal pieces were performed zealously and were received with general approval ... The works of Beethoven reported as having been performed in these concerts are the Symphony in D (in the first concert) ... the *Eroica* Symphony ... in December, and [in the] New Year, the Fourth Symphony which was also played on 15 November in the Burgtheater at a concert for the public charities. Most, if not all of these works were directed [conducted] by the composer.'[24]

Between 12 November 1807 and 27 March 1808, some twenty concerts were given in Vienna by the newly formed *Gesellschaft von Musikfreunden*. Ten of the concerts included Beethoven Symphonies: Nos. One, Two, and Three were each performed twice alongside his Piano Concerto No. 1, and the Overture *Coriolan* – also performed twice. For these performances an orchestra of 55 players assembled who included the violinist Franz Clement.[25] For these concerts the orchestra typically consisted of 13 first violins,12 second violins, 7 violas, 6 cellos, 4 double basses, and a single compliment of woodwind.[26]

1811

The Italian violinist Giuseppe Cambini lived Paris for a period and from there he contributed articles to the *Allgemeine musikalische Zeitung* and the *Tablettes de Polymnie*. Writing in the latter, in 1811, he remarked on the impression made on him after hearing Beethoven's first two symphonies:

> 'The composer Beethoven, often bizarre and baroque, sometimes sparkles with extraordinary beauties. Now he takes the majestic flight of the eagle, then he creeps along grotesque paths. After penetrating the soul with a sweet melancholy, he soon tears it by a mass of barbaric chords. He seems to harbour doves and crocodiles at the same time.'[27]

The Second Symphony was performed in Munich during May 1811 and later in December 'with general and completely deserved approval'. The correspondent of the *Allgemeine musikalische Zeitung*, however, regretted 'the works of this composer, unique in his own way, are as yet not known well enough here'. He elaborated:

> 'People are accustomed to Haydn's and Mozart's works and should not be surprised if these rare products of Beethoven, which diverge so greatly from what is customary, don't always produce their effect on the listener.'

Despite this, the *AmZ's* correspondent sought to reassure his readers by acknowledging the 'glowing fantasy and high flight of powerful, ingenious harmonies' he found prevailing in Beethoven's music. He concluded by asking: 'Why do we expect [Beethoven] always to flatter the ear, never to unsettle us, and raise us above the customary even if somewhat forcefully?'[28]

1817

A letter the Edinburgh publisher George Thomson wrote to Beethoven on 25 June 1817 offers evidence of the composer's growing international reputation. Thomson had been negotiating with Beethoven regarding his setting to music of various Scottish airs. Whilst he found the composer's piano writing 'charming' he complained 'for the Scottish people [they are] filled with too many notes, too difficult for the hand, and for the metre [tempo]'. Thomson requested Beethoven to write 'simpler and more resembling the style of the melodies'. Of greater relevance to our narrative is what Thomson later has to say:

> 'I do not need to tell you with what enthusiasm I admire your works: I am transported by them, and there is nothing in the world that I desire more than to make a pilgrimage to

Vienna to see you, and hear your Masses, your Sonatas, your Symphonies, and your Quartets performed by the great musicians of your country; for alas! most of them are too difficult for Edinburgh. In Vienna, I would believe myself in Heaven!'[29]

1819–1820

On 1 October 1819, a new concert series was started in Vienna that came to be known as the *Concerts Spirituels*. Their founder was Franz Xaver Gebauer, choir Director and organist at the Augustinian Church. The correspondent of the 5 April 1820 issue of the *Allgemeine musikalische Zeitung* noted:

'Herr Gebauer makes the proposal to form a special society of a moderate number to bring to performance only symphonies and choruses excluding all virtuoso music [pure display music] and bravura singing.'

The 'moderate number' refers to the performers who were all amateurs and who performed largely from sight. In the eighteen concerts of the first season Beethoven's first four symphonies were performed together with the *Pastoral* Symphony. The second season (1820–21) consisted of ten concerts that included the Symphonies in C minor, Op. 67, A major, Op. 92, and F major, Op. 93.

Since the players were performing from sight, it is not surprising the reviewer, commenting on the performance at the 9 April concert, felt obliged to report to Beethoven: 'I forgot to tell you that the dilettantes scraped through your symphony [unspecified] yesterday.'[30] Despite Beethoven having the satisfaction of knowing his symphonies were being performed, in a letter he wrote sometime in April 1820 to the publisher Sigmund Anton Steiner, he referred to these performances as *Winkelmusik* — a pejorative term suggesting incompetence.[31]

The *Gesellschaft von Musikfreunden* has been mentioned. Writing of its contribution to Vienna's musical scene, and the advancement of Beethoven's symphonic writing, David Wyn Jones comments:

> 'From 1819 onwards, musical life in Vienna acquired a public concert life that was at last characterised by stability and durability. The *Gesellschaft von Musikfreunden* was proving to be an institution of permanence ... with ten years of its founding it was already an institution of real consequence ... [with its] annual pattern of four vocal and orchestral concerts in the winter season. Held in the *Grosser Redoutensaal* ... Beethoven's presence as a symphonist [was] overwhelming.'[32]

For the period 1819—28, twenty performances of Beethoven's symphonies were given. The Second Symphony was performed in 1819, 1823, 1826, and 1827. The concert for 1828 was memorable for the inclusion of Schubert's Sixth Symphony alongside that of Beethoven's Fifth and Sixth Symphonies, a circumstance that would have given inestimable pleasure to Schubert had he been alive to experience the event — he passed away the previous month.

In its 22 July 1820 issue of the *Allgemeine musikalische Zeitung*, the music correspondent reported on a gathering of the Swiss Music Society in Basel. It had recently performed the Second Symphony 'with great precision by a large orchestra' (not identified). This disposed the correspondent to enthuse:

> 'The magnificent effect this direction brought forth gave proof that Beethoven's symphonies must be performed by such a large orchestra in order to unfold properly the greatness interest in them and proclaim the power of music with an irresistible rush.'[33]

1822

In the summer of 1822 the playwright and musicologist Friedrich Rochlitz was in Vienna and was eager to meet Beethoven. Following his eventual encounter with him he wrote of the experience to the publisher Gottfried Härtel. In his first letter, of 28 June, he related to Härtel he had told Beethoven of the admiration and enthusiasm felt for his symphonies in his hometown Leipzig. According to Rochlitz, Beethoven appeared to listen attentively, smiling on occasions, but It was only later Rochlitz realized Beethoven had not heard anything of what he was saying. In his second letter to Härtel, of 9 July, Rochlitz explained the two had communicated with the help of the composer's notebook that he kept close by for this purpose. It was then he learned of the composer's sense of isolation and disillusionment regarding the public perception — as he believed — of his music.

According to Rochlitz, Beethoven remarked, with some feeling:

> 'You will hear nothing of me here ... What should you hear? *Fidelio*? They cannot give it, nor do they want to listen to it. The symphonies? They

have no time for them. The concertos? Everyone grinds out only the stuff he himself has made. The solo pieces? They went out of fashion here long ago and here fashion is everything.' Despite Rochlitz thinking Beethoven may have exaggerated somewhat, on the basis of his own experience, he added 'a modicum of reason and truth remains'.[34]

In November the *Allgemeine musikalische Zeitung* included an article in which its music correspondent reflected on the nature of the symphony:

> 'The symphony is a tone painting that is produced through the collaboration of orchestral instruments. The masters who have devoted themselves to this genre, and they are the greatest composers of our nation, have elevated German orchestras greatly by the demands made on instruments in their symphonies.'

The author of the piece recognized the challenges posed by the new symphonic compositions had, in turn, served as a stimulus to the development of the virtuosity of the instrumentalists. In this regard, he cited the formative influence of the originality of Beethoven's works but he also recognised: '[The] gigantic works of *Beethoven* [*AmZ's* italics] seem to frighten off his descendants in this area.' These words proved to be prophetic when we recall how, years later, Brahms found Beethoven's symphonic legacy so intimidating — until he found the confidence to give expression to his own symphonic voice.[35]

The German music theorist and musicologist Adolf Bernhard Marx is remembered today for his pioneering biography *Ludwig van Beethoven: Leben und Schaffen* (Berlin, 1859). He was also the founder of the *Berliner Allgemeine musikalische Zeitung* — sister journal to Leipzig's contemporary Journal the *Allgemeine musikalische Zeitung.* In the 12 May 1824 issue of the Berliner *AmZ,* Marx wrote an extensive article titled 'A few words on the symphony and Beethoven's achievements in this field'. Marx first remarked on 'the numerous performances of Beethoven's symphonies in Berlin' — testimony to their having been assimilated into the symphony-concert repertoire. He acknowledged Beethoven's debt to his predecessors, notably, Haydn and Mozart of which he states:

> 'In the areas of the sonata and symphony, Beethoven began at Mozart's level, and his first outpourings can be called lyrical, even though the feeling in them was expressed more definitely and more intimately. Even if many a moment shone forth more freshly and brightly than in the more gentle Mozart and echoed the Haydn school, and even if a greater, more deeply founded unity became manifest in Beethoven's compositions.'

In his discussion of the progress of the symphony, Marx reflected on developments in its construction:

> 'Its novelty was expressed, as it were, in various directions (keys) and configurations (fragments and so forth) until it assumed its most appropriate position ... in the principal key. To this more richly developed section was added ... a conclud-

ing section, representing the principal idea. Above all, however, the minuet — usually under the name *scherzo* — was elevated to an essential part of the entire piece.'

Marx concluded by positioning Beethoven's early symphonic writing within this framework:

'To this period belong Beethoven's Symphonies in C major [No. 1, Op, 21] and D major [No.2, Op. 36]. The first can be called Mozartian without hesitation; the second is written in a similar spirit, but is expanded more and therefor goes beyond Mozartian symphonies in size.'[36]

TRANSCRIPTIONS

Transcriptions of Beethoven's symphonies began to appear soon after their composition. In the form of piano-duet arrangements (reductions), they gave access to the music to the accomplished amateur. As ensembles — in the form of arrangements for various combinations of wind and string instruments — they provided audiences with an opportunity to experience the music in venues not frequented by a full orchestra. Mozart, for example, transcribed music from his operas *Don Giovani* and *The Marriage of Figaro* for small wind ensemble.

Beethoven appears to have been content to leave transcriptions of his symphonies to others — provided they did not appear under his name. For example, in 1807 a set of seven waltzes were published by an unknown arranger, one of which was derived from the *scherzo* of the Second Symphony. In the same year, twelve short pieces were also published, now known, spuriously, as Beethoven's Twelve Ecossaises, WoO 16, the first of which is an unauthorised arrangement of part of the First Symphony. Although these compositions were not sanctioned by Beethoven, they bear testimony to the popularity of his orchestral music and the preparedness of lesser composers to exploit it.[37]

The Beethoven-Ries Trio transcription of the Second Symphony has been mentioned. In 1807 Ries followed this with an arrangement for nonet (2 violins, 2 violas, cello, double bass, flute, 2 horns) or quintet (2 violins, 2 violas, cello), both of which were published by Nikolaus Simrock. Of particular interest is that in the same year the London-based Monzani & Co. published an anonymous string-septet arrangement (2 violins, flute, 2 violas, cello and double bass) — testimony to Beethoven's growing fame overseas. Two years later Carl Friedrich Ebers followed with a further nonet arrangement (2 violins, 2 violas, double bass, 2 oboes and 2 horns) published by Johan Anton André. Anton Diabelli — of *Diabelli Variations* fame — prepared an arrangement for two pianos, published by Anton Steiner in 1810 and Breitkopf & Härtel published a similar arrangement by Friedrich Mockwitz in 1816.

The Second Symphony continued to be transcribed and arranged throughout the nineteenth century — additional testimony to the work's popularity. We list a number of these arrangements:

> string quartet (2 violins, viola, cello) by Karl Zulehner, published by Simrock 1828;
>
> quartet ensemble (flute, violin, cello, piano) by Johann Nepomuk Hummel, published by Schott 1826;
>
> quartet ensemble (piano four-hands, violin, cello) by Carl Burchard, published by Breitkoft &Härtel c. 1870;

violin and piano by Hanss Sitt, published by C.
F. Peters (unknown date);

two pianos, eight-hands by August Horn, published by Breitkopf & Härtel (unknown date);

two pianos, eight-hands by Theodor Kirchner,
published by C. F. Peters (unknown date);

two pianos, four-hands by Albert Lavignacy
Théodore Lack, published by Lemoine & Fils
(unknown date);

two pianos, four-hands by Ernst Naumann,
published by Breitkopf & Härtel 1888.[38]

Johann Nepomuk Hummel was celebrated in his day as a
virtuoso pianist and the composer of many works. His
compositions also include arrangements of Beethoven's
symphonies (Nos. 1 — 6) and several of those of Mozart.
These were typically set for piano, flute, violin, and cello
and were well received internationally by such publishers as
Simrock in Bonn, Schott in Mainz, Schlesinger in Paris, and
Chapell in London. In 1826 the Vienna journal *Musikalische Eilpost* reviewed Hummel's arrangement of the
Second Symphony, initially referring to it as 'Beethoven's
magnificent Symphony in D'. Of the arrangement the
Journal's correspondent stated:

'We ... know how exceptionally well Hummel
understands how to write and arrange for the
pianoforte. Thus, it only needs to be said that the
[Symphony No. 2] has appeared in this new form,
that the pianoforte part certainly presents difficulties in the present-day sense of the word. Also, it
certainly does require a capable player, [whereas]
the parts for the three accompanying instruments
are relatively easy.'[39]

After completing his piano studies with Beethoven, Carl Czerny remained on good terms with his teacher and rendered him many services, both personal and musical. For example, Beethoven trusted him to make a piano reduction of the score to his Opera *Fidelio* — that the present writer recalls youthfully attempting to plough through, and failing miserably! Czerny also adapted the score of the Eighth Symphony for two pianos and, rather more conventionally, premiered the *Emperor* Piano Concerto when Beethoven's loss of hearing prevented him from performing it himself. Following Beethoven's death, Czerny made four-hand arrangements of all nine Beethoven symphonies between 1827 and 1829.

Whilst Czerny was an indefatigable pioneer of the art of piano transcription, its undisputed doyen of the genre was Franz Liszt. He was in some measure fortunate. In the early part of the nineteenth century — Liszt's formative years — the piano rose in popularity and became the preferred instrument in the cultivated home for music-making. In the home it began to displace the violin and string-quartet playing — so fashionable in the time of Haydn and Mozart. Four-hand piano transcriptions became a way for amateurs and connoisseurs alike to explore orchestral music through the medium of arrangements for the keyboard. Moreover, the piano was undergoing transformation, being possessed of a more extended keyboard, a stronger frame, and, thereby, improved sonority. As regards Franz Liszt, it was a case of 'cometh the hour, cometh the man'.

In 1837, when Liszt was twenty-six, he completed transcriptions of the Fifth and Sixth Symphonies, published by Breitkopf & Härtel, and the Seventh Symphony, published by Tobias Haslinger. After hearing Liszt play his arrangements of the last three movements of the *Pastoral*

Symphony in Vienna, in November 1839, the German painter Heinrich Adam declared in the *Allgemeine Theaterzeitung* that

> 'only an artist like Liszt, who, in addition to a limitless veneration of Beethoven, possess the rare gift of understanding the great German composer, only such an artist was able, and could venture, to undertake so hazardous an undertaking'.[40]

Liszt next worked on the Third Symphony and, at the request of Breitkopf & Härtel, the First and Second Symphonies. In 1850 he completed the demanding transcription, for two pianos, of the Ninth Symphony published by Mainz B. Schott's Sôhne — a copy of which is one of the present writer's cherished possessions. Following his European tours, with their legendary performance of these and other of his compositions, Breitkopf & Härtel suggested Liszt should publish a set of all the nine symphony piano transcriptions. After some hesitation, given the artistic and intellectual challenges entailed, Liszt accepted the invitation — for which he was paid handsomely at eight francs per page. Liszt finally completed the undertaking in 1865, earning universal recognition, and admiration, for his arrangements that are still regarded as among the most technically demanding piano music ever written.

BEETHOVEN'S EARLY RECEPTION IN FRANCE: PARIS

The early reception to Beethoven's music, in France — and to his symphonies in particular — was ambivalent. His critics considered it to be bizarre and incomprehensible. His devotees, albeit initially a small number, considered it to be no less than representing 'the standard of judgement for, and gateway to, all future developments in music'.[41]

In Paris Beethoven's symphonies first found favour with young musicians — not surprisingly, being open-minded and unburdened with the weight of tradition. Students at the Conservatoire commenced a series of concerts — *Concerts Français* — that they modestly called *Exercises Publics*. Notwithstanding their amateur status, they were assisted by the forward-looking François-Antoine Habeneck. From 1804 he served as their lauréat, initially as their violinist-leader and from 1806 as their conductor. Such was the precision of the students' playing that the correspondent in a contemporary issue of *The Quarterly Music Magazine* enthused: '*The Exercises* of its [the Conservatoire's] pupils are the most brilliant concert's in Paris.'

It is a measure of Habeneck's standing that he joined the orchestra of the Opéra-Comique in 1804 and shortly after moved to the Opéra where he succeed Rudolphe Kreuzer — of Kreuzer Violin Sonata fame — as principal violin. From 1821 to 1824 he was Director of the Opéra. Habeneck's most lasting achievements, though, were the introduction of Beethoven's music to France and the founding of the Société des Concerts du Conservatoire. Adam Carse writes:

'Habeneck, judging that the time was not yet ripe for disclosing the beauties which lay in the works of the great Viennese masters, was in no hurry to force them on an unwilling public, and waited patiently for the moment when he could embark on the plan which he had so much at heart.'[42]

The Second Symphony was performed in 1821 with the *Allegretto* of the then popular Seven Symphony being substituted for the *Larghetto*. In his recollections, the ardent Beethovenian Hector Berlioz states the result was so successful that the entire symphony had to be repeated and met with great applause and that 'after this concert, Beethoven's [French] admirers began to outnumber his detractors'.[43]

During his lifetime, Hector Berlioz was known to the musically-minded public as much for his writing about music as for his own compositions. He gathered some of his writings into three books: *Les Soirées de l'orchestre* (1852), *Les Grotesques de la musique* (1859), and *À travers chants* (1862). In the latter he gives prominence to Beethoven and remarks on the composer's musicology of the Second Symphony:

'Everything in this Symphony is noble, energetic and proud; the introduction (*largo*) is a masterpiece. The most beautiful effects follow in quick succession, always in unexpected ways but without causing any confusion. The melody has a touching solemnity; from the very first bars it commands respect and sets the emotional tone. Rhythms are now more adventurous, the orchestral writing richer, more sonorous and varied. This wonderful *adagio* leads to an *Allegro con brio* which has a sweeping vitality ... The *Andante* is not treated in the same way as that of the First Symphony; instead of a theme developed in canonical imitation it consists of a pure and innocent theme, presented at first plainly by the strings, then exquisitely with delicate strokes; they faithfully reproduce the tender character of the main theme. This is the enchanting depiction of innocent joy, scarcely troubled by passing touches of melancholy. The *Scherzo* is as openly joyful in its capricious fantasy as the *Andante* was completely happy and calm. Everything in this Symphony smiles, and even the martial surges of the first *allegro* are free from any hint of violence; they only speak of the youthful ardour of a noble heart which has preserved intact the most beautiful illusions of life.[44] (See also, below: Elizabeth Csicserry-Ronay, translator and editor, *Hector Berlioz, The art of music and other essays: (À travers chants)*, Indiana University Press, 1994, pp. 12–13.)

BEETHOVEN'S RECEPTION IN ENGLAND: LONDON AND THE PHILHARMONIC SOCIETY

The Philharmonic Society of London was founded in 1813. Its stated aims were 'to promote the performance, in the most perfect manner possible, of the best and most approved instrumental music' and 'to encourage an appreciation by the public in the art of music'. The founding Directors were enterprising insofar as they resolved to promote 'that species of music which called forth the efforts and displayed the genius of the greatest masters'. These included contemporary composers such as Beethoven, Cherubini, and Carl Maria von Weber. Beethoven's pupil Ferdinand Ries was elected a Director of the Society and was active in the promotion of his teacher's symphonies. Perhaps Ries's most significant contribution, in this context, was the role he played, in 1822, in the Philharmonic Society's commissioning of Beethoven's Choral Symphony.

The Second Symphony is first mentioned in the concert programmes of the Philharmonic Society on 13 April 1818 but it was probably performed earlier under the anonymous designation 'Symphony'. Over time, Beethoven's symphonies featured regularly in the concerts of the Society through-out the nineteenth century as the following record indicates: Symphony No. 1, (19); Symphony No. 2, (39); Symphony No. 3, (52); Symphony No. 4, (54); Symphony No. 5; (77); Symphony No. 6; (69); Symphony No. 7, (65); Symphony No. 8, (47); and Symphony No. 9, (73).

The Society gave its first concert in the Argyll Rooms, Regent Street, London on Monday 8 March 1813. The impresario Johann Salomon was the Leader and Muzio Clementi directed at the piano. A Beethoven symphony was performed but was not identified in the records. At the second concert on Monday 15 March another Beethoven symphony was performed, also not identified. At the fourth concert on 3 May, the British-African violinist George Polgreen Bridget-ower took part in a performance of a Beethoven string quartet; Bridgetower is remembered today as the intended dedicatee of the *Kreutzer* Violin Sonata. In this opening season of concerts, J. B. Cramer and Charles Neate — the latter an associate of Beethoven and a founder member of the Society — performed at the pianoforte. On 21 June another Beethoven symphony was performed. Authorities consider these 'anonymous' entries in the Society's records refer to one or other of the composer's Symphonies 1–4.

The *Eroica* Symphony made its first appearance at a concert of the Philharmonic Society on Monday 28 Febru-ary 1814. This was not, though, the first English perform-ance. The Symphony had been premiered on 26 March 1807 at the Covent Garden Theatre. By way of interest, it was performed in Boston, on 17 April 1810, by the newly founded Boston Philharmonic Society. The 1815 Philhar-monic music season was significant insofar as the Society purchased from Beethoven, for the considerable sum of £200, the performing rights for three Overtures. These were, incorporating Beethoven's sub-titles: *King Stephen* — 'To

Hungary's first benefactor'; *The Ruins of Athens*, and *Overture in C— The Consecration of the House*— 'Written for the opening of the Josephstädter Theater'.

The Society performed the Fifth Symphony for the first time in England on Monday 29 April 1816. The notes accompanying the programme enthused:

> 'It is scarcely necessary to enlarge upon this important production, for it is so well known, and likely to become even more so as the symphony in which Beethoven revealed himself and his own rugged strength, having discarded the formalism which restricted his earlier works.'

Regarding its construction, the Society's music correspondent noted: 'It is orchestrally interesting as first employing trombones and double-bassoon in a symphony.' The pianist-composer Cipriani Potter received a mention in the Society's notices for 1816. He was acquainted with Beethoven who once remarked to Ries: 'Potter visited me several times; he seems to be a good man and has a talent for composition.'

The 1817 music season was noteworthy for the Society's first performance of the Seventh Symphony on 26 May, with the *Pastoral* Symphony having been presented earlier at a concert on 24 March. Of related interest is that the Directors of the Society, through the offices of Ferdinand Ries, invited Beethoven to compose and direct two symphonies for the sum of three-hundred guineas. His response was to request four-hundred and fifty guineas that the Directors declined; the outcome was Beethoven never visited England as he had planned. The 1821 season was noteworthy for the performance of no fewer than six Beethoven symphonies, namely, Nos. 1, 2, 4, 5, 6, and 7.

In the second decade of the Society's programmes it became usual for six or seven Beethoven symphonies to be performed each year. 1825 was memorable in the history of the Society for realizing, on 21 March, the first performance in England of the *Choral* Symphony. It was described as a 'New Grand Characteristic Sinfonia with Vocal Finale (composed expressly for the Society).' On the Title Page of the MS copy of the score that Beethoven sent to the Society, he inscribed the words 'Geschrieben für die Philharmonische Gesellschaft, London'.

In 1827, the Directors were informed by Ignaz Moscheles that Beethoven was ill and was in need of financial assistance. The Society undertook to give a concert for his benefit and to send him the sum of one hundred pounds. Beethoven later expressed his thanks:

'May Heaven soon restore me to health, and I will then prove to the generous English how much I appreciate the sympathy which they have shown for my condition.'

He undertook to write a new symphony for the Society — that he described as 'already sketched in outline'; his death on 26 March 1827 precluded its completion.

1929 was a significant year in the annals of the Society since it heralded the appearance of Felix Mendelsohn in its concert programmes for the first time. He would in due course exert a considerable influence on English musical taste and become a favourite of Queen Victoria and Prince Albert. On 6 February 1830 the Society's premises in the Argyll Rooms were destroyed by fire but the contents of the Library were saved — including precious Beethoven memorabilia. The Society relocated to the King's Theatre but the accommodation proved unsatisfactory. A later move in 1833, to premises in Hanover Square, offered better facilities and was the home of the Society until 1869.

The 1844 season was memorable insofar as the *thirteen*-year old boy-violinist Joseph Joachim performed Beethoven's Violin Concerto from memory — then something of an innovation — also supplying his own cadenzas. Beethoven's Overture *Leonora* No.1 was performed for the first time disposing the Society's music correspondent to enthuse 'its large proportions and grand style almost gave it the importance of a symphony'.

During his stay in London in 1856, Richard Wagner conducted the Philharmonic Society Orchestra and complimented it for being a '*strong esprit de corps*' possessed of 'superb tone' and 'the finest instruments'. He complained though of the length of the programmes that typically did not finish until after 11.00 p.m.! In 1873 the eminent interpreter of Beethoven Hans von Bülow made his debut on 28 April with a performance of Beethoven's *Emperor* Piano Concerto and would earn fame later in his capacity as an orchestral conductor — for both of which endeavours he received the Philharmonic Society's coveted Beethoven Gold Medal.

In 1885 the Society appointed Sir Arthur Sullivan as its resident conductor, a position he held for the next three years; his failing health deprived him of remaining in office for longer than he wished.

The Philharmonic Society's Centenary Year of 1912–13 provided the opportunity for a reflection of its achievements. The contributor to the records enthused:

'If the reader has the patience to wade through the pages of this long history, a history unique in the annals of musical institutions of this kind ... he will see what efforts were made to keep pace with all the changes in musical progress; what numbers of works, since acknowledged every-where as masterpieces, first made their appeal to English audiences at the Philharmonic Concerts, and what crowds of singers and players, since acclaimed great, first sang and played there.'[45]

Beethoven's connection with the Society was recalled with a performance of the *Choral* Symphony.

LATER NINETEENTH-CENTURY RECEPTION: 1850

In his study *The Orchestra from Beethoven to Berlioz*, the English-born musicologist and educator Adam von Ahnen Carse considered the changing sound of the orchestra in the first half of the nineteenth century in relation to audience expectations:

'The ears which in 1800 knew only the sounds of Haydn's and Mozart's orchestras, must have become inured by 1850 not only to an orchestral texture that had become much more complex and crowded, to more varied and richer colouring, but also to a great increase in sheer volume of sound.'

Reflecting on Beethoven's orchestral sound, as he conceived it, Carse remarks:

'[When] Beethoven gave his hearers still more notes to listen to, there were those who found the sounds too much for their ears, and set up the orchestral sound made by Haydn and Mozart as a limit which should not be exceeded.'[46]

1857

On 17 December 1857, the eighteen-year old Modest Musorgsky wrote to his teacher Mily Balakirev with whom he had commenced his studies in composition. It was with Balakirev that the two played through piano-duet arrangements of all Beethoven's symphonies and also some of the works of Schubert and their compatriot Mikhail Glinka. Balakirev pointed out to his protégé the technical structure of the compositions and how to analyse their various musical forms. The reason for Musorgsky writing to his teacher was to inform him of the arrival of a long-awaited new piano. Concerning this, he enthused:

> 'Today, thank God, the fate of the long-hoped for piano has been settled ... I am a thousand times grateful to you for the excellent choice. *La machine est parfaitement solide.*'

Unfortunately, the name of the piano maker is not revealed. Musorgsky continued:

> 'The tone is excellent and the bass very good ... I've stored away Beethoven's Second Symphony for the inauguration of the new instrument on Thursday.'[47]

1870

Richard Wagner published his *Beethoven* in 1870, the centenary year of the composer's birth. An English edition followed in 1893. Wagner's text was, in part, based upon an oration he gave as part of the centenary celebrations and takes the form of a lofty and extended encomium. Of Beethoven's approach to composition, he writes:

'[Beethoven] never altered any of the extant forms of instrumental music on principle; the same structure can be traced in his last sonatas, quartets, symphonies, etc., as in his first. But compare these works with one another: place the Eighth Symphony in F major beside the Second in D, and wonder at the entirely new world, almost in precisely the same form!'

Wagner closes with a typical flourish:

'[Beethoven's] symphonies have ... roused from the depths the new religion, the new world-redeeming announcement of sublimest innocence ... Let us then celebrate the great pathfinder ... But let us celebrate him worthily ...'.[48]

1875

On 7 May 1875, Cosima Wagner recorded Richard Wagner's thoughts on a chance hearing of part of the Second Symphony. Her Diary entry reads:

'On the 7th 'R'. encountered a group of poor blind musicians in a courtyard; they were playing the *Andante* from Beethoven's Second Symphony so wonderfully that he could not tear himself away from them, and told me about it with tears in his eyes'.

The experience disposed Wagner to remark: 'In such ways does one really feel the power of music!'[49]

1883

The Austrian pianist-composer-conductor Felix Weingartner became acquainted with Beethoven's symphonies in his student years; in later life he would have the distinction of being the first conductor to record all of the composer's symphonies. In his Autobiography *Buffets and Rewards*, he recalls a period when he was studying with the pianist-composer-pedagogue Carl Reinecke. Weingartner was just twenty at the time (1883) and, as he remarks, had fallen under the spell of the celebrated pianist-conductor Hans von Bülow.

In preparing for his examinations at the Leipzig Conservatory, Weingartner made a study of Beethoven's Second Symphony. At the first rehearsal of the work he conducted without the score — in the manner of von Bülow who was possessed of a phenomenal musical memory. Reinecke, who was present, was apparently outraged at his pupil's conduct and insisted henceforth he should always look at the score. He railed: '[It] is out of place for a pupil to imitate fashionable foolishness of certain modern conductors' — clearly a dig at von Bülow. Weingartner responded, saying he respected von Bülow 'as a model' since he was 'thoroughly acquainted with the works he conducts'. Notwithstanding that this rejoinder further enraged his teacher, Weingartner relates how he conducted the Second Symphony, at his final examination concert, without the score before him. He states:

> 'The Symphony went splendidly, received great applause and the papers were full of praise except for one friend of Reinecke's who ran me down for my "fashionable nonsense in conducting without a score".'[50]

1888–89

At the start of the concert season 1888–89, Gustav Mahler moved to Budapest to take up the post of Director of the Opera. His duties also provided him with opportunities to introduce unfamiliar works into the orchestral repertory. An anecdote from this time relates to the occasion when Mahler was preparing to give a performance of the Second Symphony. Coming from a rehearsal, he said to a friend:

> 'Today I gave the orchestra a regular sermon on the last movement of Beethoven's Second [Symphony], and they seem to have grasped my meaning. "Just look at this passage!" I told them. "Where is the 'monumental calm' [*monumentale ruhe*] and where is the 'impetus' [*schwung*] that you have been used to putting into Beethoven and often in the wrong place? Here is grace and humour; there is tenderness and restrained sentiment. But now comes a moment of passion, an unparalleled *crescendo*, and the most tremendous climax; now is the moment to change tactics, and to sweep everything before you by the intensity, the ardour and the grandeur of your playing!'[51]

1896

In 1896 Sir George Grove published *Beethoven and his Nine Symphonies*; by then he was well qualified to do so. Following a successful career as a civil engineer, he turned his gifts to musical administration. He was appointed Secretary at the Chrystal Palace, where he established an orchestra with the assistance of the conductor August Manns. Among the composers Grove introduced to the public was Franz Schubert, much of whose music was unknown at that time in England. After nearly twenty years of service at the Crystal Palace, Grove resigned the Secretaryship and joined the staff of the publishers Macmillan and Co.. Of his scholarly writings, *The Musical Times* wrote: 'His masterly biographies of Beethoven, Mendelssohn, and Schubert are models of biographical literature ...'. They eventually formed the basis of *Grove's Dictionary of Music and Musicians*. In his *Beethoven and his Nine symphonies* he writes of the composer's Op. 36:

'The Second Symphony is a great advance on the First. In the first place it is longer. Compared with the First Symphony, the Introduction is thirty-three bars long instead of twelve, and the *Allegro con brio* 328 instead of 286; the *Larghetto* is one of the longest of Beethoven's slow movements.

'The advance is more in dimensions and style, and in the wonderful fire and force of the treatment than in any really new ideas, such as its author afterwards introduced and are specially connected in our minds with the name of Beethoven.

'Another characteristic which seems to mark the historical place of the Second Symphony is that, in the slang of modern criticism, it is "pure music". No one, to our knowledge, has ever suggested a programmatic or image for any of its movements, nor is anyone likely to do so, except for the conclusion of the *Finale*, and in hearing it images certainly do crowd irresistibly on the mind. This Symphony is, in fact, the culminating point of the old, pre-Revolution world, the world of Haydn and Mozart; it was the farthest point to which Beethoven could go before he burst into that wonderful new region into which no man had before penetrated, of which no man had ever dreamed, but which is now one of our dearest possessions and will always be known by his immortal name.

'In some respects the Second Symphony is, though not the greatest, the more interesting of the nine. It shows with peculiar clearness how firmly Beethoven grasped the structural forms which had been impressed on instrumental music when he began to practice it; while it contains more than a promise of the strong individuality which possessed him, and his works caused him to stretch those forms here and there, without breaking the bounds which seem to be indispensable for really coherent and satisfactory construction.'[52]

RECEPTION IN THE TWENTIETH CENTURY

From the very many tributes to the Second Symphony, expressed throughout the twentieth century, we offer the following selection of testimonies.

1901

William Berwick Sayers was a pioneering British Librarian and a personal friend of the composer Samuel Coleridge Taylor. The latter was celebrated in his short lifetime for his setting of songs for chorus and orchestra known as *Hiawatha's Wedding Feast.* Such was his celebrity that during a tour of America, in 1904, he was introduced to President Theodore Roosevelt at the White House — a singular honour at the time for a man of African descent. Following his early death, Taylor's widow asked Sayers to write her husband's biography. This includes much of his correspondence from which we quote a letter Taylor wrote to a friend in December 1901:

'[In] this Symphony [Beethoven's Op. 36] there are none of those vivid picture-like impressions with which the following symphonies are charged, and yet what an immense advance we have here on No. 1. True, the influence of Mozart is apparent in many places, but nevertheless the work is entirely Beethoven. Moreover, to the uncultured (musically) listener, this No. 2 is perhaps the most easily followed, the most straightforward, and the most obviously *apparent* of all the nine ... Of the slow movement (*Larghetto*) some writer says "No one has ever written more beautiful, sustained, abstract music than this." Remarks are therefore superfluous, but the beautiful contrasts between wood and strings will be noticed, as will the more than usually lovely subjects ... The following movement is a real Beethoven scherzo indeed. What energy! What speed! What quiet fun pervades the music! And where is there a more charming trio than in this *scherzo*? Clear as crystal, simple as you please – but – Beethoven ... The last movement (*Allegro molto*) is a fine finale – charged with an abundance of fire and strenuous energy ... The movement is full of the "Great Man to be," and is a magnificent example of a symphonic movement in one tempo, without any interruptions from beginning to end.'[53]

Sir Herbert Beerbohm Tree was an English character actor who was celebrated for his leading roles in the theatre repertory and for his dramatizations of figures from popular nineteenth-century novels. Generations of actors also have him to thank for founding The Royal Academy of Dramatic Art (RADA) in 1904. In his extensive repertoire Tree occasionally depicted celebrated figures from the past, and it is in this connection we learn, albeit somewhat indirectly, of the wider public's growing awareness of Beethoven at this time. On 27 November 1909, the illustrated London weekly newspaper *The Graphic* depicted a scene from a play about Beethoven by the French dramatist and librettist René Fauchois. This depicted Tree as the composer. The cover illustration, by the artist Steven Spurrier, portrays Beethoven in a state of torment at not being able to hear the sounds of his music. His patron Karl Lichnowsky, and others, look on in manifest despair as Beethoven presses his hands to his ears — melodramatic, perhaps, but poignantly indicative of the composer's misfortune. The Caption to the cover reads:

'The play by René Fauchois, adapted by Mr. Louis Napoleon Parker, was produced on November 25, with Sir Herbert Tree as the great composer. This picture represents the moment when Beethoven realizes that he is becoming deaf — the greatest tragedy for a master of sound — for he has not heard a note of the violin. The figure in the background at the left is that of Beethoven's aristocratic patron.'[54]

1916

Ernest Markham Lee was a composer, lecturer and pianist-organist whose discourses and popular writings contributed to the better understanding of classical music for many young people of his generation. His books included: *The Music Lover's Ear Tests — On Listening to Music* (1918); *A Course in Music* and *Musical Theory and Knowledge* (1923); *The Man and his Music* (1915); and *The Story of the Symphony* (1916). In the latter he makes reference to the Second Symphony, suggesting that it did not form a part of the regular repertoire in the first decade or so of the last century — at least for English audiences: 'One seldom hears the Second Symphony nowadays, except in a series of concerts where the whole nine are played *seriatim*.' Of the work itself, he remarks:

'The orchestra employed is the same as in the C major [Symphony], and the form adopted is similar, except that a *scherzo* takes the place of the minuet. The introductory *adagio* is larger and more developed, but in many places the themes suggest an even earlier school of composition than does the First Symphony. This is noticeably the case in the main idea of the opening *allegro*, which is very square cut, and to our minds today, unimaginative. The second movement is a *larghetto*, with a charming theme, lyrical in style, happy and serene, with some beautiful examples of orchestral effects. Yet even here we have little of the real Beethoven, who shows us more of his individuality in the bright and wayward *scherzo* which follows. In the finale we find a force and abruptness which are much more characteristic, and which are at once apparent in the chief theme of the movement. This is a great finale even today, with its wonderful coda, and its evidence of emancipation from the formality which lurks behind so many of the noblest works of earlier composers.'[55]

1917

Notwithstanding his celebrity as a philosopher, dramatist, novelist, essayist, art historian and Nobel Laureate (prize for literature in 1915) Romain Rolland wrote extensively on music and was appointed to the first chair of music history at the Sorbonne in 1903. His passion for music — he was an accomplished pianist — found expression in several studies of Beethoven who for Rolland was 'the universal musician above all the others'. His writings about the composer and his works include: *Beethoven and Handel* (1917); *Goethe and Beethoven* (1930); and *Beethoven the Creator* (1937). In the former of these, he wrote briefly about the Second Symphony:

'In the Second Symphony, which is a great advance on the composer's First, Beethoven's hold of his subject is much firmer and the objects themselves are more striking. The *Larghetto* is full of lovely curves, and there is some charming conversational work between the woodwind instruments. The horn passage is the precursor of many fine symphony subjects of a martial nature for horns.

'Whilst the chromatic harmony is purely Mozartian, the *Scherzo* is a genuine Beethovenian outburst full of verve and piquant in touch.

'There is a feeling of broadness about the brilliant and energetic Finale which is absent from the Finale of the First Symphony.'[56]

1925

In his pioneering study *Beethoven* (1925), the German-born musicologist Paul Bekker considered the contemporary reception of the Second Symphony:

'The markedly cool reception of the Second Symphony had some justification according to the existing standard of taste. The means of expression which Beethoven employed were distinctly "futuristic"' for those days; the character and content of the work, on the contrary, were confined, for the most part, within the limits hitherto observed. It was one of those rare cases in which Beethoven's development as a technical musician outran his development as an imaginative composer. The "effort after the new and striking", upon which the [*Allgemeine musikalische Zeitung*] contemporary critic commented so derogatorily, is indeed perceptible, but the clearly conceived goal which could justify these efforts is lacking. Beethoven does not here steer his ship into uncharted seas, seeking undiscovered lands, but cruises about erratically in well-known waters. It is not surprising that, with his musical genius, he has been able to improve upon his First Symphony in freedom of treatment of the symphonic form and of the means of expression which it offers; but the fact that he merely experiments with these means, and does not employ them to any very exalted end, gives the D major Symphony a curious and uneasy position between past and future, and makes it, perhaps, inferior to the First as a symphonic entity.'[57]

1927

In 1927 *The Musical Times* invited the Irish composer, conductor, and pianist. Sir Herbert Hamilton Harty to contribute to its *Special Issue*, published to commemorate Beethoven's Death Centenary (1827–1927). He did so in an article titled *Beethoven's Orchestra: A Conductor's Reflections*. He makes the following general remarks concerning Beethoven's orchestration:

> 'Beethoven's general habit and manner in orchestration is fully exemplified in his symphonies, and it is not necessary to go further afield, even if, in other works, he makes use of some instrument which does not appear in his scores. If we take the nine symphonies and regard them from a merely technical point of view, they reveal, to an impartial eye, that the strings are always used with the greatest fullness and resource, the bassoons and drums with a special originality. And the flutes, oboes, clarinets, horns, trumpets, and trombones in a way we might expect (and that we get) from any well-equipped typical musician of those days. There are obscurities and miscalculations in certain places, some of which appear to be due to the impatience and brusqueness which were part of the composer's character, others which are undoubtedly the result of simple errors in questions of balance. Instances of both will occur to the minds of those familiar with the scores.'

Harty next considered the detrimental changes he considered some orchestral instruments had undergone since Beethoven's time:

'[Nowadays] we use a very much larger body of strings than was the general custom in Beethoven's lifetime [and] there is no doubt that many of the wind instruments have undergone since then a considerable change, and have gained in ease of manipulation at the expense of beauty of tone. The flute, for instance, must have frequently possessed a much sweeter and more characteristic tone before it was furnished with the ingenious mechanism in use today, and there is no doubt that the horn has also suffered in this respect by the addition of valves, and the trumpet, probably for the same reason. The oboe and bassoon, on the other hand, were rougher and coarser in quality, and the timpani less accurate and shallower in tone. It is likely that the trombone is the only wind instrument which has not altered in timbre, for there has been no change in its mechanism. Keeping these considerations in mind, it is interesting to imagine how Beethoven's symphonies may have sounded to his audiences, and, at the same time, it may give some justification for the readjustments it is felt necessary to make in modern performances.'

Harty concluded his essay:

'It is worthwhile to consider whether over-caution is in the best interest of these bold and unconventional masterpieces, or whether, in reality, it does not cripple freedom and candour of interpretation. What Beethoven would have said to our modern methods of preforming his works it is

111

impossible to tell. Wagner was not above taking the advice of Richter, nor Brahms of a Joachim, and, on the whole, it seems probable that Beethoven, great autocrat as he was, would not have rejected without consideration any suggestions made to him by a qualified craftsman who revered his music, and who disclaimed any wish or intention to interfere with essentials ... In the end, this is all that anyone entitled to the name of good musician has ever proposed, or ever will propose in connection with the music of Beethoven — "To amend the letter so that the spirit may shine forth more brightly".'[58]

1934

Marion Scott was an English violinist, music critic, and writer on music. She is remembered today for her pioneering study *Beethoven* that was first published in 1934 as one of J. M. Dent & Sons publications about the life and work of the great composers — originally titled *Music Masters Series*. It is a measure of her work's standing — it received both critical and public acclaim — that it was reprinted many times under the modified, over-arching title of *The Master Musicians*. In this guise, Scott's study of Beethoven has subsequently been reworked and expanded by the pianist-musicologist Denis Matthews and, following him, by the scholar-musicologist-pedagogue Barrie Cooper.

Scott's writing is characterised by a blend of deep respect for Beethoven 'the man', tempered with the objectivity of a professional musician; Scott founded her own string quartet and was a pioneer in introducing contemporary music to London audiences. With regard to the Second Symphony, she suggests Beethoven found in the writing of it 'a refuge in its Elysian beauty from the tragedy in his heart' — a reference, of course, to his encroaching deafness. She continues:

'It is a greater work than the First Symphony in every way save the balanced design. Beethoven has expanded the constructive scheme of the eighteenth-century symphony to something larger than the strains which it had been built to carry. As a result, he had much trouble with his architecture — it is said he rewrote the Symphony three times. The work is a hybrid. But how loveable! Think of that long, fine introduction — *Adagio-molto* — larger than anything designed by Haydn (though not so close-knit as Beethoven's later work), with its prophetic vision of the Ninth Symphony.

'The *Allegro con brio*, with its crisp *gruppetti* in the first subject and its fiery string passages, belongs partly to the old world, yet is touched by Beethoven's own power.

'The slow movement — *Larghetto* — is a long dream of beauty where Beethoven lavishes his unmatched skill on displaying, developing, and adorning his lovely subjects. Generally speaking, when experimenting at this period upon a fusion of sonata form with lyricism, he poured lyricism into weightier form; here he reversed the process, and wrote his lyric movement in sonata form.

'The *Scherzo* is the most significant part of the Symphony, with its characteristic explosions of energy and the remarkable forecast of the Ninth Symphony in the Trio. The explosive element appears again in the Finale, also another forecast of the Ninth Symphony.'[59]

1935

The British musicologist, composer, pedagogue and conductor Sir Donald Francis Tovey is perhaps best known for his *Essays in Musical Analysis*. They had their origins as programme notes written by him to accompany the concerts given by the Ried Orchestra, Edinburgh — performed largely under Tovey's direction. The *Essays* were published in six volumes with each volume focusing on a particular category of Beethoven's music. Volumes I and II were devoted to the symphonies; Volume III, the concertos; Volume IV, illustrative music, Volume V, vocal music; and Volume VI, supplementary essays. A seventh volume was published posthumously dealing with chamber music. Of Beethoven's Op. 36 Tovey states"

> 'Beethoven's Second Symphony was evidently larger and more brilliant than any that had been heard up to 1801; and people who could understand the three great symphonies that Mozart had poured out, in the six weeks between the end of June and the 10th of August 1788, would have found Beethoven's language less abstruse, though the brilliance and breadth of his design and the dramatic vigour of his style were so exciting that it was thought advisable to warn young persons against so "subversive" (*sittenverderblich*) a work. What the effect of such warnings might be is a bootless inquiry; but Beethoven's Second Symphony, and his next opus, the Concerto in C minor (Op. 37), have produced a greater number of definite echoes from later composers than any other of his works before the Ninth Symphony. And the echoes are by no means confined to imitative or

classical efforts: they are to be found in things like Schubert's Grand Duo and Schuman's Fourth Symphony, works written at high noon-tide of their composer's powers and quite unrestrained in the urgency of important new developments. Indeed, Beethoven's Second Symphony itself seems almost classist in the neighbourhood of such works as his profoundly dramatic Sonata in D minor, Op. 31, No. 2; while we can go back as far as the C minor Trio, Op. 1, No. 3, and find Beethoven already both as mature and as *sittenverderblich* in style and matter.'

Of the second movement Tovey is unequivocal"

'The *Larghetto* is one of the most luxurious slow movements in the world ... To many a child in musical matters, this movement has brought about the first awakening to a sense of beauty in music.'[60]

1936

In his Biography of the British conductor and cellist Sir John Barbirolli, the music critic Michael Kennedy recalls the period when Barbirolli had just been engaged as the permanent conductor of the Philharmonic Orchestra at Carnegie Hall. He had succeeded non-other than Arturo Toscanini. On 11 November 1936, Barbirolli wrote home to his wife the oboist Evelyn Rothwell. He enthused:

'The orchestra continues to work splendidly for me ... I would like to tell you of one thing that happened today, which did make me rather happy. I had been rehearsing the Beethoven Second Symphony, and all through it seemed as if I was shedding rather a new light on it for them, but just before the end I asked them to do something which seemed quite natural and simple to me, when, led by some of the wind, the whole orchestra broke out into a "Bravo Maestro", which I must say, coming from this particular bunch and their experience with Toscanini, touched me greatly.'[61]

In their *A Dictionary of Musical Quotations*, Ian Crofton and Donald Fraser include reflections on music-making in war-time America. Their survey includes the review of a concert that took place in the Carnegie Hall on 19 November 1942. Beethoven's Second Symphony was performed by the Philharmonic Symphony Orchestra under the direction of the Polish conductor Arthur Rodzinski. The reviewer of the concert, identified only as 'GP' was evidently not impressed by the interpretation of the piece nor the standard of the playing. He complained:

'Last night Beethoven's lovely Second Symphony came out violent, mechanical, fast and accurate. The strings messed up all the rapid figures and short notes. The horns gurgled as if they were playing under water. The oboes buzzed and bleated. The heavy accents sounded as if someone had suddenly pinched the whole violin section. The music was clear in its essential outlines but soiled and unlovely, as in a good edition that has been carelessly handled.'[62]

1954

Gordon Jacob is known to concert-goers as a prolific composer; his compositions include symphonies, concertos, suites, chamber works, pieces for solo instrumentalists, as well as orchestral arrangements of the works of other composers. In his long career as professor of composition at the Royal College of Music (1924–66) he published several books on aspects of orchestration and contributed introductions to the Penguin *Miniature Score* series of publications, of which he was also the editor. Writing of the Second Symphony he states:

'The *Allegro con brio* is cast in regular sonata form. The first subject, on violas and cellos provides a good example of Beethoven's fondness for basing his principal themes on the arpeggios of the common chord, a predilection which was to be shared by Brahms ... The second movement, *Larghetto,* is one of Beethoven's most beautiful slow movements. His metronome mark shows that he wishes it to move along delicately and lightly and without "sweetness long drawn out" [*L'Allegro,* John Milton]. It is important that this indication should be observed as otherwise the movement would be too long ... The *Scherzo* gives a foretaste of the later Beethoven in its violent contrasts, sudden explosions, and boisterous humour. Its abrupt changes of key must have caused a good deal of surprise to contemporary listeners by their boldness and unexpectedness ... The finale carries on the rumbustious spirit of the *Scherzo* in its opening subject, but a smoother and more tranquil feeling pervades the subsidiary first subject (bar 26) and the second subject (bar

117

52) though the rhythm and vitality of the music are never allowed to flag.'[63]

In his *Masterworks of the Orchestral Repertoire: A Guide for Listeners* (1954) the American musicologist Donald Nivison Ferguson placed the Second Symphony in the context of the *Heiligenstadt Testament*:

'About two years elapsed between the First Symphony and the Second. They were eventful years, both for the great and little world in which Beethoven lived. Napoleon was already a mighty figure in that great world – a figure out of which Beethoven's imagination was soon to evoke the ideal of a hero. In the world of music Beethoven was as yet by no means the all-conqueror, but was advancing towards that position by steps that were to prove more sure than those of the man-of-arms.

'Within himself, however, he confronted one appalling prospect. Unmistakably. He was growing deaf. He had tried to hide that misfortune from the world, and even from himself; but in 1802 he could, and would, no longer disguise it. He avowed it in that strangely incoherent and despairing letter which he called the *Heiligenstadt Testament* – "The Will". The new Symphony, composed at Heiligenstadt in the summer of that year 1802, was probably finished by that time. From the tone of the music one can only infer "The Will" was written in an exceptional fit of despondency, for he must have been aware of his disability throughout the composition of the music, and must have struggled valiantly against it.'[64]

Although the interpretation on record of Beethoven's music is outside our terms of reference, we make an exception here to consider the views of the British musician Spike Hughes in his consideration of the manner in which the Italian conductor Arturo Toscanini approached the Second Symphony in his recordings. He writes:

'Although the listener who had heard Toscanini conduct the First Symphony of Beethoven, the Second did not come as a surprise so much as a confirmation of the status of a composer whose début had been arresting and whose future would certainly command attention and respect.

'In the Introduction to the Second Symphony, Toscanini stressed particularly that element of drama which Beethoven was beginning to bring to the symphony; and for all that we have been brought up to regard Beethoven's even-numbered symphonies as "relaxed", compared with the violence and intensity of the "odd-numbered" works, for Toscanini to have regarded the Second Symphony as anything but the extremely vigorous and urgent piece it is would have been entirely out of character. [There] was nothing in the score to tell Toscanini that this would eventually be regarded as one of the "even-numbered" symphonies.

'Certainly, the Second Symphony includes elements that we have come to regard as typical of the "even-numbered" works. There is a certain tenderness, for instance, in the very first phrase of the *Adagio* introduction, but Toscanini did not in any way emphasize this lyrical passage at the expense of the dramatic sequence that follows it on the grounds that this was an "even-numbered" symphony. As always, while he saw "what was there", he saw a great deal more besides, including how to make Beethoven's reiterated scale-passages sound like music instead of technical exercises.'[65]

1961

The German-born orchestral conductor Otto Klemperer contributed an essay to accompany his 1961 complete recordings of Beethoven's symphonies. This was later published in 1964 as his *Minor Recollections.* In these he writes how he had often conducted cycles of the Beethoven symphonies in such concert venues as Los Angeles (1933), Milan (1935), Strasbourg (1936), Budapest (1947), Amsterdam (1949), London (1957 and 1959), and Vienna (1960). As a consequence, he declared: 'The result was that, as time went by, I found myself wearing a sort of dog-collar marked "Beethoven Specialist".' He protested: 'I am neither a Beethoven specialist nor a "modern conductor". My aim has always been to conduct competently in all musical styles.' Of Beethoven's symphonies he states:

'Beethoven was a revolutionary, and nothing could be more erroneous than to imagine that the great revolutionary arrived on the German scene like some well-behaved and docile lapdog. His symphonies are four-handed affairs, to say the least. Few people are familiar with Beethoven's metronome markings, though they sometimes appear to be very fast and provide only a rough indication of the tempo at which his music should be played.'

He adds:

'Most people think of Beethoven as a melancholy, tragic, gloomy character, but this is a crude distinction. He was, particularly in his youthful years, a happy-natured, cheerful person. The language of the First and Second Symphonies is unmistakable, and even the Fourth conveys a mood of exaltation ... It was not until the Sixth Symphony that the clouds began to gather. His hearing deteriorated progressively, but he put up a stout fight: "I shall seize Fate by the throat. It will never humble me" [Beethoven's words of defiance].'[66]

1968

In the late 1960s, the American conductor and writer on music Robert Craft made diary notes of an interview he had with his close friend Igor Stravinsky. He asked him if he would identify some of his favourite events in Beethoven's symphonies. Stravinsky made reference to the Second Symphony, albeit in somewhat convoluted terms: 'Schuman is a composer for whom I have a personal weakness, but the symphony is not his domain.' [By way of added interest, Stravinsky met Schuman's wife Clara when he was a boy of thirteen — describing her then as "an old lady with a walking stick"]. He continues:

'If I compare a symphony of his, say, the D minor, which I have just heard, with the Schubert Fourth (admittedly an invidious comparison like all such), the Schuman seems not to be a symphony at all, in the Beethoven sense. It is naïve in construction and it was not conceived instrumentally ... But, however far from Beethoven, the theme at measure 305 must have been derived from the *Larghetto* in Beethoven's Second Symphony.'

For good measure, Stravinsky added: 'The Trio of the *Scherzo* is my favourite episode in the Fourth Symphony.'[67]

1970

Robert Simpson is perhaps best remembered for being a prolific composer; between 1951 and 1990 he composed nine symphonies alongside four concertos and fifteen string quartets. A generation of music-lovers (the present writer included) will also remember Simpson for his contributions to the BBC both as producer and broadcaster. It was for the BBC that he published *Beethoven Symphonies* (1970) in which he writes:

'Having realised that Beethoven's First Symphony is already a new type, we are in a position to grasp the greater dimensions of the Second. If we accept that the first two symphonies belong to the eighteenth century, in that their motivation is entirely musical, we must hear clearly that beneath the formal gestures, and the fact that much of the material is from common stock, [there is] a new kind of stirring that is, in fact manifest. The thrilling *élan* of No. 2 is caused by the way Beethoven propels the thematic tags of his forebears upon a tonal current of unprecedented breadth and force. A first movement of considerable power and size rises from the largest slow introduction yet composed by anyone; not even Mozart's *Prague* Symphony displays a prelude of such scope and variety, ranging from simple lyricism to an imposing D minor unison climax prophesying the Ninth Symphony.'[68]

Sometime in 1970, the composer, pianist, conductor, and radio broadcaster Anthony Hopkins shared his thoughts on music with the German-American pianist, composer, and conductor Andre Previn. These were subsequently published as *Music Face to Face*. He writes:

'[The] only classical recording that I was given — I think it was as late as my fifteenth birthday — was Beecham's performance of Beethoven's Second Symphony, and this was an absolute revelation to me. I used to play it over and over, but I loved to conduct it too.'

Hopkins further recalls watching the British-born, conductor Leopold Stokowski conducting a performance of Tchaikovsky's Fifth Symphony and being captivated when, at a moment of climax, he raised four fingers towards the brass section. Such was the impression made on Hopkins he reveals:

'I don't know what he meant, but I felt this was a deeply significant gesture and I know that at any climax in this Beethoven Symphony [Op. 36] I always used to raise four fingers.'[69]

In his later writing *The Concertgoer's Companion* (1984), Hopkins writes of the Heiligenstadt-period in Beethoven's life and his response to the onset of deafness:

'Such inner torment in a Romantic composer would undoubtedly have produced an equally harrowing piece of music, a literally Tragic symphony.

Beethoven, it seems, was able to exorcise despair by the act of composition, for the Second Symphony is an exuberant and optimistic work that bubbles over with high spirits. Only in the slow introduction do we find the occasional sorrowful phrase, even so, it appears to be more a conventional expressive gesture than a revelation of private grief.'[70]

1972

Joseph Braunstein was an American musicologist, teacher and Senior Programme annotator for the Chamber Music Society of the Lincoln Center. Over his long career — he attained the great age of 104 — Braunstein wrote more than 500 programme notes for the Chamber Orchestra *Musica Aeterna* that he had co-founded. His collected writings were published in three volumes, in the second volume of which he discussed the Second Symphony within the wider context of Beethoven's symphonies:

'Viewed in the context of Beethoven's entire symphonic work, and also in that of his stylistic development, the Second Symphony occupies a particular position: it stands between two worlds. Beethoven's First Symphony symbolises, with Mozart's and Haydn's last symphonies, the peak of the eighteenth-century type and the nineteenth-century symphony as created in the Third (*Eroica*, 1804). The step Beethoven made from the Second to the Third Symphony was paralleled half a century later by Richard Wagner in the evolution from *Lohengrin* to *Rheingold*. Although Beethoven's Second Symphony shows new traits, it is basically oriented in the concept of the eighteenth century ... If the Symphony, viewed as a whole, kept to the Haydn-Mozart tradition, it went beyond the eighteenth-century technique in the orchestral treatment. The alternation between wind and string instruments, sometimes applied from measure to measure — and the distribution of one melody among several instruments — anticipate the technique used in the *Eroica*. It may have confused the musicians around 1804 and later on. As Berlioz records, even in the 1820s incredible cuts were inflicted on the score of the Second Symphony to make it performable in Paris. This was not necessary in Vienna. There the Symphony soon won the favour of the public and critics, who implored Beethoven, after the first public reading of the Third Symphony (*Eroica*), "to give us works that resemble the First and Second Symphonies ... that will always place Beethoven among the first-rate instrumental composers".'[71]

1973

In his study of Beethoven's orchestral music, the Irish musicologist and academic Basil Deane writes about the Second Symphony in the following terms:

'In its final version the *Adagio molto* introduction is at once traditional and original: traditional in that, unlike that of the First Symphony, it establishes the tonic harmony at the outset; and original in its subsequent harmonic and thematic range ... In its colour and lyricism, the A minor *Larghetto* far surpasses its predecessor ...

Throughout the movement there is a wealth of melodic invention that Tovey rightly observed was plundered by Schubert [Tovey, 1935, *Essays in Musical Analysis*, Vol. 1, pp. 27–28] ... By wilful fragmentation of texture, rhythmic displacement, and harmonic expectations, Beethoven creates a scherzo which is both explosive and witty. The same qualities characterise the concluding *Allegro molto.*'

Deane concludes:

'One of the outstanding features of the Symphony as a whole is its orchestration. Beethoven employs the same orchestral forces as in his First Symphony: double woodwind, horns and trumpets, drums, and strings. Yet the effect is quite different. Berlioz, a connoisseur, wrote of the Scherzo: "To hear the different instruments disputing the possession of some portion of a motive, which no one of them executes entirely, but of which each fragment becomes in this way coloured with a thousand different tints from one to another, one might easily indulge the fancy of being present at the fairy gambols of the graceful spirits of [Weber's] *Oberon.*'[72]

Louise Elvira Cuyler was an American musicologist recognised for her scholarly writings — she held the title 'Distinguished Professor' at Smith College, Massachusetts. Her book publications include *The Symphony* (1973, 1995) in which she comments:

'The plausible and obvious relationship between

the First and Second Symphonies is the more notable because it does not happen again: each subsequent symphony is highly individual and apparently independently conceived. Beethoven expands several devices that he merely experimented with in the earlier work. He employs much more daring key digressions and expands the scope of the basic sonata-allegro design. The orchestra required for this work is the same as that for the First Symphony: pairs of flutes, oboes, clarinets, bassoons, horns, and trumpets; and the usual string choir. Burt the composer's gift for deploying the instruments with flexibility and imagination is especially marked in this Second Symphony; frequent use of louvered texture and colourful antiphonal disposition of the choirs, signal Beethoven's increasing ease with the large ensemble. In later works, Beethoven depended on instrumental colour to provide much of the lively sense of ebb and flow that characterise his mature works.'[73]

1977

Following a successful career as a music executive the American-born Maynard Solomon achieved international renown as a musicologist for his biographical studies of Beethoven, Mozart and Schubert. Of Beethoven's Second Symphony he remarks:

'Completed in 1802, during a turbulent period in Beethoven's life, the Second Symphony, in D major, Op. 36, is already the work of a mature master who is settling accounts — or making peace — with the high-Classic symphonic tradition before embarking on an unprecedented musical voyage. It is a work which has both retrospective and prospective characteristics. It is firmly rooted in Mozart's and Haydn's last symphonies while anticipating Beethoven's later development by its dynamic contrasts, unexpected modulations, and propulsive movement, all of which are controlled by a confident and flowing Classicism.'[74]

1979

The American music-educator William Preston Stedman considers Beethoven's use of instruments in the Second Symphony:

'This work uses the same instrumentation as that found in the First Symphony. It emphasises some sections of the wind instruments, an orchestral treatment that differs markedly from the wind colour employed by both Haydn and Mozart. Much of the past melodic emphasis in wind sections had been assigned to flutes and oboes, with the oboe becoming the soprano member of the wind section. In the Second Symphony it is the clarinet that becomes as increasingly important solo woodwind instrument, at times more important and useful than the oboe ... The Symphony itself is a continuation of the Haydn-Mozart approach with many Beethoven departures. Three of the movements are in sonata-allegro form (I, II, and IV). Finally, Beethoven added a scherzo and advertised it truthfully as that. The coda of the first and final movements are both larger and longer than

those corresponding movements in the First
Symphony.'[75]

1985

Denis Matthews is remembered for being both a concert
pianist and musicologist, the latter in his capacity as professor of music at the University of Newcastle. His *Beethoven*,
published in Dent's *Master Musician Series* (1985), followed
on from Marion Scott's pioneering study of the composer
(1935 with subsequent reprintings) and has in turn been
followed by Barry Cooper's study of the same title (1985).
In his reflections on Beethoven's Op. 36, Matthews writes:

'The Second Symphony (1802) establishes a
grandeur manner in the size and scope of its slow
introduction, though it begins with a direct call-
to-arms and affirms its key of D major in a theme
given to wind and strings in turn. Before long, a
series of abrupt modulations presages
Beethoven's dramatic middle-period style, and a
powerful unison climax in D *minor* is often cited
as a prophecy of the first movement of the Ninth
Symphony ... The second subject has an unusu-
ally martial character, perhaps a Revolutionary
influence, and plays an important part in the
development ... Yet the Symphony still casts
backward glances at the eighteenth century,
especially in the lyrical outpouring of the
Larghetto, where many turns of phrase suggest
Haydn or Mozart, and Haydn certainly in the
bucolic cadence-theme with its notoriously high
asides from the horns. The *Scherzo* is wholly
Beethovenish throwing its three-note figure
around the orchestra in humorous fashion.'[76]

1987

The English conductor Sir Roger Norrington is respected for his historically informed performances of Beethoven's symphonies. In his liner notes to his recording of the Second Symphony (1987), he remarks:

> 'Beethoven's point of departure for his D major Symphony is that of Haydn in his last twelve symphonies, composed for London: a four-movement work, with a slow introduction and rondo finale, that makes a vivid and aggressive use of the full orchestra. In comparison with the First Symphony what strikes the listener about Beethoven's Second Symphony is its complete lack of deference; there is a humour verging on the grotesque. Only a minute into the work the formalities of the opening are deflected into a grand, expansive paragraph (here, perhaps, the stimulus is Mozart's *Prague* Symphony).'[77]

1988

In their survey of *A History Western Music* (1998), the American musicologists Donald Jay Grout and Claude Victor Palisca position the Second Symphony on the verge of Beethoven's second period and remark:

> 'The long *Adagio* that introduces the first movement announces a work conceived on a scale hitherto unknown in symphonic music ... The first movement has a long coda, which includes extensive new development of the principal material. The rest of the Symphony has correspondingly large dimensions, with a profusion of thematic material held together in perfect formal

balance. The *Larghetto* is especially remarkable for the multiplicity of themes, and for its rich cantabile character. The *Scherzo* and finale, like the first movement, are full of energy and fire. The Finale is written in an enlarged sonata form, with suggestions of rondo in extra recurrences of the first theme, one at the beginning of the development section and one at the beginning of the coda; the coda itself is twice as long as the development section, and introduces a new theme.'[78]

1989

The British musicologist Barrie Cooper is perhaps best known to Beethovenians for his study of the composer in the *Master Musicians* series of publications (2000), to admirers of Beethoven for his *Beethoven and the Creative process* (1990), and, in collaboration with fellow musicologists, *The Beethoven Compendium* (1991). He is also known for his realization of Beethoven's sketches for his unfinished Tenth Symphony and for his critical edition of Beethoven's piano sonatas for the Associated Board of the Royal Schools of Music) — that for a generation of students was dominated by the edition of Harold Craxton and Donald Francis Tovey. Cooper has also contributed introductions to the urtext editions of the Beethoven symphonies revised and edited by the Beethoven scholar and conductor Jonathan del Mar. Of the Second Symphony, Cooper writes:

'The work shows striking advances on the First Symphony in terms of scale and complexity. Although later to be overshadowed by the mighty *Eroica* Symphony, the Second Symphony was at its time of composition the longest and most powerful symphony ever written. Its enlarged dimensions are evident from the slow introduction, which is more than twice as long as that of the First Symphony, and modulates to the remote key of B-flat major (bar 12) before returning to the tonic. When the main allegro theme eventually arrives (bar 34), it is played not by the first violins but by violas and cellos, with the violins mereley accompanying — a most unusual scoring for a main theme (though it foreshadows a similar texture in the main theme of the *Eroica*) ...' .

'The second movement is, like the first, in sonata form, and the exposition is endlessly lyrical in character, with a series of melodies that follow one another in a seemingly effortless flow. Again there is some remarkable orchestration, particularly in the closing theme of the exposition (bar 82 onwards), which is scored for second violins and cellos in octaves, accompanied by the remaining strings ...'.

'For the first time in a symphony, the third movement is actually entitled *Scherzo* rather than *Minuet*, although there are precedents amongst the chamber works of both Beethoven and Haydn. It exhibits typical scherzo characteristics such as a fast tempo, light textures and much staccato, while its sudden lurch to B-flat major (bar 21) subtly recalls the use of this key in the introduction to the first movement ...' .

'The finale is once again in sonata form, and begins with a scrappy opening gesture that seems introductory but recurs frequently as an integral part of the movement ... The most remarkable structural feature of the finale, however, is the enormous coda, starting around bar 282—90 and occupying more than a third of the entire movement. This section was extended in length several times during the course of much sketching, and although it remains close to the home key throughout, it intensively develops motifs from earlier in the movement ... Beethoven sensed that his themes possessed so many possibilities for exploration that only a lengthy coda would suffice to round off the movement with a conclusion that was thoroughly satisfying,'[79]

1990

The Austrian conductor Nikolaus Harnoncourt shared with the Sir Roger Norrington a reputation for historically informed performances of music from the Classical era. Between June and July 1990, he recorded Beethoven's Second and Fifth Symphonies. Mindful of Harnoncourt's reputation for historic performance-practice, he was asked about his approach to the interpretation of Beethoven's orchestral music by professor Hartmut Krones — Head of the Department of Musical Studies and Performing Practice at the Vienna College of Fine Arts. Krones raised the question of what he referred to as 'one of the most controversial issues in the whole of Beethoven interpretation', namely the composer's original metronome markings. Harnoncourt responded:

'When I read Beethoven's scores without actually playing them, I arrive at almost the same metronome markings as he did. However, a tempo measured as the same can vary greatly in effect according to the circumstances — the size of the orchestra here is just as decisive as the size and resonance of the hall. The tempo as measured in one's mind is certainly the fastest of all; with just a piano or string quartet, I am still very close to my "imagined tempo", but with a huge orchestra I may find I have to move away from it. Perhaps it depends on whether one is playing in the morning, afternoon or evening: the pulse-frequency and the attitude of musicians and audience alike is different every time. If you fail to take all these factors into account and simply judge tempo with a metronome, then this is inhuman and unreal. But, notwithstanding, Beethoven did mean his tempi as he wrote them down. One just has to modify them all the time, and nobody knew how to do that better then Beethoven himself.'[80]

1991

The Cambridge University musicologist Nicholas Marston singles out for comment particular features of the Second Symphony:

'The slow introduction is much more substantial and foreshadows those of the Fourth and Seventh Symphonies; also, the finale already exhibits very clearly that sense of irresistible drive which is so characteristic of Beethoven (again compared with the finale of the Seventh Symphony). Prophetic too is the massive developmental coda of the finale: in scope it heralds that in the first movement of the *Eroica,* and its force is such that it grounds not only the last movement but the entire work. The sense of a psychological "journey" from beginning to end which is thus created became an essential feature of Beethoven's symphonic style.'[81]

In his *Classical Music: The Era of Haydn, Mozart, and Beethoven*, musicologist Philip Downs writes:

'The Second Symphony is a formally orthodox work, and breaks little new ground. The tonal device of the slow introduction, that Beethoven had used so successfully in the First Symphony, could not be repeated without becoming stale. Here, he writes an introduction that is longer, richer, and more self-contained than in any of his other symphonies with the exception of the Seventh, and much closer in style to the ideal of Mozart than Haydn. He continues to expand his resources, making the orchestral palette richer and more sumptuous than anything dreamed of earlier (except perhaps by Mozart in the slow movement of Symphony No. 38). Early critics praised the slow movement, but found the third and fourth movements were very hard to accept although they recognized the humorous intent. The self-confidence expressed in this work is at the opposite pole from the mood of the *Heiligenstadt Testament*, and yet these two documents existed side by side in the mind of their creator.'[82]

The American translator Elizabeth Csicserry-Ronay is known and respected for her scholarly English-language editions of the writings of Hector Berlioz. From these we have selected the following passage in which Berlioz discusses the Second Symphony:

'This Symphony is all nobility, energy, and pride. The introductory *Largo* is a masterpiece, wherein the most beautiful and unexpected effects follow one another without creating confusion. The melody is touchingly solemn from the outset; it inspires and sets the stage emotionally. Soon the rhythm grows bolder; the orchestration becomes richer, more sonorous, and more varied. This wonderful *Adagio* leads into an *Allegro con brio* of irresistible spirit. The gruppetto [turn], which is played in unison by the violas and cellos in the first measure of the theme, reappears on its own to establish either progressions or crescendo imitations between the winds and strings — all this as original as it is as full of life ... The *Andante* is quite unlike that of the First Symphony. Instead of a subject developed by canonic imitation, the theme is a pure and ingenious song, presented by the quartet of strings and then embellished with rare elegance by delicate runs that are always in keeping with the feeling of tenderness which characterises the main theme. This *Andante* is a lovely image of innocent happiness scarcely clouded by a few melancholy accents.

'The *Scherzo* is as openly cheerful and playful in its fantasy as the *Andante* was happily serene, for this Symphony is cheerful throughout. Even the warrior-like verve of the first *Allegro* is entirely free of violence; one can sense only the youthful ardour of a noble heart that keeps intact the finest illusions of life. The composer still believes in immortal glory, love, and self-sacrifice. What gay abandon! What flashes of wit! What high spirits! To hear all the instruments challenging each other over fragments of a motif which none plays in its entirety, each portion shimmering with a thousand colours as it passes from one instrument to the other, you would think you were watching [Weber's] *Oberon's* graceful sprites at play. The finale belongs to the same world.'[83]

1995

Richard Osborne, the British writer and former presenter to BBC Radio 3, contributed the chapter *Beethoven* to Robert Layton's *A Guide to the Symphony* (1985). He opens his account:

'If the First Symphony is a comically subversive work, the Second Symphony, no less fiery if properly conducted, is on an altogether grander scale. It is by no means lacking in wit and humour. (The last two movements are uproarious in their rough-hewn way.) What a difference here is the long-range planning of this *dramma giocoso*. In particular, the flat sixth (B flat) of the home key of D major stalks through the Symphony like Till Eulenspiegel, turning over apple-carts wherever he can find them. It first appears in bar 12 of the Symphony's slow movement, it strikes again in the *Scherzo* shortly after the double bar, and finally frightens the wits out of everyone at bar 372 during the finale's enormously extended coda. Paralleling this new preoccupation with long-term thinking is a complimentary preoccupation with sonata form and internal musical developments (even the *Scherzo* and its Trio have vestigial development sections). Though we expect the first movement to be in sonata form, and, possibly, the finale as well, it is more surprising to find the slow movement also in fully worked-out sonata form — and worked out with a prodigality of theme, sub-theme, and variant scoring that must have made even Schubert gaze.'[84]

1997

David Wyn Jones is a Welsh musicologist and a recognised authority on the music of the Classical period, notably that of Haydn (*The Life of Haydn,* 2009), and also the music of Beethoven (*The Life of Beethoven,* 1998). Writing of Beethoven's Second Symphony Jones draws attention to the work's innovative features:

'The *Allegro con brio* has a nervous energy greater than any previous symphonic first movement, and the way in which the march-like tune on clarinets, that serves as the second subject, is greeted by an avid *fortissimo* is only one of many exaggerated gestures in the movement. The *Larghetto* provides a relaxing interlude, abundantly tuneful in the manner of the contemporary Romances for violin and orchestra with a sentiment that crucially stops short of suavity. In the *Scherzo,* sudden dynamics unsettle the phrasing pattern, while the tuneful Trio neatly points up the eccentricity of the main section. From the gruff opening of the finale it is clear that the movement is going to be an explosive conclusion to the Symphony, gaining towards the end an intensity of expression that would have shocked Haydn.'[85]

William Kinderman is recognised for both his prowess as a concert pianist and for his scholarly writings on music. These include *Beethoven's Diabelli Variations* (1987), *Beethoven's Compositional Process* (1991) and *Beethoven* (1995). In the latter he discusses the Second Symphony in the following terms — quoted here in summary form:

'In this Symphony, especially in its outer movements, Beethoven brought the full scope of his imagination to bear on the orchestral genre for the first time. A link with the legacy of Haydn and Mozart is still tangible, to be sure: certain features of the slow introduction to the first movement are reminiscent of Mozart's *Prague* Symphony K 504, in the same key, whereas the coda of the finale has Haydnesque touches ... Central to Beethoven's conception is the association of stark, unharmonized unison gestures with the minor mode of D ... This is one of the moments in Beethoven's earlier music that reminds us forcefully of the Ninth Symphony ... Some early critics had difficulty with the Second Symphony, preferring the milder manners of the First. Exasperated denunciation of the music as bizarre, confused, or incomprehensible was directed especially at the finale, an *Allegro molto* in sonata form. The style is clearly Haydnesque, but it is even more audaciously impertinent than Haydn would have allowed ... The *Allegro molto* of Beethoven's Second

Symphony is a heightened comedy, capable of absorbing disruptive elements and even an excessiveness bordering on the absurd. This is comedy sublime.'[86]

RECEPTION NEARER OUR OWN TIME

The reader is reminded (see 'Author's Note') that the author's cut-off date for his researches was 2007, consequently no texts are included here beyond that time.

2000

The American musicologist and scholar Scott Burnham collaborated with the music critic Michael Steinberg in their survey of Beethoven's music and the context within which it was composed. Of the Second Symphony they write:

'Beethoven begins with a slow introduction, one without precedent in sheer size. In the opening *Adagio* of the First Symphony, Beethoven had followed Haydn's practice of compressing much dramatic event into few notes. Now, seeking to create something spacious and varied, he returned to Mozart for a model, specifically to the *Prague* Symphony, which is in the same key of D major ... Beethoven's introduction to the Second Symphony encompasses large and bold harmonic excursions, as well as comprehending a wide range of musical characters, from pliant lyricism to the stern D minor unison fortissimo that so startlingly anticipates the Ninth Symphony ... The *Larghetto* brings a sweetness that is new in Beethoven's language. The music unfolds in a leisurely way that seems far from the worlds of both Haydn and Mozart. It does point to the future, though: what would Schuman have done without this music to lean on?

'In the First Symphony, Beethoven still called his very fast one-in-bar third movement a minuet; here he admits that he is writing a scherzo, actually using the word in his tempo / character designation. We should note that he flirts with D minor and makes a delightfully surprising and quite extended excursion into B-flat major. The Trio is oboe-tinged and passionate. The sonority and the melody's smooth contour have often evoked comparisons with the corresponding page in the Ninth Symphony; the tempi, however, are very different, that in the Ninth being much faster.

'The finale begins with a gesture of captivating impudence, a two-note flick up high, followed by a dismissive growl down below. This has splendid comic possibilities, and Beethoven neglects none of them.'[87]

2002

In his survey *The first Golden Age of the Viennese Symphony*, the American musicologist Alfred Peter Brown cites the advances the D major Symphony, Op. 36 made over its predecessor the C major Symphony, Op. 21:

'The assertiveness of the Second Symphony, when compared to the First, is immediately realized; rather than beginning timidly on a chord removed from its tonality, Beethoven now confronts the audience with a tutti *coup d'archet* on D major, just as Haydn had done in his D major "London" Symphony, No. 98 ... In nearly every way, the first movement of Symphony No. 2 is a more compelling piece than its predecessor. The thematic working-out is based on a logic not previously present; the long-term harmonic plan is more convincing, in setting up and resolving conflicts; and the texture, fabrics, and orchestration have a brilliance not previously heard ... The middle section (mm 12–22) is extraordinary not only for its tonal rhetoric but also for its pointillistic orchestration ... as pitches are tossed from one to another ... Yet, beneath the deep originality of this section lurks the ghost of the introduction to Mozart's Symphony K. 504 (*Prague*) and the slow movement of Mozart's Symphony K. 551 (*Jupiter*) with its expressive thirty-second note figures.'[88]

2003

The Scottish-born music critic and musicologist Conrad Wilson identified twenty compositions of Beethoven that he considered reveal significant progress in the composer's development. One of these was the Second Symphony, of which he remarks:

' "Artists are fiery by nature and do not weep", declared Beethoven [in his *Heiligenstadt Testament*] around the time he composed the Second of his Nine Symphonies. And there is much fire, and little weeping, in this remarkable work, which shows no dwindling of inspiration no loss of nerve, after the impact made by its predecessor, the Symphony No. 1 in C major, indeed, as the voice of a new century, it speaks far more potently than that infinitely less daring work. For all the lyrical, pastoral sweetness of its slow movement, the Second Symphony contains

142

music quite startlingly progressive and idiosyn-
cratic, often volcanic in energy and humour, a
true prelude to the *Eroica* and an abundantly
assured, brilliantly devised masterpiece in its
own right.

'Though often described as "early" Beethoven,
and descended though it is from Haydn and
Mozart, the Second Symphony needs to be heard
in the context of his own music. Like the Third
Piano Concerto and *Moonlight* Sonata, which
date from the same period, it displays the hand
of a vanguard composer for whom the eighteenth
century was a thing of the past. The scale of the
writing, conspicuously bigger than that of the First
Symphony, shows how aware the young
Beethoven already was that symphonic form was
capable of unprecedented expansion.'[89]

2005

In 2005, during the week Sunday 5 June to Friday 10 June,
BBC Radio 3 performed *all* Beethoven's music in a contin-
uous sequence that it titled *The Beethoven Experience.* On
Thursday 9 June, the Second Symphony was performed in
'authentic performance' by the Chamber Orchestra of
Europe conducted by Nikolaus Hnoncourt. For this occasion, the British musicologist and educator Terry Barfoot
contributed the programme notes from which the following
extract is derived:

'The first years of the new century were a time of
torment and even despair for Beethoven. In
October 1802 he wrote the famous *Heiligenstadt
Testament*, a lengthy letter to his brothers which,
though never actually sent, expressed most elo-

quently the trauma of increasing deafness which he had to endure. In this moving and highly personal document Beethoven contemplates suicide, but rejects it because his sense of mission prevails: "Only it, my art, held me back. It seemed to me impossible to quit the world until I had produced all I felt it in me to produce; and so I reprieved my wretched life".

'Since Symphony No. 2 is contemporary with this crisis, it makes a particularly interesting example of the relationship between a composer's life and his art. If viewed in this way, the Symphony confirms Beethoven as a classical rather than a romantic artist, for only in the first movement's slow introduction is a sense of passionate intensity approaching personal grief to be found. Instead the Symphony, taken as a whole, is an exuberant and lively composition of not inconsiderable power; if it proves anything, it proves that creativity can drive out despair.'[90]

Although not connected directly with the Second Symphony in D major, Op. 36, we give the last words to the doyen of Beethovenians, Sir Donald Francis Tovey:

'To measure Beethoven's influence is like measuring Shakespeare's. It is an influence either too vague or too profound to define ... It is as [however] certain as anything in the history of art that there will never be a time when Beethoven's work does not occupy the central place in a sound musical mind. When Beethoven's work is out of fashion, that is because people are afraid of drama and of sublime emotions.'[91]

1   For accounts of Potter's and Russell's recollections of Beethoven, see: Oscar
    George Theodore Sonneck, *Beethoven: Impressions of Contemporaries*,
    Oxford University Press, 1927, p. 101 and p. 108; Peter Clive, 2001, pp.
    269–70 and pp. 298–99; and Anne-Louise Coldicott, *Reception* in: Barry
    Cooper, *The Beethoven Compendium: A Guide to Beethoven's Life and
    Music*, Thames and Hudson, 1991, p. 294.
2   Emily Anderson editor and translator, Macmillan, 1961, Vol. 1, Letter No, 69
    and Letter No. 70, p. 87.
3   Beethoven House, Digital Archives, *Sinfonie Nr. 2 (D-Dur), Op. 36*.
4   Elliot Forbes editor, *Thayer's Life of Beethoven*, Princeton University Press,
    1967 pp. 328–30 and H. C. Robbins Landon, *Haydn: Chronicle and
    Works: Haydn, The Late Years, 1801–1809*, Indiana University Press, 1977,
    pp. 256–57.
5   Franz Wegeler, *Remembering Beethoven: The Biographical Notes of Franz
    Wegeler and Ferdinand Ries*, Andre Deutsch, 1988, p. 75 and Elliot Forbes
    editor, *Thayer's Life of Beethoven*, Princeton University Press, 1967.
6   *Ibid*, Franz Wegeler, pp. 66–67.
7   Barry Cooper, *Beethoven and the Creative Process*, Clarendon Press, 1990,
    p. 30.
8   H. C. Robbins Landon, *Haydn: Chronicle and Works: Haydn, The Late Years,
    1801–1809*, 1977, p. 257 and also cited in Landon, *Beethoven*, 1970, p.
    147.
9   *Ibid*.
10 Wayne M. Senner, Robin Wallace and William Meredith editors, *The
    Critical Reception of Beethoven's Compositions by his German
    Contemporaries,* Lincoln: University of Nebraska Press, in association
    with the American Beethoven Society and the Ira F. Brilliant Center
    for Beethoven Studies, San José State University, 1999, Vol. 2, pp.
    164–65.
11 Elliot Forbes editor, *Thayer's Life of Beethoven*, Princeton University Press,
    1967 pp. 361–62.
12 Barry Cooper, *Beethoven: The Master Musicians Series*, Oxford University
    Press, 2000, p. 139.
13 Wayne M. Senner, Robin Wallace and William Meredith editors, 1999, Vol.
    1, p. 196. See also: David Wyn Jones, *The Symphony in Beethoven's
    Vienna*, Cambridge University Press, 2006, pp. 165–66.
14 Anton Felix Schindler, *Beethoven as I Knew Him*, edited by Donald W.
    MacArdle and translated by Constance S. Jolly from the German edition of
    1860, Faber and Faber, 1966, pp. 110–11.
15 Wayne M. Senner, Robin Wallace and William Meredith editors, 1999, Vol.
    1, pp. 101–02. See also: H. C. Robbins Landon, *Beethoven: A Documen-
    tary Study*, Thames and Hudson, 1970. p. 74. For Ries's account of the
    concert see: Franz Wegeler and Ferdinand Ries, Andre Deutsch, 1988
    (reprint), pp. 101–02.
16 Wayne M. Senner et al (see endnote 15) Vol. 1, p. 199.
17 *Ibid*, p. 200.
18 Quoted, with adaptation, form: H. C. Robbins Landon, *Beethoven: A
    Documentary Study*, Thames and Hudson, 1970, p. 92. See also: Landon,
    1991, p. 109.

19 Emily Anderson editor and translator, Macmillan, 1961, Vol. 1, Letter No. 130, pp. 148—49.
20 Wayne M. Senner, Robin Wallace and William Meredith editors, 1999, Vol. 1, p. 201.
21 Franz Wegeler, *Remembering Beethoven: The Biographical Notes of Franz Wegeler and Ferdinand Ries*, Andre Deutsch, 1988, p. 94.
22 Emily Anderson editor and translator, 1961, Vol. 2, Letter No. 534, pp. 502—04.
23 Peter Clive, *Beethoven and his World*, Oxford University Press, 2001, p. 73 and pp. 149—50. See also: Barry Cooper, *The Beethoven Compendium: A Guide to Beethoven's Life and Music*, Thames and Hudson, 1991, p. 19.
24 Elliot Forbes editor, *Thayer's Life of Beethoven*, Princeton University Press, 1967 p. 428.
25 Theodore Albrecht editor and translator, University of Nebraska Press, 1996, Vol. 1, Letter No. 128, pp. 197—99.
26 Otto Biba, *Concert Life in Beethoven's Vienna*, in: Robert Winter, editor, *Beethoven, Performers, and Critics: the International Beethoven Congress, Detroit*, 1977, Wayne State University Press, 1980, p. 88.
27 Leo Schrade, *Beethoven in France: The Growth of an Idea*, Yale University Press, and Oxford University Press, 1942. Schrade discusses Beethoven at some length beyond the words quoted, see: pp. 3—6, and p. 29, p, 31, and p. 38.
28 Wayne M. Senner, Robin Wallace and William Meredith editors, 1999, Vol. 1, p. 203.
29 Theodore Albrecht editor and translator, University of Nebraska Press, 1996, Vol. 2, Letter No. 240, pp. 125—127.
30 Elliot Forbes editor, *Thayer's Life of Beethoven*, Princeton University Press, 1967, pp. 770—71.
31 Emily Anderson editor and translator, 1961, Vol. 2, Letter No. 1022, pp. 893—4.
32 David Wyn Jones, *The Symphony in Beethoven's Vienna*, Cambridge University Press, 2006, p. 185.
33 Wayne M. Senner, Robin Wallace and William Meredith editors, 1999, Vol. 1, p. 204.
34 Elliot Forbes editor, *Thayer's Life of Beethoven*, Princeton University Press, 1967 pp. 800—01.
35 Wayne M. Senner, Robin Wallace and William Meredith editors, 1999, Vol. 1, p. 55—60.
36 *Ibid*, p. 59 and p. 64.
37 Nicholas Marston, *Symphonies*, in: Barry Cooper, *The Beethoven Compendium: A Guide to Beethoven's Life and Music*, Thames and Hudson, 1991, p. 224.
38 With acknowledgment, with adaptations, to *Cultural Activities Department Juan March Foundation.*
39 Wayne M. Senner, Robin Wallace and William Meredith editors, 1999, Vol. 1, p. 205.
40 The quotation is derived from Peter Clive, *Beethoven and his World*, Oxford University Press, 2001, pp. 210—11.
41 Peter Brown, *Critical Reaction to Beethoven in France*, website article.
42 Adam von Ahnen Carse, *The Orchestra from Beethoven to Berlioz: A History*

of the Orchestra in the first half of the 19th century, and of the Development of Orchestral Baton-Conducting, W. Heffer, 1948, p. 90.

43 Robin Wallace, *Beethoven's Critics: Aesthetic Dilemmas and Resolutions during the Composer's Lifetime*, Cambridge University Press, 1986, p. 108.

44 Hector Berlioz, *The Art of Music and other Essays, A Tavers Chants*, derived from *The Hector Berlioz website*, translation by Michel Austin.

45 Cyril Ehrlich, *First Philharmonic: A History of the Royal Philharmonic Society*, Clarendon Press, 1995.

46 Adam von Ahnen Carse, 1948, pp. 478–79.

47 Leyda Jay and Sergi Bertensson, *The Musorgsky Reader: A Life of Modeste Petrovich Musorgsky in Letters and Documents*, W.W. Norton, 1947, pp. 3–4.

48 Richard Wagner, *Beethoven: With [a] Supplement from the Philosophical Works of A. Schopenhauer*, translated by E. Dannreuther, Reeves, 1893, p. 42 and pp. 112–13.

49 Gregor-Dellin and Dietrich Mack, editors, *Cosima Wagner's diaries*, Vol. 1, 1869 - 1877, Collins, 1978–80, p. 845.

50 Felix Weingartner, *Buffets and Rewards: A Musician's Reminiscences*, Hutchinson & Co., 1937, pp. 89–90.

51 Natalie Bauer-Lechner, *Recollections of Gustav Mahler*, Faber Music, 1980, pp. 136–37.

52 Sir George Grove, *Beethoven and his Nine Symphonies*, Novello, Ewer, 1896, pp. 23–24 and p. 41.

53 W. C. Berwick Sayers, *Samuel Coleridge-Taylor, Musician: His Life and Letters*, Cassell and Co., 191, pp. 129–30.

54 The image of the tormented Beethoven accompanies the website article: 'Sir Herbert Beerbohm Tree as Beethoven at his Majesty's Theatre.'

55 Ernest Markham Lee, *The Story of the Symphony*, Scott Publishing Co., 1916, pp. 48–50.

56 Romain Rolland, *Beethoven and Handel*, Waverley Book Co., 1917, pp. 110–11.

57 Paul Bekker, *Beethoven*, J. M. Dent & Sons, 1925., pp. 151–52.

58 Hamilton Harty, *Beethoven's Orchestra: A Conductor's Reflections* in: *Beethoven*: Special Number, *Music & Letters*, 1927, pp. 172–77.

59 Marion M. Scott, *Beethoven: The Master Musicians*, Dent, 1940, pp. 158–59.

60 Donald Francis Tovey, *Essays in Musical Analysis*, Oxford University Press, H. Milford, Vol. 1, 1935, pp. 25–27.

61 Michael Kennedy, *Barbirolli, Conductor Laureate: The Authorised Biography*. Hart-Davis, MacGibbon, 1973, pp. 117–18.

62 Ian Crofton and Donald Fraser editors, *A Dictionary of Musical Quotations*, Croom Helm, 1985, pp. 69–70.

63 Gordon Jacob, Introduction to, *Beethoven, Symphony No. 2 in D major, Op. 36*, Penguin Scores, 1954.

64 Donald Nivison Ferguson, *Masterworks of the Orchestral Repertoire: A Guide for Listeners*, University of Minnesota Press, 1954, pp. 42–43.

65 Spike Hughes, *The Toscanini Legacy: A Critical Study of Arturo Toscanini's Performances of Beethoven, Verdi, and Other Composers*, Putnam, 1959, p. 32.

66 Martin Anderson editor, *Klemperer on Music: Shavings from a Musician's Workbench*, Toccata Press, 1986, pp. 97—99.

67 Igor Stravinsky and Robert Craft, *Dialogues and a Diary*, Faber and Faber 1968, pp. 112—16.

68 Robert Simpson, *Beethoven Symphonies*, British Broadcasting Corporation, 1970, p. 16.

69 Antony Hopkins. *Andre Previn, Music Face to Face*, Hamish Hamilton, 1971, pp. 3—4.

70 Antony Hopkins, *The Concertgoer's Companion*, J.M. Dent & Sons Ltd., 1984, p. 64.

71 Joseph Braunstein, *Musica Aeterna; Program Notes for 1961—1971, Musica Aeterna*, 1972, pp. 31—32.

72 Basil Deane, *The Symphonies and Overtures* in: Denis Arnold and Nigel Fortune editors, *The Beethoven Companion*, Faber and Faber, 1973, pp. 285—86.

73 Louise Elvira Cuyler, *The Symphony*, Harcourt Brace Jovanovich, 1973, p. 56.

74 Maynard Solomon, *Beethoven*, Schirmer, 1977, pp. 103—4.

75 William Preston Stedman, *The Symphony*, Prentice-Hall, 1979, p. 66.

76 Denis Matthews, *Beethoven; Master Musicians*, J. M. Dent, 1985, pp. 154—55.

77 Sir Roger Norrington, Introduction to *Ludwig van Beethoven: Sinfonie Nr. 2, Op. 36*, London Classic Players, EMI Records Ltd., 1987.

78 Donald Jay Grout and Claude V. Palisca editors, *A History of Western Music*, J. M. Dent, 1988, p. 635.

79 Barry Cooper, Introduction to: *Ludwig van Beethoven, Symphony No. 2 in D major*, Urtext, Herausgegben, edited by Jonathan Del Mar, undated (c 1990?).

80 Nikolaus Harnoncourt, Introductory notes to the recording of Beethoven's Symphony No. 2 by the Chamber Orchestra of Europe, conducted by Nikolaus Harnoncourt, June—July, 1990.

81 Nicholas Marston, *Symphonies*, in: Cooper, Barry. *The Beethoven Compendium: A Guide to Beethoven's Life and Music*, Thames and Hudson, 1991, p. 214.

82 Philip G. Downs, *Classical Music: The Era of Haydn, Mozart, and Beethoven*, W.W. Norton, 1992, p. 593.

83 Elizabeth Csicserry-Ronay, translator and editor, *Hector Berlioz, The Art of Music and other Essays: (À travers chants)*, Indiana University Press, 1994, pp. 12—13.

84 Richard Osborne, *Beethoven* in: Robert Layton, editor. *A Guide to the Symphony*, Oxford University Press, 1995, p. 84.

85 David Wyn Jones, Liner notes (Introduction) to, *Beethoven, Second Symphony*, London Classical Players conducted by Sir Roger Norrington, EMI Records, 1997.

86 William Kinderman, *Beethoven*, Oxford University Press, 1997, pp. 80—85.

87 Scott G. Burnham and Michael P. Steinberg, editors, *Beethoven and his World*, Princeton University Press, 2000, pp. 8—11.

88 Alfred Peter Brown, *The Symphonic Repertoire*, Vol. 2: *The First Golden Age of the Viennese Symphony; Haydn, Mozart, Beethoven, and Schubert*, Indiana University Press, 2002, p. 453 and p. 458.

148

[89] Conrad Wilson, *Notes on Beethoven: 20 crucial works*, Saint Andrew Press, 2003, pp. 25–26.

[90] Terry Barfoot, *Symphony No. 2 in D major, The Beethoven Experience*, BBC, Radio Three, 7 June, 2005.

[91] Donald Francis Tovey, *Ludwig van Beethoven* in: *The Classics of Music*, Michael Tilmouth editor, Oxford University Press 2001, p. 341.

BIBLIOGRAPHY

The author has individually consulted all the publications listed in this bibliography and can confirm that each makes reference, in some way or other, to Beethoven and his works. It will be evident from their titles which of these are publications devoted exclusively to the composer. Others that make only passing reference to Beethoven and his compositions, nevertheless unfailingly bear testimony to his genius and humanity. The diversity of the titles listed testifies to the centrality of Beethoven to western culture and beyond; the mere survey of these should be of itself a rewarding experience for a lover of so-called classical music. The entries are confined to book publications, reflecting the scope of the author's researches. The cut-off date for this was 2007; no works after this date are listed, notwithstanding the author is mindful that Beethoven musicology, and related publication, continue to be a major field of endeavour.

Abraham, Gerald. *Beethoven's second-period quartets*. London: Oxford University Press: Humphrey Milford, 1944.

Abraham, Gerald. *Essays on Russian and East European music*. Oxford: Clarendon Press: New York: Oxford University Press, 1985.

Abraham, Gerald, Editor. *The age of Beethoven, 1790-1830*. London: Oxford University Press, 1982.

Abraham, Gerald. *The tradition of Western music*. London: Oxford University Press, 1974.

Abse, Dannie and Joan. *The Music lover's literary companion*. London: Robson Books, 1988.

Adorno, Theodor W., Translator. *Alban Berg: master of the smallest link*. Cambridge: Cambridge University Press, 1991.

Adorno, Theodor W. *Beethoven: the philosophy of music; fragments and texts*. Cambridge: Polity Press, 1998.

Albrecht, Daniel, Editor. *Modernism and music: an anthology of sources*. Chicago; London: University of Chicago Press, 2004.

Albrecht, Theodore, Translator and Editor. *Letters to Beethoven and other correspondence*. Lincoln, New England: University of Nebraska Press, 3 vols., 1996.

Allsobrook, David Ian. *Liszt: my travelling circus life*. London: Macmillan, 1991.

Anderson, Christopher, Editor and Translator. *Selected writings of Max Reger*. New York; London: Routledge, 2006.

Anderson, Emily, Editor and Translator. *The letters of Beethoven*. London: Macmillan, 3 vols.,1961.

Anderson, Martin, Editor. *Klemperer on music: shavings from a musician's workbench*. London: Toccata Press, 1986.

Antheil, George. *Bad boy of music*. London; New York: Hurst & Blackett Ltd., 1945.

Appleby, David P. *Heitor Villa-Lobos: a bio-bibliography*. New York: Greenwood Press, 1988.

Aprahamian, Felix, Editor. *Essays on music: an anthology from The Listener*. London, Cassell, 1967.

Armero, Gonzalo and Jorge de Persia. *Manuel de Falla : his life & works*. London: Omnibus Press, 1999.

Arnold, Ben, Editor. *The Liszt companion*. Westport, Connecticut; London: Greenwood Press, 2002.

Arnold, Denis and Nigel Fortune, Editors. *The Beethoven companion*. London: Faber and Faber, 1973.

Ashbrook, William. *Donizetti*. London: Cassell, 1965.

Auner, Joseph Henry. *A Schoenberg reader: documents of a life*. New Haven Connecticut; London: Yale University Press, 2003.

Avins, Styra, Editor. *Johannes Brahms: life and letters*. Oxford: Oxford University Press, 1997.

Azoury, Pierre H. *Chopin through his contemporaries: friends, lovers, and rivals*. Westport, Connecticut: Greenwood Press, 1999.

Badura-Skoda, Paul. *Carl Czerny: On the Proper Performance of all Beethoven's Works for the Piano*. Universal Edition: A. G. Wien, 1970.

Bailey, Cyril. *Hugh Percy Allen*. London: Oxford University Press, 1948.

Bailey, Kathryn. *The life of Webern.* Cambridge: Cambridge University Press, 1998.

Barenboim, Daniel. *A life in music.* London: Weidenfeld & Nicolson, 1991.

Barlow, Michael. *Whom the gods love: the life and music of George Butterworth.* London: Toccata Press, 1997.

Barrett-Ayres, Reginald. *Joseph Haydn and the string quartet.* New York: Schirmer Books, 1974.

Bartos, Frantisek. *Bedrich Smetana: Letters and reminiscences.* Prague: Artia, 1953.

Barzun, Jacques. *Pleasures of music: an anthology of writing about music and musicians.* London: Cassell, 1977.

Bauer-Lechner, Natalie. *Recollections of Gustav Mahler.* London: Faber Music, 1980.

Bazhanov, N. Nikolai. *Rakhmaninov.* Moscow: Raduga, 1983.

Beaumont, Antony, Editor. *Ferruccio Busoni: Selected letters.* London: Faber and Faber, 1987.

Beaumont, Antony, Editor. *Gustav Mahler, letters to his wife.* London: Faber and Faber, 2004.

Beecham, Thomas. *A mingled chime: an autobiography.* New York: Da Capo Press, 1976.

Bekker, Paul. *Beethoven.* London: J. M. Dent & Sons, 1925.

Bellasis, Edward. *Cherubini: memorials illustrative of his life.* London: Burns and Oates, 1874.

Bennett, James R. Sterndale. *The life of William Sterndale Bennett.* Cambridge: University Press, 1907.

Benser, Caroline Cepin. *Egon Wellesz (1885–1974): chronicle of twentieth-century musician.* New York: P. Lang, 1985.

Berlioz, Hector. *Evenings in the orchestra.* Harmondsworth: Penguin Books, 1963.

Berlioz, Hector. *The musical madhouse (Les grotesques de la musique).* Rochester, New York: University of Rochester Press, 2003.

Bernard, Jonathan W., Editor. *Elliott Carter: collected essays and lectures, 1937-1995.* Rochester, New York; Woodbridge: University of Rochester Press, 1998.

Bernstein, Leonard. *The joy of music.* New York: Simon and Schuster, 1959.

Bertensson, Sergei. *Sergei Rachmaninoff: a lifetime in music.* London: G. Allen & Unwin, 1965.

Biancolli, Louis. *The Flagstad manuscript.* New York: Putnam, 1952.

Bickley, Nora, Editor. *Letters from and to Joseph Joachim.* London: Macmillan, 1914.

Bie, Oskar. *A history of the pianoforte and pianoforte players.* New York: Da Capo Press, 1966.

Blaukopf, Herta. *Mahler's unknown letters.* London: Gollancz, 1986.

Blaukopf, Kurt and Herta. *Mahler: his life, work and world.* London: Thames and Hudson, 1991.

Bliss, Arthur. *As I remember.* London: Thames Publishing, 1989.

Block, Adrienne Fried. *Amy Beach, passionate Victorian: the life and work of an American composer, 1867–1944.* New York: Oxford University Press, 1998.

Bloch, Ernst. *Essays on the philosophy of music.* Cambridge: Cambridge University Press, 1985.

Blocker, Robert. *The Robert Shaw reader.* New Haven; London: Yale University Press, 2004.

Blom, Eric. *A musical postbag.* London: J. M. Dent, 1945.

Blom, Eric. *Beethoven's pianoforte sonatas discussed.* London: J. M. Dent, 1938.

Blom, Eric. *Classics major and minor: with some other musical ruminations.* London: J. M. Dent, 1958.

Blum, David. *The art of quartet playing: the Guarneri Quartet in conversation with David Blum.* London: Gollancz, 1986.

Blume, Friedrich. *Classic and Romantic music: a comprehensive survey.* London: Faber and Faber, 1972.

Boden, Anthony. *The Parrys of the Golden Vale: background to genius.* London: Thames Publishing, 1998.

Bonavia, Ferruccio. *Musicians on music.* London: Routledge & Kegan Paul, 1956.

Bonds, Mark Evan *After Beethoven: imperatives of originality in the symphony.* Cambridge, Massachusetts; London: Harvard University Press, 1996.

Bonis, Ferenc, Editor. *The selected writings of Zoltán Kodály.* London; New York: Boosey & Hawkes, 1974.

Bookspan, Martin. *André Previn: a biography.* London: Hamilton, 1981.

Boros, James and Richard Toop, Editors. *Brian Ferneyhough: Collected writings.* Amsterdam: Harwood Academic, 1995.

Boulez, Pierre. *Stocktakings from an apprenticeship.* Oxford: Clarendon Press, 1991.

Boult, Adrian. *Boult on music: words from a lifetime's communication.* London: Toccata Press, 1983.

Boult, Adrian. *My own trumpet.* London, Hamish Hamilton, 1973.

Boult, Adrian with Jerrold Northrop Moore. *Music and friends: seven decades of letters to Adrian Boult from Elgar, Vaughan Williams, Holst, Bruno Walter, Yehudi Menuhin and other friends.* London: Hamish Hamilton, 1979.

Bovet, Marie Anne de. *Charles Gounod: his life and his works.* London: S. Low, Marston, Searle & Rivington, Ltd., 1891.

Bowen, Catherine Drinker. *Beloved friend: the story of Tchaikowsky and Nadejda von Meck.* London: Hutchinson & Co., 1937.

Bowen, Meiron, Editor. *Gerhard on music: selected writings.* Brookfield, Vermont: Ashgate, 2000.

Bowen, Meirion. *Michael Tippett.* London: Robson Books, 1982.

Bowen, Meiron, Editor. *Music of the angels: essays and sketchbooks of Michael Tippett.* London: Eulenburg, 1980.

Bowen, Meiron, Editor. *Tippett on music.* Oxford: Clarendon Press, 1995.

Bowers, Faubion. *Scriabin: a biography.* Mineola: Dover; London: Constable, 1996.

Boyden, Matthew. *Richard Strauss.* London: Weidenfeld & Nicolson, 1999.

Bozarth, George S., Editor. *Brahms*

studies: analytical and historical perspectives; papers delivered at the International Brahms Conference, Washington, DC, 5-8 May 1983. Oxford: Clarendon Press, 1990.

Brand, Juliane, Christopher Hailey and Donald Harris, Editors. The Berg-Schoenberg correspondence: selected letters. Basingstoke: Macmillan, 1987.

Brandenbugh, Sieghard, Editor. Haydn, Mozart, & Beethoven: studies in the music of the classical period: essays in honor of Alan Tyson. Oxford: Clarendon Press, 1998.

Braunstein, Joseph. Musica Æterna, program notes for 1961–1971. New York: Musica Æterna, 1972.

Braunstein, Joseph. Musica Æterna, program notes for 1971–1976. New York: Musica Æterna, 1978.

Brendel, Alfred. Alfred Brendel on music: collected essays. Chicago, Iliinois: A Cappella Books, 2001.

Brendel, Alfred. The veil of order: Alfred Brendel in conversation with Martin Meyer. London: Faber and Faber, 2002.

Breuning, Gerhard von. Memories of Beethoven: from the house of the black-robed Spaniards. Cambridge: Cambridge University Press, 1992.

Briscoe, James R., Editor. (Brief Description): Debussy in performance. New Haven: Yale University Press, 1999.

Brott, Alexander Betty Nygaard King. Alexander Brott: my lives in music. Oakville, Ontario; Niagara Falls, New York: Mosaic Press, 2005.

Brown, Alfred Peter. The symphonic repertoire. Vol. 2, The first golden age of the Viennese symphony: Haydn, Mozart, Beethoven, and Schubert. Bloomington, Indiana: Indiana University Press, 2002.

Brown, Maurice John Edwin. Schubert: a critical biography. London: Macmillan; New York: St. Martin's Press, 1958.

Broyles, Michael. Beethoven: the emergence and evolution of Beethoven's heroic style. New York: Excelsior Music Publishing Co., 1987.

Brubaker, Bruce and Jane Gottlieb, Editors. Pianist, scholar, connoisseur: essays in honor of Jacob Lateiner. Stuyvesant, N.Y., Pendragon Press, 2000.

Buch, Esteban. Beethoven's Ninth: a political history. Chicago; London: University of Chicago Press, 2003.

Burk, John N., Editor. Letters of Richard Wagner: the Burrell collection. London: Gollancz, 1951.

Burnham, Scott G. Beethoven hero. Princeton, New Jersey: Princeton University Press, 1995.

Burnham, Scott G and Michael P. Steinberg, Editors. Beethoven and his world. Princeton, New Jersey; Oxford: Princeton University Press, 2000.

Burton, William Westbrook, Editor. Conversations about Bernstein. New York; Oxford: Oxford University Press, 1995.

Busch, Fritz. Pages from a musician's life. London: Hogarth Press, 1953.

Busch, Hans, Editor. Verdi's Aida: the history of an opera in letters and documents. Minneapolis: University of Minnesota Press, 1978.

Busch, Hans, Editor. Verdi's Falstaff in letters and contemporary reviews. Bloomington: Indiana University Press, 1997.

Busch, Marie, Translator. Memoirs of Eugenie Schumann. London: W. Heinemann, 1927.

Bush, Alan Dudley. In my eighth decade and other essays. London: Kahn & Averill, 1980.

Busoni, Ferruccio. Letters to his wife. Translated by Rosamond Ley. New York: Da Capo Press, 1975.

Byron, Reginald. Music, culture, & experience: selected papers of John Blacking. Chicago: University of Chicago Press, 1995.

Cairns, David. Responses: musical essays and reviews. New York: Da Capo Press, 1980.

Cardus, Neville. Talking of music. London: Collins, 1957.

Carley, Lionel. Delius: a life in letters. London: Scolar Press in association with the Delius Trust, 1988.

Carley, Lionel. Grieg and Delius: a chronicle of their friendship in letters. London: Marion Boyars, 1993.

Carner, Mosco. Major and minor. London: Duckworth, 1980

Carner, Mosco. Puccini: a critical biography. London: Duckworth, 1958.

Carroll, Brendan G. The last prodigy: a biography of Erich Wolfgang Korngold. Portland, Oregon: Amadeus Press, 1997.

Carse, Adam von Ahn. The life of Jullien: adventurer, showman-conductor and establisher of the Promenade Concerts in England, together with a history of those concerts up to 1895. Cambridge England: Heffer, 1951.

Carse, Adam von Ahn. The orchestra from Beethoven to Berlioz: a history of the orchestra in the first half of the 19th century, and of the development of orchestral baton-conducting. Cambridge: W. Heffer, 1948.

Casals, Pablo. Joys and sorrows: reflections by Pablo Casals as told to Albert E. Kahn. London: Macdonald, 1970.

Casals, Pablo. The memoirs of Pablo Casals as told to Thomas Dozier. London: Life en Español, 1959.

Chappell, Paul. Dr. S. S. Wesley, 1810–1876: portrait of a Victorian musician. Great Wakering: Mayhew-McCrimmon, 1977.

Chasins, Abram. Leopold Stokowski, a profile. New York: Hawthorn Books, 1979.

Charlton, Davi, Editor and Martyn Clarke Translator. E.T.A. Hoffmann's musical writings: Kreisleriana, The Poet and the Composer. Cambridge: Cambridge University Press, 1989.

Chávez, Carlos. Musical thought. Cambridge: Harvard University Press, 1961.

Chesterman, Robert, Editor. Conversations with conductors: Bruno Walter, Sir Adrian Boult, Leonard Bernstein, Ernest Ansermet, Otto Klemperer, Leopold Stokowski. Totowa, New Jersey: Rowman and Littlefield, 1976.

Chissell, Joan. Clara Schumann: a dedicated spirit; a study of her life and work. London: Hamilton, 1983.

Chua, Daniel K. L. *The "Galitzin" quartets of Beethoven: Opp.127, 132, 130*. Princeton: Princeton University Press, 1995.

Citron, Marcia, Editor. *The letters of Fanny Hensel to Felix Mendelssohn*. Stuyvesant, New York: Pendragon Press, 1987.

Clark, Walter Aaron. *Enrique Granados: poet of the piano*. Oxford, England; New York, N.Y.: Oxford University Press, 2006.

Clark, Walter Aaron. *Isaac Albéniz: portrait of a romantic*. Oxford; New York: Oxford University Press, 1999.

Clive, Peter. *Beethoven and his world*. Oxford University Press, 2001.

Closson, Ernest. *History of the piano*. Translated by Delano Ames and edited by Robin Golding. London: Paul Elek, 1947.

Cockshoot, John V. *The fugue in Beethoven's piano music*. London: Routledge & Kegan Paul, 1959.

Coe, Richard N, Translator. *Life of Rossini by Stendhal*. London: Calder & Boyars, 1970.

Coleman, Alexander, Editor. *Diversions & animadversions: essays from The new criterion*. New Brunswick, New Jersey; London: Transaction Publishers, 2005.

Colerick, George. *From the Italian girl to Cabaret: musical humour, parody and burlesque*. London: Juventus, 1998.

Coleridige, A. D. *Life of Moscheles, with selections from his diaries and correspondence by his wife*. London: Hurst & Blackett, 1873.

Colles, Henry Cope. *Essays and lectures*. London: Humphrey Milford, Oxford University Press, 1945.

Cone, Edward T., Editor. *Roger Sessions on music: collected essays*. Princeton, New Jersey: Princeton University Press, 1979.

Cone, Edward T. *The composer's voice*. Berkeley; London: University of California Press, 1974.

Cook, Susan and Judy S. Tsou, Editors. *Cecilia reclaimed: feminist perspectives on gender and music*. Urbana: University of Illinois Press, 1994.

Cooper, Barry. *Beethoven: The master musicians series*. Oxford: Oxford University Press, 2000.

Cooper, Barry. *Beethoven and the creative process*. Oxford: Clarendon Press, 1990.

Cooper, Barry. *Beethoven's folksong settings: chronology, sources, style*. Cambridge: Cambridge University Press, 1991.

Cooper, Barry. *The Beethoven compendium: a guide to Beethoven's life and music*. London: Thames and Hudson, 1991.

Cooper, Martin. *Beethoven: the last decade, 1817–1827*. London: Oxford University Press, 1970.

Cooper, Martin. *Judgements of value: selected writings on music*. Oxford; New York: Oxford University Press, 1988.

Cooper, Martin. *Ideas and music*. London: Barrie and Rockliff, 1965.

Cooper, Victoria L. *The house of Novello: the practice and policy of a Victorian music publisher, 1829–1866*. Aldershot, Hants: Ashgate, 2003.

Coover, James. *Music at auction: Puttick and Simpson (of Lon-*

don), *1794–1971: being an annotated, chronological list of sales of musical materials*. Warren, Michigan: Harmonie Park Press, 1988.

Copland, Aaron. *Copland on music*. London: Deutsch, 1961.

Corredor, J. Ma. *Conversations with Casals*. London: Hutchinson, 1956.

Cott, Jonathan. *Stockhausen: conversations with the composer*. London: Picador, 1974.

Cottrell, Stephen. *Professional music making in London: ethnography and experience*. Aldershot: Ashgate, 2004.

Cowell, Henry. *Charles Ives and his music*. New York: Oxford University Press, 1955.

Cowling, Elizabeth. *The cello*. London: Batsford, 1983.

Crabbe, John. *Beethoven's empire of the mind*. Newbury: Lovell Baines, 1982.

Craft, Robert. *An improbable life: memoirs*. Nashville: Vanderbilt University Press, 2002.

Craft, Robert, Editor. *Stravinsky: selected correspondence*. London: Faber and Faber, 3 Vols. 1982–1985.

Craw, Howard Allen. *A biography and thematic catalog of the works of J. L. Dussek: 1760–1812*. Ann Arbor: Michigan, 1965.

Crawford, Richard, R. Allen Lott and Carol J. Oja, Editors. *A Celebration of American music: words and music in honor of H. Wiley Hitchcock*. Ann Arbor: University of Michigan Press, 1990.

Craxton, Harold and Tovey, Donald Francis. *Beethoven: Sonatas for Pianoforte*. London: The Associated Board, [1931].

Crichton, Ronald: Editor. *The memoirs of Ethel Smyth*. New York: Viking, 1987.

Crist, Stephen A. and Roberta M. Marvin, Editors. *Historical musicology: sources, methods, interpretations*. Rochester, New York: University of Rochester Press, 2004.

Crofton, Ian and Donald Fraser, Editors. *A dictionary of musical quotations*. London: Croom Helm, 1985.

Crompton, Louis, Editor. *Shaw, Bernard: The great composers: reviews and bombardments*. Berkeley; London: University of California Press, 1978.

Csicserry-Ronay, Elizabeth, Translator and Editor. *Hector Berlioz: The art of music and other essays: (A travers chants)*. Bloomington: Indiana University Press, 1994.

Curtiss, Mina Kirstein. *Bizet and his world*. London: Secker & Warburg, 1959.

Cuyler, Louise Elvira. *The symphony*. New York: Harcourt Brace Jovanovich, 1973.

Dahlhaus, Carl. *Ludwig van Beethoven: approaches to his music*. Oxford: Clarendon Press, 1991.

Dahlhaus, Carl. *Nineteenth-century music*. Translated by J. Bradford Robinson. Berkeley; London: University of California Press, 1989.

Daniels, Robin. *Conversations with Cardus*. London: Gollancz, 1976.

Daniels, Robin. Conversations with Menuhin. London: Macdonald General Books, 1979.

Day, James. *Vaughan Williams*. London: Dent, 1961.

Davies, Peter Maxwell. *Studies from two decades*. Selected and introduced by Stephen Pruslin. London: Boosey & Hawkes, 1979.

Dean, Winton. *Georges Bizet: his life and work*. London: J.M. Dent, 1965.

Deas, Stewart. *In defence of Hanslick*. London: Williams and Norgate, 1940.

Debussy, Claude. *Debussy on music*. London: Secker & Warburg, 1977.

Delbanco, Nicholas. *The Beaux Arts Trio*. London: Gollancz, 1985.

Demény, Janos, Editor. *Béla Bartók: letters*. London: Faber and Faber, 1971.

Dent, Edward Joseph. *Selected essays*. Edited by Hugh Taylor. Cambridge; New York: Cambridge University Press, 1979.

Deutsch, Otto Erich. *Mozart: a documentary biography*. London: Adam & Charles Black, 1965.

Deutsch, Otto Erich. *Schubert: a documentary biography*. London: J.M. Dent, 1946

Deutsch, Otto Erich. *Schubert: memoirs by his friends*. London: Adam & Charles Black, 1958.

Dibble, Jeremy. *C. Hubert H. Parry: his life and music*. Oxford: Clarendon Press, 1992.

Dibble, Jeremy. *Charles Villiers Stanford: man and musician*. Oxford: Oxford University Press, 2002.

Donakowski, Conrad L. *A muse for the masses: ritual and music in an age of democratic revolution, 1770–1870*. Chicago: University of Chicago Press, 1977.

Dower, Catherine. *Alfred Einstein on music: selected music criticisms*. New York: Greenwood Press, 1991.

Downs, Philip G. *Classical music: the era of Haydn, Mozart, and Beethoven*. New York: W.W. Norton, 1992.

Drabkin, William. *Beethoven: Missa Solemnis*. Cambridge: Cambridge University Press, 1991.

Dreyfus, Kay. *The farthest north of humanness: letters of Percy Grainger, 1901–1914*. South Melbourne; Basingstoke: Macmillan, 1985.

Dubal, David, Editor. *Remembering Horowitz: 125 pianists recall a legend*. New York: Schirmer Books, 1993.

Dubal, David. *The world of the concert pianist*. London: Victor Gollancz, 1985.

Dvořák, Otakar. *Antonín Dvořák, my father*. Spillville, Iowa: Czech Historical Research Center, 1993.

Dyson, George. *The progress of music*. London: Oxford University Press, Humphrey Milford, 1932.

Eastaugh, Kenneth. *Havergal Brian: the making of a composer*. London: Harrap, 1976.

Edwards, Allen. *Flawed words and stubborn sounds: a conversation with Elliott Carter*. New York: Norton & Company, 1971.

Edwards, Frederick George. *Musical haunts in London*. London: J. Curwen & Sons, 1895.

Ehrlich, Cyril. *First philharmonic: a history of the Royal Philharmonic Society*. Oxford: Clarendon Press, 1995.

Einstein, Alfred. *A short history of music*. London: Cassell and Company Ltd., 1948.

Einstein, Alfred. *Essays on music*. London: Faber and Faber, 1958.

Einstein, Alfred. *Mozart: his character, his work*. London: Cassell and Company Ltd., 1946.

Einstein, Alfred. *Music in the Romantic era*. London: J.M. Dent Ltd., 1947.

Ekman, Karl. *Jean Sibelius, his life and personality*. New York: Tudor Publishing. Co., 1945.

Elgar, Edward. *A future for English music: and other lectures*, Edited by Percy M. Young. London: Dobson, 1968.

Elkin, Robert. *Queen's Hall, 1893–1941*. London: Rider, 1944.

Ella, John. *Musical sketches, abroad and at home: with original music by Mozart, Czerny, Graun, etc., vocal cadenzas and other musical illustrations*. London: Ridgway, Vol. 1., 1869.

Ellis, William Ashton. *The family letters of Richard Wagner*. Edited and translated by William Ashton Ellis and enlarged with introduction and notes by John Deathridge. Basingstoke: Macmillan, 1991.

Ellis, William Ashton. *Richard Wagner's prose works: Vol. 1, The art-work of the future*. Edited and translated by William Ashton Ellis. London: Kegan Paul, Trench, Trübner, 1895.

Ellis, William Ashton. *Richard Wagner's prose works: Vol. 2, Opera and drama*. Edited and translated by William Ashton Ellis. London: Kegan Paul, Trench, Trübner, 1900.

Ellis, William Ashton. *Richard Wagner's prose works: Vol. 3, The theatre*. Edited and translated by William Ashton Ellis. London: Kegan Paul, Trench, Trübner, 1907.

Ellis, William Ashton. *Richard Wagner's prose works: Vol. 4, Art and politics*. Edited and translated by William Ashton Ellis. London: Kegan Paul, Trench, Trübner, 1895.

Ellis, William Ashton. *Richard Wagner's prose works: Vol. 5, Actors and singers*. Edited and translated by William Ashton Ellis. London: Kegan Paul, Trench, Trübner, 1896.

Ellis, William Ashton. *Richard Wagner's prose works: Vol. 6, Religion and art*. Edited and translated by William Ashton Ellis. London: Kegan Paul, Trench, Trübner, 1897.

Ellis, William Ashton. *Richard Wagner's prose works: Vol. 7, In Paris and Dresden*. Edited and translated by William Ashton Ellis. London: Kegan Paul, Trench, Trübner, 1898.

Ellis, William Ashton. *Richard Wagner's prose works: Vol. 8, Posthumous*. Edited and translated by William Ashton Ellis. London: Kegan Paul, Trench, Trübner, 1899.

Elterlein, Ernst von. *Beethoven's pianoforte sonatas: explained for the lovers of the musical art*. London: W. Reeves, 1898.

Engel, Carl. *Musical myths and facts*. London: Novello, Ewer & Co.; New York: J.L. Peters, 1876.

Eosze, László. *Zoltán Kodály: his life and work*. London: Collet's, 1962.

Etter, Brian K. *From classicism to modernism: Western musical culture and the metaphysics of order*. Aldershot: Ashgate, 2001.

Ewen, David. *From Bach to Stravinsky: the history of music by its* foremost critics. New York, Greenwood Press, 1968.

Ewen, David. *Romain Rolland's Essays on music.* New York: Dover Publications, 1959.

Fay, Amy. *Music-study in Germany: from the home correspondence of Amy Fay.* New York: Dover Publications, 1965.

Fenby, Eric. *Delius as I knew him.* London: Quality Press, 1936.

Ferguson, Donald Nivison. *Masterworks of the orchestral repertoire: a guide for listeners.* Minneapolis: University of Minnesota Press, 1954.

Fétis, François-Joseph. *Curiosités historiques de la musique: complément nécessaire de la Musique mise à la portée de tout le monde.* Paris: Janet et Cotelle, 1830.

Fifield, Christopher. *Max Bruch: his life and works.* London: Gollancz, 1988.

Fifield, Christopher. *True artist and true friend: a biography of Hans Richter.* Oxford: Clarendon Press, 1993.

Finson, Jon and R. Larry Todd, Editors. *Mendelssohn and Schumann: essays on their music and its context.* Durham, N.C.: Duke University Press, 1984.

Fischer, Edwin. *Beethoven's pianoforte sonatas: a guide for students & amateurs.* London: Faber and Faber, 1959.

Fischer, Edwin. *Reflections on music.* London: Williams and Norgate, 1951.

Fischer, Hans Conrad and Erich Kock. *Ludwig van Beethoven: a study in text and pictures.* London: Macmillan; New York, St. Martin's Press, 1972.

Fischmann, Zdenka E. *Janácˇek-Newmarch correspondence. 1st limited and numbered edition.* Rockville, MD: Kabel Publishers, 1986.

Fitzlyon, April. *Maria Malibran: diva of the romantic age.* London: Souvenir Press, 1987.

FitzLyon, April. *The price of genius: a life of Pauline Viardot.* London: John Calder, 1964.

Forbes, Elliot, Editor. *Thayer's life of Beethoven.* Princeton, New Jersey: Princeton University Press, 1967.

Foreman, Lewis. *Bax: a composer and his times.* London: Scolar Press, 1983.

Foreman, Lewis, Editor. *Farewell, my youth, and other writings by Arnold Bax.* Aldershot: Scolar Press, 1992.

Foster, Myles Birket. *History of the Philharmonic Society of London, 1813–1912: a record of a hundred years' work in the cause of music.* London: Bodley Head, 1912.

Foulds, John. *Music today: its heritage from the past, and legacy to the future.* London: I. Nicholson and Watson, limited, 1934.

Frank, Mortimer H. *Arturo Toscanini: the NBC years.* Portland, Oregon: Amadeus Press, 2002.

Fraser, Andrew Alastair. *Essays on music.* London: Oxford University Press, H. Milford, 1930.

Frohlich, Martha. *Beethoven's Appassionata' sonata.* Oxford: Clarendon Press, 1991.

Gal, Hans. *The golden age of Vienna.* London: Max Parrish & Co. Limited, 1948.

Gal, Hans. *The musician's world:*

great composers in their letters. London: Thames and Hudson, 1965.

Galatopoulos, Stelios. *Bellini: life, times, music.* London: Sanctuary, 2002.

Garden, Edward and Nigel Gottrei, Editors. *'To my best friend': correspondence between Tchaikovsky and Nadezhda von Meck, 1876–1878.* Oxford: Clarendon Press, 1993.

Geck, Martin. Beethoven. London: Haus, 2003.

Gerig, Reginald. *Famous pianists & their technique.* Washington: R. B. Luce, 1974.

Gilliam, Bryan. *The life of Richard Strauss.* Cambridge: Cambridge University Press, 1999.

Gilliam, Bryan, Editor. *Richard Strauss and his world.* Princeton, New Jersey: Princeton University Press, 1992.

Gillies, Malcolm and Bruce Clunies Ross, Editors. *Grainger on music.* Oxford; New York: Oxford University Press, 1999.

Gillies, Malcolm and David Pear, Editors. *The all-round man: selected letters of Percy Grainger, 1914–1961.* Oxford: Clarendon Press, 1994.

Gillies, Malcolm, Editor. *The Bartók companion.* London: Faber and Faber, 1993.

Gillmor, Alan M. *Erik Satie.* Basingstoke: Macmillan Press, 1988.

Glehn, M. E. *Goethe and Mendelssohn : (1821–1831).* London: Macmillan, 1874.

Glowacki, John, Editor. *Paul A. Pisk: Essays in his honor.* Austin, Texas: University of Texas, 1966

Gollancz, Victor. *Journey towards music: a memoir.* London: Victor Gollancz Ltd., 1964.

Good, Edwin Marshall. *Giraffes, black dragons, and other pianos: a technological history from Cristofori to the modern concert grand.* Stanford, California: Stanford University Press, 1982.

Gordon, David. *Musical visitors to Britain.* London: Routledge, 2005.

Gordon, Stewart. *A history of keyboard literature: music for the piano and its forerunners.* Schirmer Books: New York: London : Prentice Hall International, 1996.

Gorrell, Lorraine. *The nineteenth-century German lied.* Portland, Oregon: Amadeus Press, 1993.

Goss, Glenda D. *Jean Sibelius: the Hämeenlinna letters: scenes from a musical life, 1875–1895.* Esbo, Finland: Schildts, 1997.

Goss, Madeleine. *Bolero: the life of Maurice Ravel.* New York: Tudor, 1945.

Gotch, Rosamund Brunel, Editor. *Mendelssohn and his friends in Kensington: letters from Fanny and Sophy Horsley, written 1833–36.* London: Oxford University Press, 1938.

Gounod, Charles. *Charles Gounod; autobiographical reminiscences: with family letters and notes on music; from the French.* London: William Heinemann, 1896.

Grabs, Manfred, Editor. *Hanns Eisler: a rebel in music; selected writings.* Berlin: Seven Seas Publishers, 1978.

Grace, Harvey. *A musician at large.* London: Oxford University Press, H. Milford, 1928.

(La) Grange, Henry-Louis de. *Gustav Mahler*. Oxford: Oxford University Press, 1995.

Graves, Charles L. *Hubert Parry: his life and works*. London: Macmillan, 1926.

Graves, Charles L. *Post-Victorian music: with other studies and sketches*. London: Macmillan and Co., limited, 1911.

Graves, Charles L. *The life & letters of Sir George Grove, Hon. D.C.L. (Durham), Hon. LL.D. (Glasgow), formerly director of the Royal college of music*. London: Macmillan and Co., Ltd.; New York: The Macmillan Co., 1903.

Gray, Cecil. *Musical chairs, or, between two stools: being the life and memoirs of Cecil Gray*. London: Home & Van Thal, 1948.

Gregor-Dellin and Dietrich Mack, Editors. *Cosima Wagner's diaries.: Vol. 1, 1869 - 1877*. London: Collins, 1978-1980.

Griffiths, Paul. *Modern music: the avant-garde since 1945*. London: J. M. Dent & Sons Ltd., 1981.

Griffiths, Paul. *Olivier Messiaen and the music of time*. London: Faber and Faber, 1985.

Griffiths, Paul. *Peter Maxwell Davies*. London: Robson Books, 1988.

Griffiths, Paul. *The sea on fire: Jean Barraqué*. Rochester, New York: Woodbridge: University of Rochester Press, 2003.

Griffiths, Paul. *The string quartet*. London: Thames and Hudson, 1983.

Grout, Donald Jay and Claude V. Palisca, Editors. *A history of Western music*. London: J. M. Dent, 1988.

Grove, George. *Beethoven and his nine symphonies*. London: Novello, Ewer, 1896.

Grover, Ralph Scott. *Ernest Chausson: the man and his music*. London: The Athlone Press, 1980.

Grover, Ralph Scott. *The music of Edmund Rubbra*. Aldershot: Scolar Press, 1993.

Grun, Bernard. *Alban Berg: letters to his wife*. Edited and translated by Bernard Grun. London: Faber and Faber, 1971.

Gutman, David. *Prokofiev*. London: Omnibus Press, 1990.

Hadow, William Henry. *Collected essays*. London: H. Milford at the Oxford University Press, 1928.

Hadow, William Henry. *Beethoven's Op. 18 Quartets*. London: H. Milford at the Oxford University Press, 1926.

Haggin, Bernard H. *Music observed*. New York: Oxford University Press, 1964.

Hailey, Christopher. *Franz Schreker, 1878–1934: a cultural biography*. Cambridge: Cambridge University Press, 1993.

Hall, Michael. *Leaving home: a conducted tour of twentieth-century music with Simon Rattle*. London: Faber and Faber, 1996.

Hall, Patricia and Friedemann Sallis, Editors. (Brief Description): *A handbook to twentieth-century musical sketches*. Cambridge: Cambridge University Press, 2004.

Hallé, C. E. *Life and letters of Sir Charles Hallé: being an autobiography (1819–1860) with correspondence and diaries*. London: Smith, Elder & Co., 1896.

162

Halstead, Jill. *The woman composer: creativity and the gendered politics of musical composition.* Aldershot: Ashgate, 1997.

Hamburger, Michael, Editor and Translator. *Beethoven letters, journals, and conversations.* New York: Thames and Hudson, 1951.

Hammelmann, Hanns A. and Ewald Osers. *The correspondence between Richard Strauss and Hugo von Hofmannsthal.* London: Collins, 1961.

Hanson, Lawrence and Elisabeth Hanson. *Tchaikovsky: the man behind the music.* New York: Dodd, Mead & Co, 1967.

Harding, James. *Massenet.* London: J. M. Dent & Sons Ltd., 1970.

Harding, James. *Saint-Saëns and his circle.* London: Chapman & Hall, 1965.

Harding, Rosamond E. M. *Origins of musical time and expression.* London: Oxford University Press, 1938.

Harman, Alec with Anthony Milner and Wilfrid Mellers. *Man and his music: the story of musical experience in the West.* London: Barrie & Jenkins, 1988.

Harper, Nancy Lee. *Manuel de Falla: his life and music.* Lanham, Maryland; London: The Scarecrow Press, 2005.

Hartmann, Arthur. *'Claude Debussy as I knew him' and other writings of Arthur Hartmann.* Edited by Samuel Hsu, Sidney Grolnic, and Mark Peters. Rochester, New York; Woodbridge: University of Rochester Press, 2003.

Haugen, Einar and Camilla Cai. *Ole Bull: Norway's romantic musician and cosmopolitan patriot.*

Madison: The University of Wisconsin Press, 1993.

Headington, Christopher. *The Bodley Head history of Western music.* London: The Bodley Head, 1974.

Heartz, Daniel. *Music in European capitals: the galant style, 1720–1780.* New York; London: W. W. Norton, 2003.

Hedley, Arthur, Editor. *Selected correspondence of Fryderyk Chopin: abridged from Fryderyk Chopin's correspondence.* London: Heinemann, 1962.

Heiles, Anne Mischakoff. *Mischa Mischakoff: journeys of a concertmaster.* Sterling Heights, Michigan: Harmonie Park Press, 2006.

Henderson, Sanya Shoilevska. *Alex North, film composer: a biography, with musical analyses of a Streetcar named desire, Spartacus, The misfits, Under the volcano, and Prizzi's honor.* Jefferson, N.C.; London: McFarland, 2003.

Henschel, George. *Personal recollections of Johannes Brahms: some of his letters to and pages from a journal kept by George Henschel.* Boston: R G. Badger, 1907.

Henze, Hans Werner. *Bohemian fifths: an autobiography.* London: Faber and Faber, 1998.

Henze, Hans Werner. *Music and politics: collected writings 1953–81.* London: Faber and Faber, 1982.

Herbert, May, Translator. *Early letters of Robert Schumann.* London: George Bell and Sons, 1888.

Heyman, Barbara B. *Samuel Barber:*

the composer and his music. New York: Oxford University Press, 1992.

Heyworth, Peter. *Otto Klemperer, his life and times.* Cambridge: Cambridge University Press, 2 Vols. 1983–1996.

Hildebrandt, Dieter. *Pianoforte: a social history of the piano.* London: Hutchinson, 1988.

Hill, Peter. *The Messiaen companion.* London: Faber and Faber, 1995.

Hill, Peter and Nigel Simeone. *Messiaen.* New Haven Connecticut; London: Yale University Press, 2005.

Hiller, Ferdinand. *Mendelssohn: Letters and recollections.* New York: Vienna House, 1972.

Hines, Robert Stephan. *The orchestral composer's point of view: essays on twentieth-century music by those who wrote it.* Norman: University of Oklahoma Press, 1970.

Ho, Allan B. *Shostakovich reconsidered.* London: Toccata Press, 1998.

Hodeir, André. *Since Debussy: a view of contemporary music.* New York: Da Capo Press, 1975.

Holmes, Edward. *The life of Mozart: including his correspondence.* London: Chapman and Hall, 1845.

Holmes, John L. *Composers on composers.* New York: Greenwood Press, 1990.

Hopkins, Anthony. *The concertgoer's companion.* London: J.M. Dent & Sons Ltd., 1984.

Hopkins, Anthony. *The seven concertos of Beethoven.* Aldershot: Scolar Press, 1996.

Holt, Richard. *Nicolas Medtner*

(1879–1951): a tribute to his art and personality. London: D. Dobson, 1955.

Honegger, Arthur. *I am a composer.* London: Faber and Faber, 1966.

Hoover, Kathleen and John Cage. *Virgil Thomson: his life and music.* New York; London: T. Yoseloff, 1959.

Horgan, Paul. *Encounters with Stravinsky: a personal record.* London: The Bodley Head, 1972.

Horowitz, Joseph. *Conversations with Arrau.* London: Collins, 1982.

Horowitz, Joseph. Understanding Toscanini. London: Faber and Faber, 1987.

Horwood, Wally. *Adolphe Sax, 1814–1894: his life and legacy.* Bramley: Bramley Books, 1980.

Howie, Crawford. *Anton Bruckner: a documentary biography.* Lewiston, N.Y.; Lampeter: Edwin Mellen Press, 2002.

Hueffer, Francis. *Correspondence of Wagner and Liszt.* New York: Greenwood Press, 2 Vols.1969.

Hughes, Spike. *The Toscanini legacy: a critical study of Arturo Toscanini's performances of Beethoven, Verdi, and other composers.* London: Putnam, 1959.

Hullah, Annette. *Theodor Leschetizky.* London and New York: J. Land & Co., 1906.

Le Huray, Peter and James Day, Editors. *Music and aesthetics in the eighteenth and early-nineteenth centuries.* Cambridge: Cambridge University Press, 1988.

D' Indy, Vincent. *César Franck.* New York: Dover Publications, 1965.

Jacobs, Arthur. *Arthur Sullivan: A*

Victorian musician. Aldershot: Scolar Press, 1992.

Jahn, Otto. *Life of Mozart.* London: Novello, Ewer & Co., 1882.

Jefferson, Alan. *Sir Thomas Beecham: a centenary tribute.* London: World Records Ltd., 1979.

Jezic, Diane. *The musical migration and Ernst Toch.* Ames: Iowa State University Press, 1989.

Johnson, Douglas Porter, Editor. *The Beethoven sketchbooks: history, reconstruction, inventory.* Oxford: Clarendon, 1985.

Johnson, Stephen. *Bruckner remembered.* London: Faber and Faber, 1998.

Jones, David, Wyn. *Beethoven: Pastoral symphony.* Cambridge: Cambridge University Press, 1995.

Jones, David Wyn. *The life of Beethoven.* Cambridge: Cambridge University Press, 1998.

Jones, David Wyn. *The symphony in Beethoven's Vienna.* Cambridge: Cambridge University Press, 2006.

Jones, J. Barrie, Editor. *Gabriel Fauré: a life in letters.* London: Batsford, 1989.

Jones, Peter Ward, Editor and Translator. *The Mendelssohns on honeymoon: the 1837 diary of Felix and Cécile Mendelssohn Bartholdy, together with letters to their families.* Oxford: Clarendon Press, 1997.

Jones, Timothy. *Beethoven, the Moonlight and other sonatas, Op. 27 and Op. 31.* Cambridge; New York, N.Y.: Cambridge University Press, 1999.

Kalischer, A. C., Editor. *Beethoven's letters: a critical edition.* London: J. M. Dent, 1909.

Kárpáti, János. *Bartók's chamber music.* Stuyvesant, New York: Pendragon Press, 1994.

Keefe, Simon P. *The Cambridge companion to the concerto.* Cambridge, New York, N.Y.: Cambridge University Press, 2005.

Keller, Hans. *The great Haydn quartets: their interpretation.* London: J. M. Dent, 1986.

Keller, Hans, Editor. *The memoirs of Carl Flesch.* New York: Macmillan, 1958.

Keller, Hans, and Christopher Wintle. *Beethoven's string quartets in F minor, Op. 95 and C minor, Op. 131: two studies.* Nottingham: Department of Music, University of Nottingham, 1995.

Kelly, Thomas Forrest. *First nights at the opera: five musical premiers.* New Haven: Yale University Press, 2004.

Kennedy, Michael. *Adrian Boult.* London: Hamish Hamilton, 1987.

Kennedy, Michael. *Barbirolli, conductor laureate: the authorised biography.* London: Hart-Davis, MacGibbon, 1973.

Kennedy, Michael, Editor. *The autobiography of Charles Hallé; with correspondence and diaries.*

London: Paul Elek, 1972.

Kennedy, Michael. *Hallé tradition: a century of music.* Manchester: Manchester University Press, 1960.

Kennedy, Michael. *The works of Ralph Vaughan Williams.* London: Oxford University Press, 1964.

Kemp, Ian. *Tippett: the composer and his music.* London; New York: Eulenburg Books, 1984.

Kerman, Joseph. *The Beethoven quartets.* London: Oxford University Press, 1967, c1966.

Kerman, Joseph. *Write all these down: essays on music.* Berkeley, California; London: University of California Press, 1994.

Kildea, Paul, Editor. *Britten on music.* Oxford: Oxford University Press, 2003.

Kinderman, William. *Beethoven.* Oxford: Oxford University Press, 1997.

Kinderman, William. *Beethoven's Diabelli variations.* Oxford: Clarendon Press; New York: Oxford University Press, 1987.

Kinderman, William, Editor. *The string quartets of Beethoven.* Urbana, Ilinois: University of Illinois Press, 2005.

King, Alec Hyatt. *Musical pursuits: selected essays.* London: British Library, 1987.

Kirby, F. E. *Music for piano: a short history.* Amadeus Press: Portland, 1995.

Kirkpatrick, John, Editor. *Charles E. Ives: Memos.* New York: W.W. Norton, 1972.

Knapp, Raymond. *Brahms and the challenge of the symphony.* Stuyvesant, N.Y.: Pendragon Press, c.1997.

Knight, Frida. *Cambridge music: from the Middle Ages to modern times.* Cambridge, England.: New York: Oleander Press, 1980.

Knight, Max, Translator. *A confidential matter: the letters of Richard Strauss and Stefan Zweig, 1931–1935.* Berkeley; London: University of California Press, 1977.

Kok, Alexander. *A voice in the dark: the philharmonia years.* Ampleforth: Emerson Edition, 2002.

Kopelson, Kevin. *Beethoven's kiss: pianism, perversion, and the mastery of desire.* Stanford, California: Stanford University Press, 1996.

Kostelanetz, Richard, Editor. *Aaron Copland: a reader; selected writings 1923–1972.* New York; London: Routledge, 2003.

Kostelanetz, Richard. *Conversing with Cage.* New York; London: Routledge, 2003.

Kostelanetz, Richard. *On innovative musicians.* New York: Limelight Editions, 1989.

Kostelanetz, Richard, Editor. *Virgil Thomson: a reader ; selected writings, 1924–1984.* New York; London: Routledge, 2002.

Kowalke, Kim H. *Kurt Weill in Europe.* Ann Arbor, Michigan: UMI Research Press, 1979.

Krehbiel, Henry Edward. *The pianoforte and its music.* New York: Cooper Square Publishers, 1971.

Kruseman, Philip, Editor. *Beethoven's own words.* London: Hinrichsen Edition, 1948.

Kurtz, Michael. *Stockhausen: a biography.* London: Faber and Faber, 1992.

Lam, Basil. *Beethoven string quartets.* Seattle: University of Washington Press, 1975.

Lambert, Constant. *Music ho!: a study of music in decline.* London: Faber and Faber, Ltd. 1934.

Landon, H. C. Robbins. *Beethoven: a documentary study.* London: Thames and Hudson, 1970.

Landon, H. C. Robbins. *Beethoven: his life, work and world.*

London: Thames and Hudson, 1992.

Landon, H. C. Robbins. *Essays on the Viennese classical style: Gluck, Haydn, Mozart, Beethoven.* London: Barrie & Rockliff The Cresset Press, 1970.

Landon, H. C. Robbins. *Haydn: chronicle and works/Haydn, the late years, 1801–1809.* Bloomington: Indiana University Press, 1977.

Landon, H. C. Robbins. *Haydn: his life and music.* London: Thames and Hudson, 1988.

Landon, H. C. Robbins. *Haydn in England, 1791–1795.* London: Thames and Hudson, 1976.

Landon, H. C. Robbins. *Haydn: the years of 'The creation', 1796–800.* London: Thames and Hudson, 1977.

Landon, H. C. Robbins. *Mozart: the golden years, 1781–1791.* New York: Schirmer Books, 1989.

Landon, H. C. Robbins. *1791, Mozart's last year.* London: Thames and Hudson, 1988.

Landon, H. C. Robbins *The collected correspondence and London notebooks of Joseph Haydn.* London: Barrie and Rockliff, 1959.

Landon, H. C. Robbins: Editor. *The Mozart companion. London: Faber, 1956.*

Landowska, Wanda. *Music of the past.* London: Geoffrey Bles, 1926.

Lang, Paul Henry. *Musicology and performance.* New Haven: Yale University Press, 1997.

Lang, Paul Henry. *The creative world of Beethoven.* New York: W. W. Norton 1971.

Laurence, Dan H., Editor. *Shaw's music: the complete musical criticism in three volumes.* London: Max Reinhardt, the Bodley Head, 1981.

Lawford-Hinrichsen, Irene. *Music publishing and patronage: C. F. Peters, 1800 to the Holocaust.* Kenton: Edition Press, 2000.

Layton, Robert, Editor. *A guide to the concerto.* Oxford: Oxford University Press, 1996.

Layton, Robert, Editor. *A guide to the symphony.* Oxford: Oxford University Press, 1995.

Lebrecht, Norman. *The maestro myth: great conductors in pursuit of power.* London: Simon & Schuster, 1991.

Lee, Ernest Markham. *The story of the symphony.* London: Scott Publishing Co., 1916.

Leibowitz, Herbert A., Editor. *Musical impressions: selections from Paul Rosenfeld's criticism.* London: G. Allen & Unwin, 1970.

Lenrow, Elbert, Editor and Translator. *The letters of Richard Wagner to Anton Pusinelli.* New York: Vienna House, 1972.

Leonard, Maurice. *Kathleen: the life of Kathleen Ferrier: 1912–1953.* London: Hutchinson, 1988.

Lesure, François and Roger Nichols, Editors. *Debussy, letters.* London: Faber and Faber, 1987.

Letellier, Robert Ignatius, Editor and Translator. *The diaries of Giacomo Meyerbeer.* Madison: Fairleigh Dickinson University Press; London: Associated University Presses, 4 Vols., 1999–2004.

Levas, Santeri. *Sibelius: a personal portrait.* London: J. M. Dent, 1972.

Levy, Alan Howard. *Edward Mac-Dowell, an American master.* Lanham, Md. & London: Scarecrow Press, 1998.

Levy, David Benjamin. *Beethoven: the Ninth Symphony.* New Haven, Connecticut; London: Yale University Press, 2003.

Leyda, Jay and Sergi Bertensson. *The Musorgsky reader: a life of Modeste Petrovich Musorgsky in letters and documents.* New York: W.W. Norton, 1947.

Lewis, Thomas P., Editor. *Raymond Leppard on music: an anthology of critical and personal writings.* White Plains, N.Y.: Pro/Am Music Resources, 1993.

Liébert, Georges. *Nietzsche and music.* Chicago: University of Chicago Press, 2004.

Liszt, Franz. *An artist's journey: lettres d'un bachelier ès musique, 1835–1841.* Chicago: University of Chicago Press, 1989.

Litzmann, Berthold, Editor. *Clara Schumann: an artist's life, based on material found in diaries and letters.* London: Macmillan; Leipzig: Breitkopf & Härtel, 2 Vols. 1913.

Litzmann, Berthold, Editor. *Letters of Clara Schumann and Johannes Brahms, 1853–1896. New York, Vienna House. 2 Vols.* 1971.

Lloyd, Stephen. *William Walton: muse of fire.* Woodbridge, Suffolk: The Boydell Press, 2001.

Locke, Ralph P. and Cyrilla Barr, Editors. *Cultivating music in America: women patrons and activists since 1860.* Berkeley: University of California Press, 1997.

Lockspeiser, Edward. *Debussy: his life and mind.* London: Cassell. 2 Vols. 1962–1965.

Lockspeiser, Edward. *The literary clef: an anthology of letters and writings by French composers.* London: J. Calder. 1958.

Lockwood, Lewis, Editor. *Beethoven essays: studies in honor of Elliot Forbes.* Cambridge, Massachusetts: Harvard University Department of Music: Distributed by Harvard University Press, 1984.

Lockwood, Lewis and Mark Kroll, Editors. *The Beethoven violin sonatas: history, criticism, performance.* Urbana: University of Illinois Press, 2004.

Loft, Abram. *Violin and keyboard: the duo repertoire.* New York: Grossman Publishers. 2 Vols. 1973.

Longyear, Rey Morgan. *Nineteenth-century romanticism in music.* Englewood Cliffs: Prentice-Hall, 1969.

Lowe, C. Egerton. *Beethoven's pianoforte sonatas: hints on their rendering, form, etc., with appendices on definition of sonata, music forms, ornaments, pianoforte pedals, and how to discover keys.* London: Novello, 1929.

Macdonald, Hugh, Editor. *Berlioz: Selected letters.* London: Faber and Faber, 1995.

Macdonald, Malcolm, Editor. *Havergal Brian on music: selections from his journalism: Volume One, British music.* London: Toccata Press, 1986.

MacDonald, Malcolm. *Varèse: astronomer in sound.* London: Kahn & Averill, 2003.

MacDowell, Edward. *Critical and historical essays: lectures delivered at Columbia University.* Edited by W. J. Baltzell. London: Elkin; Boston: A.P. Schmidt, 1912.

MacFarren, Walter. Memories: an autobiography. London: Walter Scott Publishing Co.,1905.

Mackenzie, Alexander Campbell. *A musician's narrative.* London: Cassell and company, Ltd, 1927.

McCarthy, Margaret William, Editor. *More letters of Amy Fay: the American years, 1879–1916.* Detroit: Information Coordinators, 1986.

McClary, Susan. *Feminine endings: music, gender, and sexuality.* Minneapolis: University of Minnesota Press, 1991.

McClatchie, Stephen, Editor and Translator. *The Mahler family letters.* Oxford: Oxford University Press, 2006.

McVeigh, Simon. *Concert life in London from Mozart to Haydn.* Cambridge: Cambridge University Press, 1993.

Mahler, Alma. *Gustav Mahler: memories and letters.* Enlarged edition revised and edited and with and introduction by Donald Mitchell. London: John Murray, 1968.

Mai, François Martin. *Diagnosing genius: the life and death of Beethoven.* Montreal; London: McGill-Queen's University Press, 2007.

Del Mar, Norman. *Orchestral variations: confusion and error in the orchestral repertoire.* London: Eulenburg, 1981.

Del Mar, Norman. *Richard Strauss: a critical commentary on his life and works.* London: Barrie & Jenkins. 3 Vols. 1978.

(La) Mara [pseudonym]. *Letters of Franz Liszt.* London: H. Grevel & Co., 2 Vols. 1894.

Marek, George Richard. *Puccini.* London: Cassell & Co., 1952.

Marek, George Richard. *Toscanini.* London: Vision, 1976.

(De) Marliave, Joseph. *Beethoven's quartets.* New York: Dover Publications (reprint), 1961.

Martin, George Whitney. *Verdi: his music, life and times.* London: Macmillan, 1965.

Martner, Knud, Editor. *Selected letters of Gustav Mahler.* London; Boston: Faber and Faber, 1979.

Martyn, Barrie. *Nicolas Medtner: his life and music.* Aldershot: Scolar Press, 1995.

Martyn, Barrie. *Rachmaninoff: composer, pianist, conductor.* Aldershot: Scolar, 1990.

Massenet, Jules. *My recollections.* Westport, Connecticut: Greenwood Press.1970.

Matheopoulos, Helena. *Maestro: encounters with conductors of today.* London: Hutchinson, 1982.

Matthews, Denis. *Beethoven.* London: J. M. Dent, 1985.

Matthews, Denis. *Beethoven piano sonatas.* London: British Broadcasting Corporation, 1967.

Matthews, Denis. *In pursuit of music.* London: Victor Gollancz Ltd., 1968.

Matthews, Denis. *Keyboard music.* Newton Abbot: London David & Charles, 1972.

Mellers, Wilfrid Howard. *Caliban reborn: renewal in twentieth-century music.* London: Victor Gollancz, 1967.

Mellers, Wilfrid Howard. *The sonata principle (from c. 1750).* London: Rockliff, 1957.

Mendelssohn Bartholdy. *Letters from Italy and Switzerland.* London: Longman, Green, Longman, and Roberts, 1862.

Mendelssohn Bartholdy, Paul. *Letters of Felix Mendelssohn Bartholdy, from 1833 to 1847.* London: Longman, Green, Longman, Roberts, & Green, 1864.

Menuhin, Yehudi and Curtis W. Davis. *The music of man.* London: Macdonald and Jane's, 1979.

Menuhin, Yehudi. *Theme and variations.* London: Heinemann Educational Books Ltd., 1972.

Menuhin, Yehudi. *Unfinished journey.* London: Macdonald and Jane's, 1977.

Messian, Olivier. *Music and color: conversations with Claude Samuel.* Portland, Oregon: Amadeus, 1994.

Miall, Anthony. *Musical bumps.* London: J.M. Dent & Sons Ltd, 1981.

Michotte, Edmond. *Richard Wagner's visit to Rossini (Paris 1860): and, An evening at Rossini's in Beau-Sejour (Passy), 1858.* Chicago; London: University of Chicago Press, 1982.

Mies, Paul. *Beethoven's sketches: an analysis of his style based on a study of his sketchbooks.* New York: Johnson Reprint, 1969.

Milhaud, Darius. *My happy life.* London: Boyars, 1995.

Miller, Mina. *The Nielsen companion.* London: Faber and Faber, 1994.

Milsom, David. *Theory and practice in late nineteenth-century violin performance: an examination of style in performance, 1850–1900.* Aldershot: Ashgate, 2003.

Mitchell, Donald, Editor. *Letters from a life: the selected letters and diaries of Benjamin Britten 1913–1976.* London: Faber and Faber. 3 Vols., 1991.

Mitchell, Donald and Hans Keller, Editors. *Music survey: new series 1949–1952.* London: Faber Music in association with Faber & Faber, 1981.

Mitchell, Jon C. *A comprehensive biography of composer Gustav Holst, with correspondence and diary excerpts: including his American years.* Lewiston, New York: Edwin Mellen Press, 2001.

Moldenhauer, Hans. *Anton von Webern: a chronicle of his life and work.* London: Victor Gollancz, 1978.

Monrad-Johansen. Edvard Grieg. New York: Tudor Publishing Co., 1945.

Moore, Gerald. *Am I too loud?: memoirs of an accompanist.* London: Hamish Hamilton, 1962.

Moore, Gerald. *Farewell recital: further memoirs.* Harmondsworth: Penguin Books, 1979.

Moore, Gerald. *Furthermoore: interludes in an accompanist's life.* London: Hamish Hamilton, 1983.

Moore, Jerrold Northrop. *Edward Elgar: a creative life.* Oxford: Oxford University Press, 1984.

Moore, Jerrold Northrop. *Elgar, Edward. The windflower letters: correspondence with Alice Caroline Stuart Wortley and her family.* Oxford: Clarendon

Press; New York: Oxford University Press, 1989.

Moore, Jerrold Northrop. *Elgar, Edward. Edward Elgar: letters of a lifetime.* Oxford: Clarendon Press; New York: Oxford University Press, 1990.

Moore, Jerrold Northrop. *Elgar, Edward. Elgar and his publishers: letters of a creative life.* Oxford: Clarendon, 1987.

Moreux, Serge. *Béla Bartók.* London: Harvill Press, 1953.

Morgan, Kenneth. *Fritz Reiner, maestro and martinet.* Urbana: University of Illinois Press, 2005.

Cone, Edward T., Editor. *Music, a view from Delft: selected essays.* Chicago: University of Chicago Press, 1989.

Morgan, Robert P. *Twentieth-century music: a history of musical style in modern Europe and America.* New York: Norton, 1991.

Morgenstern, Sam., Editor. *Composers on music: an anthology of composers' writings.* London: Faber & Faber, 1956.

Morrow, Mary Sue. *Concert life in Haydn's Vienna: aspects of a developing musical and social institution.* Stuyvesant, New York: Pendragon Press, 1989.

Moscheles, Felix, Editor and Translator. *Letters from Felix Mendelssohn-Bartholdy to Ignaz and Charlotte Moscheles.* London: Trübner and Co., 1888.

Mudge, Richard B., Translator. *Glinka, Mikhail Ivanovich: Memoirs.* Norman: University of Oklahoma Press, 1963.

Munch, Charles. *I am a conductor.* New York: Oxford University Press, 1955.

Mundy, Simon. *Bernard Haitink: a working life.* London: Robson Books, 1987.

Musgrave, Michael. *The musical life of the Crystal Palace.* Cambridge: Cambridge University Press, 1995.

Music & Letters. *Beethoven: special number.* London: Music & Letters, 1927.

Musical Times. *Special Issue.* John A. Fuller-Maitland London: Vol. VIII, No. 2, 1927.

Myers, Rollo H., Editor. *Twentieth-century music.* London: Calder and Boyars, 1960.

National Gallery (Great Britain). *Music performed at the National Gallery concerts, 10th October 1939 to 10th April 1946.* London: Privately printed, 1948.

Nattiez, Jean-Jacques, Editor. *Orientations: collected writings — Pierre Boulez.* London: Faber and Faber, 1986.

Nauhaus, Gerd, Editor. *The marriage diaries of Robert & Clara Schumann.* London: Robson Books, 1994.

Nectoux, Jean Michel. *Gabriel Fauré: a musical life.* Translated by Roger Nichols. Cambridge: Cambridge University Press, 1991.

Nettl, Paul. *Beethoven handbook.* Westport, Connecticut: Greenwood Press, 1975.

Neumayr, Anton. *Music and medicine.* Bloomington, Illinois: Medi-Ed Press, 1994–1997

Newbould, Brian. *Schubert and the symphony: a new perspective.* Surbiton: Toccata Press, 1992.

Newlin, Dika. *Schoenberg remembered: diaries and recollections (1938–76).* New York: Pendragon Press, 1980.

Newman, Ernest. *From the world of music: essays from 'The Sunday Times'*. London: J. Calder, 1956.

Newman, Ernest. Hugo Wolf. New York: Dover Publications, 1966.

Newman, Ernest, Annotated and Translated. *Memoirs of Hector Berlioz from 1803 to 1865, comprising his travels in Germany, Italy, Russia, and England*. New York: Knopf, 1932.

Newman, Ernest. *More essays from the world of music: essays from the 'Sunday Times'*. London: John Calder, 1958.

Newman, Ernest. *Musical studies*. London; New York: John Lane, 1910.

Newman, Ernest. *Testament of music: essays and papers*. London: Putnam, 1962.

Newman, Richard. *Alma Rosé: Vienna to Auschwitz*. Portland, Oregon: Amadeus Press, 2000.

Newman, William S. *The sonata in the classic era*. Chapel Hill: University of North Carolina Press 1963.

Newman, William S. *The sonata in the Classic era*. New York; London: W.W. Norton, 1983.

Newmarch, Rosa Harriet. *Henry J. Wood*. London & New York: John Lane, 1904.

Nicholas, Jeremy. *Godowsky: the pianists' pianist; a biography of Leopold Godowsky*. Hexham: Appian Publications & Recordings, 1989.

Nichols, Roger. *Debussy remembered*. London: Faber and Faber, 1992.

Nichols, Roger. *Mendelssohn remembered*. London: Faber and Faber, 1997.

Nichols, Roger. *Ravel remembered*. London: Faber and Faber, 1987.

Niecks, Frederick. *Robert Schumann*. London: J. M. Dent, 1925.

Nielsen, Carl. *Living music*. Copenhagen, Wilhelm Hansen, 1968.

Nielsen, Carl. *My childhood*. Copenhagen, Wilhelm Hansen, 1972.

Nikolska, Irina. *Conversations with Witold Lutoslawski, (1987–92)*. Stockholm: Melos, 1994.

Nohl, Ludwig. *Beethoven depicted by his contemporaries*. London: Reeves, 1880.

De Nora, Tia. *Beethoven and the construction of genius: musical politics in Vienna, 1792–1803*. Berkeley: University of California Press, 1997.

Norton, Spencer, Editor and Translator. *Music in my time: the memoirs of Alfredo Casella*. Norman: University of Oklahoma Press, 1955.

Nottebohm, Gustav. *Two Beethoven sketchbooks: a description with musical extracts*. London: Gollancz, 1979.

Oakeley, Edward Murray. *The life of Sir Herbert Stanley Oakeley*. London: George Allen, 1904.

Lucas, Brenda and Michael Kerr. *Virtuoso: the story of John Ogdon*. London: H. Hamilton, 1981.

Oliver, Michael, Editor. *Settling the score: a journey through the music of the twentieth century*. London: Faber and Faber, 1999.

Olleson, Philip. *Samuel Wesley: the man and his music*. Woodbridge: Boydell Press, 2003.

Olleson, Philip, Editor. *The letters of Samuel Wesley: professional* and social correspondence, *1797–1837.* Oxford; New York: Oxford University Press, 2001.

Olmstead, Andrea. *Conversations with Roger Sessions.* Boston: Northeastern University Press, 1987.

Orenstein, Arbie, Editor. *A Ravel reader: correspondence, articles, interviews.* New York: Columbia University Press, 1990.

Orenstein, Arbie. *Ravel: man and musician.* New York: Columbia University Press, 1975.

Orledge, Robert. *Charles Koechlin (1867–1950): his life and works.* New York: Harwood Academic Publishers, 1989.

Orledge, Robert. *Gabriel Fauré.* London: Eulenburg Books, 1979.

Orledge, Robert. *Satie remembered.* London: Faber and Faber, 1995.

Orledge, Robert. *Satie the composer.* Cambridge: Cambridge University Press, 1990.

Orlova, Alexandra. *Glinka's life in music: a chronicle.* Ann Arbor: UMI Research Press, 1988.

Orlova, Alexandra. *Musorgsky's days and works: a biography in documents.* Ann Arbor: UMI Research Press, 1983.

Orlova, Alexandra. *Tchaikovsky: a self-portrait.* Oxford: Oxford University Press, 1990.

Osborne, Charles, Editor and Translator. *Letters of Giuseppe Verdi.* London: Victor Gollancz, 1971.

Osmond-Smith David, Editor and Translator. *Luciano Berio: Two interviews with Rossana Dalmonte and Bálint András Varga.* New York; London: Boyars, 1985.

Ouellette, Fernand. *Edgard Varèse.* London: Calder & Boyars, 1973.

Paderewski, Ignacy Jan and Mary Lawton. *The Paderewski memoirs.* London: Collins, 1939.

Page, Tim: Editor. *The Glenn Gould reader.* London: Faber and Faber, 1987.

Page, Tim. *Music from the road: views and reviews, 1978–1992.* New York; Oxford: Oxford University Press, 1992.

Page, Tim and Vanessa Weeks, Editors. *Selected letters of Virgil Thomson.* New York: Summit Books, 1988.

Page, Tim. *Tim Page on music: views and reviews.* Portland, Oregon: Amadeus Press, 2002.

Palmer, Christopher. *Herbert Howells, (1892–1983): a celebration.* London: Thames, 1996.

Palmer, Christopher, Editor. *Sergei Prokofiev: Soviet diary 1927 and other writings.* London: Faber and Faber, 1991.

Palmer, Fiona M. *Domenico Dragonetti in England (1794–1846): the career of a double bass virtuoso.* Oxford: Clarendon, 1997.

Palmieri, Robert, Editor. *Encyclopedia of the piano.* New York: Garland, 1996.

Panufnik, Andrzej. *Composing myself.* London: Methuen, 1987.

Parsons, James, Editor. *The Cambridge companion to the Lied.* Cambridge: Cambridge University Press, 2004.

Paynter, John, Editor. *Between old worlds and new: occasional writings on music by Wilfrid Mellers.* London: Cygnus Arts, 1997.

Pestelli, Giorgio. *The age of Mozart and Beethoven.* Cambridge:

Cambridge University Press, 1984.

Peyser, Joan. *Bernstein: a biography: revised & updated.* New York: Billboard Books, 1998.

Phillips-Matz, Mary Jane. *Verdi: a biography.* Oxford: Oxford University Press, 1993.

Piggott, Patrick. *The life and music of John Field, 1782–1837: creator of the nocturne.* London: Faber and Faber, 1973.

Plantinga, Leon. *Beethoven's concertos: history, style, performance.* New York: Norton, 1999.

Plantinga, Leon. *Clementi: his life and music.* London: Oxford University Press, 1977.

Plantinga, Leon. *Romantic music: a history of musical style in nineteenth-century Europe.* New York; London: Norton, 1984.

Plaskin, Glenn. *Horowitz: a biography of Vladimir Horowitz.* London: Macdonald, 1983.

Pleasants, Henry, Editor and Translator. *Hanslick, Eduard: Music criticisms, 1846–99.* Baltimore: Penguin Books, 1963.

Pleasants, Henry, Editor and Translator. *Hanslick's music criticisms.* New York: Dover Publications, 1988.

Pleasants, Henry, Editor and Translator. *The music criticism of Hugo Wolf.* New York: Holmes & Meier Publishers, 1978.

Pleasants, Henry, Editor and Translator. *The musical journeys of Louis Spohr.* Norman: University of Oklahoma Press, 1961.

Pollack, Howard. *Aaron Copland: the life and work of an uncommon man.* New York: Henry Holt, 1999.

Poulenc, Francis. *My friends and myself.* London: Dennis Dobson, 1978.

Powell, Richard, Mrs. *Edward Elgar: memories of a variation.* Aldershot, Hants, England: Scolar Press; Brookfield, Vermont, USA: Ashgate Publishing. Co., 1994.

Poznansky, Alexander, Editor. *Tchaikovsky through others' eyes.* Bloomington: Indiana University Press, 1999.

Praeger, Ferdinand. *Wagner as I knew him.* London; New York: Longmans, Green, 1892.

Previn, Andre. *Anthony Hopkins. Music face to face.* London, Hamish Hamilton, 1971.

Prieberg, Fred K. *Trial of strength: Wilhelm Furtwängler and the Third Reich.* London: Quartet, 1991.

Procter-Gregg, Humphrey. *Beecham remembered.* London: Duckworth, 1976.

Prokofiev, Sergey. *Prokofiev by Prokofiev: a composer's memoir.* London: Macdonald and Jane's, 1979.

Rachmaninoff, Sergei. *Rachmaninoff's recollections told to Oskar von Riesemann.* London: George Allen & Unwin, 1934.

Radcliffe, Philip. *Beethoven's string quartets.* Cambridge: Cambridge University Press, 1978.

Radcliffe, Philip. *Piano Music in: The Age of Beethoven, The New Oxford History of Music, Vol. VIII.* Gerald Abraham, (Editor), 1988, p. 340.

Ratner, Leonard G. *Romantic music: sound and syntax.* New York: Schirmer Books, 1992.

Raynor, Henry. *A social history of music: from the middle ages to*

Beethoven. London: Barrie & Jenkins, 1972.

Rees, Brian. *Camille Saint-Saëns: a life.* London: Chatto & Windus, 1999.

Reich, Willi, Editor. *Anton Webern: The path to the new music.* London; Bryn Mawr: Theodore Presser in association with Universal Edition, 1963.

Reid, Charles. *John Barbirolli: a biography.* London, Hamish Hamilton, 1971.

Reid, Charles. *Malcolm Sargent: a biography.* London: Hamilton, 1968.

Rennert, Jonathan. *William Crotch (1775–1847): composer, artist, teacher.* Lavenham: Terence Dalton, 1975.

Rice, John A. *Antonio Salieri and Viennese Opera.* Chicago, Illinois: University of Chicago Press, 1998.

Rice, John A. *Empress Marie Therese and music at the Viennese court, 1792–1807.* Cambridge: Cambridge University Press, 2003.

Richards, Fiona. *The Music of John Ireland.* Aldershot: Ashgate, 2000.

Rigby, Charles. *Sir Charles Hallé: a portrait for today.* Manchester: Dolphin Press, 1952.

Ringer, Alexander, Editor. *The early Romantic era: between Revolutions; 1789 and 1848.* Basingstoke: Macmillan, 1990.

Roberts, John P.L. and Ghyslaine Guertin, Editors. *Glenn Gould: Selected letters.* Toronto; Oxford: Oxford University Press, 1992.

Robertson, Alec. *More than music.* London: Collins, 1961.

Robinson, Harlow, Editor and Translator. *Selected letters of Sergei Prokofiev.* Boston: Northeastern University Press, 1998.

Robinson, Harlow. *Sergei Prokofiev: a biography.* London: Hale, 1987.

Robinson, Paul A. *Ludwig van Beethoven, Fidelio.* Cambridge: Cambridge University Press, 1996.

Robinson, Suzanne, Editor. *Michael Tippett: music and literature.* Aldershot: Ashgate, 2002.

Rochberg, George. *The aesthetics of survival: a composer's view of twentieth-century music.* Ann Arbor, Michigan: University of Michigan Press, 2004.

Rodmell, Paul. *Charles Villiers Stanford.* Aldershot: Ashgate, 2002.

Roeder, Michael Thomas. *A history of the concerto.* Portland, Oregon: Amadeus Press, 1994.

Rohr, Deborah Adams. *The careers of British musicians, 1750–1850: a profession of artisans.* Cambridge: Cambridge University Press, 2001.

Rolland, Romain. *Goethe and Beethoven.* New York; London: Blom, 1968.

Rolland, Romain. *Beethoven and Handel.* London: Waverley Book Co., 1917.

Rolland, Romain. *Beethoven the creator.* Garden City, New York: Garden City Pub., 1937.

Roscow, Gregory, Editor. *Bliss on music: selected writings of Arthur Bliss, 1920–1975.* Oxford: Oxford University Press, 1991.

Rosen, Charles. *Beethoven's piano sonatas: a short companion.* New Haven, Connecticut:

London: Yale University Press, 2002.

Rosen, Charles. *Critical entertainments: music old and new.* Cambridge, Massachusetts; London: Harvard University Press, 2000.

Rosen, Charles. *The classical style: Haydn, Mozart, Beethoven.* London: Faber and Faber, 1976.

Rosen, Charles. *The romantic generation.* Cambridge, Massachusetts: Harvard University Press, 1995.

Rosenthal, Albi. *Obiter scripta: essays, lectures, articles, interviews and reviews on music, and other subjects.* Oxford: Offox Press; Lanham: Scarecrow Press, 2000.

Rostal, Max. *Beethoven: the sonatas for piano and violin; thoughts on their interpretation.* London: Toccata Press, 1985.

Rostropovich, Mstislav and Galina Vishnevskaya. *Russia, music, and liberty.* Portland, Oregan: Amadeus Press, 1995.

Rubinstein, Arthur. *My many years.* London: Jonathan Cape, 1980.

Rubinstein, Arthur. *My young years.* London: Jonathan Cape, 1973.

Rumph, Stephen C. *Beethoven after Napoleon: political romanticism in the late works.* Berkeley; London: University of California Press, 2004.

Rye, Matthew Rye. *Notes to the BBC Radio Three Beethoven Experience, Friday 10 June 2005,* www.bbc.co.uk/radio3/Beethoven

Sachs, Harvey. *Toscanini.* London: Weidenfeld and Nicholson, 1978.

Sachs, Joel. *Kapellmeister Hummel in England and France.* Detroit: Information Coordinators, 1977.

Saffle, Michael, Editor. *Liszt and his world: proceedings of the International Liszt Conference held at Virginia Polytechnic Institute and State University, 20–23 May 1993.* Stuyvesant, New York: Pendragon Press, 1998.

Safránek, Milos. *Bohuslav Martinu, his life and works.* London: Allan Wingate, 1962.

Saint-Saëns, Camille. *Outspoken essays on music.* Westport, Connecticut: Greenwood Press, 1970.

Saussine, Renée de. *Paganini.* Westport, Connecticut: Greenwood Press, 1976.

Sayers, W. C. Berwick. *Samuel Coleridge-Taylor, musician: his life and letters.* London; New York: Cassell and Co., 1915.

Schaarwächter, Jürgen. *HB: aspects of Havergal Brian.* Aldershot: Ashgate, 1997.

Schafer, R. Murray. *E.T.A. Hoffmann and music.* Toronto: University of Toronto Press, 1975.

Schafer, R. Murray, Editor. *Ezra Pound and music: the complete criticism.* London: Faber and Faber, 1978.

Schat, Peter. *The tone clock.* Chur, Switzerland; Langhorne, Pa.: Harwood Academic Publishers, 1993.

Schenk, Erich. *Mozart and his times.* Edited and Translated by Richard and Clara Winstin. London: Secker & Warburg, 1960.

Schindler, Anton Felix. *Beethoven as I knew him.* Edited by Donald W. MacArdle and Translated by Constance S. Jolly from the

German edition of 1860 London: Faber and Faber, 1966.

Schlosser, Johann. *Beethoven: the first biography, 1827.* Edited by Barry Cooper. Portland, Oregon: Amadeus Press, 1996.

Schnabel, Artur. *My life and music.* London: Longmans, 1961.

Schnittke, Alfred. *A Schnittke reader.* Bloomington: Indiana University Press, 2002.

Scholes, Percy Alfred. *Crotchets: a few short musical notes.* London: John Lane, 1924.

Schonberg, Harold C. *The great pianists.* London: Victor Gollancz, 1964.

Schrade, Leo. *Beethoven in France: the growth of an idea.* New Haven; London: Yale University Press, H. Milford, Oxford University Press, 1942.

Schrade, Leo. *Tragedy in the art of music.* Cambridge, Massachusetts: Harvard University Press, 1964.

Schuh, Willi. *Richard Strauss: a chronicle of the early years 1864–1898.* Cambridge: Cambridge University Press, 1982.

Schuh, Willi, Editor. *Richard Strauss: Recollections and reflections.* London; New York: Boosey & Hawkes, 1953.

Schuller, Gunther. *Musings: the musical worlds of Gunther Schuller.* New York: Oxford University Press, 1986.

Schumann, Robert. *Music and musicians: essays and criticisms.* London: William Reeves, 1877.

Schuttenhelm, Editor. *Selected letters of Michael Tippett.* London: Faber and Faber, 2005.

Schwartz, Elliott. *Music since 1945: issues, materials, and literature.*

New York: Schirmer Books, 1993.

Scott, Marion M. *Beethoven: (The master musicians).* London: Dent, 1940.

Scott-Sutherland, Colin. *Arnold Bax.* London: J. M. Dent, 1973.

Searle, Muriel V. *John Ireland: the man and his music.* Tunbridge Wells: Midas Books, 1979.

Secrest, Meryle. *Leonard Bernstein: a life.* London: Bloomsbury, 1995.

Seeger, Charles. *Studies in musicology II, 1929–1979.* Edited by Anne M. Pescatello. Berkeley; London: University of California Press, 1994.

Selden-Goth, Gisela, Editor. *Felix Mendelssohn: letters.* London: Paul Elek Publishers Ltd, 1946.

Senner, Wayne M., Robin Wallace and William Meredith, Editors. *The critical reception of Beethoven's compositions by his German contemporaries.* Lincoln: University of Nebraska Press, in association with the American Beethoven Society and the Ira F. Brilliant Center for Beethoven Studies, San José State University, 1999.

Seroff, Victor I. *Rachmaninoff.* London: Cassell & Company, 1951.

Sessions, Roger. *Questions about music.* Cambridge, Massachusetts: Harvard University Press, 1970.

Sessions, Roger. *The musical experience of composer, performer, listener.* New York: Atheneum, 1966, 1950.

Seyfried, Ignaz von. *Louis van Beethoven's Studies in thorough-bass, counterpoint and the art of scientific composition.* Leipzig; New-York: Schuberth and Company, 1853.

Sharma, Bhesham R. *Music and culture in the age of mechanical reproduction.* New York: Peter Lang, 2000.

Shaw, Bernard. *How to become a musical critic.* London: R. Hart Davis, 1960.

Shaw, Bernard. *London music in 1888–89 as heard by Corno di Bassetto (later known as Bernard Shaw): with some further autobiographical particulars.* London: Constable and Company, 1937.

Shaw, Bernard. *Music in London, 1890–1894.* London: Constable and Company Limited, 3 Vols., 1932.

Shedlock, John South. *Beethoven's pianoforte sonatas: the origin and respective values of various readings.* London: Augener Ltd., 1918.

Shedlock, John South. *The pianoforte sonata: its origin and development.* London: Methuen, 1895.

Shepherd, Arthur. *The string quartets of Ludwig van Beethoven.* Cleveland: H. Carr, The Printing Press, 1935.

Sheppard, Leslie and Herbert R. Axelrod. *Paganini: containing a portfolio of drawings by Vido Polikarpus.* Neptune City, New Jersey: Paganiniana Publications, 1979.

Short, Michael. *Gustav Holst: the man and his music.* Oxford: Oxford University Press, 1990.

Shostakovich, Dmitry. *Dmitry Shostakovich: about himself and his times.* Moscow: Progress Publishers, 1981.

Simpson, John Palgrave. *Carl Maria von Weber: the life of an artist, from the German of his son Baron, Max Maria von Weber.* London: Chapman and Hall, 1865.

Simpson, Robert. *Beethoven symphonies.* London: British Broadcasting Corporation, 1970.

Sipe, Thomas. *Beethoven: Eroica symphony.* Cambridge: Cambridge University Press, 1998.

Sitwell, Sacheverell. *Mozart.* Edinburgh: Peter Davies Limited, 1932.

Skelton, Geoffrey. *Paul Hindemith: the man behind the music; a biography.* London: Victor Gollancz, 1975.

Smallman, Basil. *The piano trio: its history, technique, and repertoire.* Oxford: Clarendon Press; Oxford; New York: Oxford University Press, 1990.

Smidak, Emil. *Isaak-Ignaz Moscheles: the life of the composer and his encounters with Beethoven, Liszt, Chopin, and Mendelssohn.* Aldershot, Hampshire, England: Scolar Press; Brookfield, Vermont, USA: Gower Publishing Co., 1989.

Smith, Barry. *Peter Warlock: the life of Philip Heseltine.* Oxford: Oxford University Press, 1994.

Smith, Joan Allen. *Schoenberg and his circle: a Viennese portrait.* New York: Schirmer Books, London: Collier Macmillan, 1986.

Smith, Richard Langham, Editor. *Debussy on music: the critical writings of the great French composer Claude Debussy.* London: Secker & Warburg, 1977.

Smith, Ronald. *Alkan.* London: Kahn and Averill, 1976.

Snowman, Daniel. *The Amadeus Quartet: the men and the music.* London: Robson Books, 1981.

Solomon, Maynard. *Beethoven.* New York: Schirmer, 1977.

Solomon, Maynard. *Beethoven essays.* Cambridge, Massachusetts; London: Harvard University Press, 1988.

Solomon, Maynard. *Late Beethoven: music, thought, imagination.* Berkeley; London: University of California Press, 2003.

Solomon, Maynard. *Mozart: a life.* London: Hutchinson, 1995.

Sonneck, Oscar George Theodore. *Beethoven: impressions of contemporaries.* London: Oxford University Press, 1927.

Spalding, Albert. *Rise to follow: an autobiography.* London: Frederick Muller Ltd., 1946.

Spohr, Louis. *Louis Spohr's autobiography.* London: Longman, Green, Longman, Roberts, & Green, 1865.

Stafford, William. *Mozart myths: a critical reassessment.* Stanford, California: Stanford University Press, 1991.

Stanford, Charles Villiers. *Interludes: records and reflections.* London: John Murray, 1922.

Stanley, Glen, Editor. *The Cambridge companion to Beethoven.* Cambridge; New York: Cambridge University Press, 2000

Stedman, Preston. *The symphony.* Englewood Cliffs, New Jersey; London: Prentice-Hall, 1979.

Stedron, Bohumír, Editor and Translator. *Leos Janácek: letters and reminiscences.* Prague: Artia, 1955.

Stein, Erwin, Editor. *Arnold Schoenberg: letters.* London: Faber and Faber, 1964.

Stein, Erwin. *Orpheus in new guises.* London: Rockliff, 1953.

Stein, Jack Madison. *Poem and music in the German lied from Gluck to Hugo Wolf.* Cambridge, Massachusetts: Harvard University Press, 1971.

Stein, Leonard, Editor. *Style and idea: selected writings of Arnold Schoenberg.* London: Faber and Faber, 1975.

Steinberg, Michael P. *Listening to reason: culture, subjectivity, and nineteenth-century music.* Princeton, New Jersey: Princeton University Press, 2004.

Steinberg, Michael. *The concerto: a listener's guide.* New York: Oxford University Press, 1998.

Steinberg, Michael. *The symphony: a listener's guide.* Oxford; New York: Oxford University Press, 1995.

Sternfeld, Frederick William. *Goethe and music: a list of parodies and Goethe's relationship to music; a list of references.* New York: Da Capo Press, 1979.

Stivender, David. *Mascagni: an autobiography compiled, edited and translated from original sources.* New York: Pro/Am Music Resources; London: Kahn & Averill, 1988.

Stone, Else and Kurt Stone, Editors. *The writings of Elliott Carter: an American composer looks at modern music.* Bloomington: Indiana University Press, 1977.

Stowell, Robin. *Beethoven: violin concerto.* Cambridge: Cambridge University Press, 1998.

Stowell, Robin: Editor. *The Cambridge companion to the cello.*

Cambridge: Cambridge University Press, 1999.

Stowell, Robin: Editor. *The Cambridge companion to the string quartet.* Cambridge: Cambridge University Press, 2003.

Stratton, Stephen Samuel. *Mendelssohn.* London: J.M. Dent & Co.; New York: E.P. Dutton & Co., 1901.

Straus, Joseph N. *Remaking the past: musical modernism and the influence of the tonal tradition.* Cambridge, Massachusetts: Harvard University Press, 1990.

Stravinsky, Igor. *An autobiography.* London: Calder and Boyars, 1975.

Stravinsky, Igor. *Themes and conclusions.* London: Faber and Faber, 1972.

Stravinsky, Igor and Robert Craft. *Conversations with Igor Stravinsky.* London: Faber and Faber, 1959.

Stravinsky, Igor and Robert Craft. *Dialogues and a diary.* London: Faber and Faber 1968.

Stravinsky, Igor and Robert Craft. *Memories and commentaries.* London: Faber and Faber, 2002.

Strunk, Oliver. *Source readings in music history, 4: The Classic era.* London: Faber and Faber 1981.

Sullivan, Blair, Editor. *The echo of music: essays in honor of Marie Louise Göllner.* Warren, Michigan: Harmonie Park Press, 2004.

Sullivan, Jack, Editor. *Words on music: from Addison to Barzun.* Athens: Ohio University Press, 1990.

Symonette, Lys and Kim H. Kowalke, Editors and Translators. *Speak low (when you speak love): the letters of Kurt Weill and Lotte Lenya.* London: Hamish Hamilton, 1996.

Swalin, Benjamin F. *The violin concerto: a study in German romanticism.* New York, Da Capo Press, 1973.

Szigeti, Joseph. *With strings attached: reminiscences and reflections.* London: Cassell & Co. Ltd, 1949.

Tanner, Michael, Editor. *Notebooks, 1924–1954: Wilhelm Furtwängler.* London: Quartet Books, 1989.

Taylor, Robert, Editor. *Furtwängler on music: essays and addresses.* Aldershot: Scolar, 1991.

Taylor, Ronald. *Kurt Weill: composer in a divided world.* London: Simon & Schuster, 1991.

Tchaikovsky, Peter Ilich. *Letters to his family: an autobiography.* Translated by Galina von Meck. London: Dennis Dobson, 1981.

Tertis, Lionel. *My viola and I: a complete autobiography; with, 'Beauty of tone in string playing', and other essays.* London: Paul Elek, 1974.

Thayer, Alexander Wheelock. *Salieri: rival of Mozart.* Edited by Theodore Albrecht. Kansas City, Missouri: Philharmonia of Greater Kansas City, 1989.

Thomas, Michael Tilson. *Viva voce: conversations with Edward Seckerson.* London: Faber and Faber 1994.

Thomson, Andrew. *Vincent d'Indy and his world.* Oxford: Clarendon Press, 1996.

Thomson, Virgil. *The musical scene.* New York: Greenwood Press, 1968.

Thomson, Virgil. Virgil Thomson.

London: Weidenfeld & Nicolson, 1967.

Tillard, Françoise. *Fanny Mendelssohn.* Amadeus Press: Portland, 1996.

Tilmouth, Michael, Editor. *Donald Francis Tovey: The classics of music: talks, essays, and other writings previously uncollected.* Oxford: Oxford University Press, 2001

Tippett, Michael. *Moving into Aquarius.* London: Routledge and Kegan Paul, 1959.

Tippett, Michael. *Those twentieth century blues: an autobiography.* London: Hutchinson, 1991.

Todd, R. Larry, Editor. *Nineteenth-century piano music.* New York; London: Routledge, 2004.

Todd, R. Larry, Editor. *Schumann and his world.* Princeton: Princeton University Press, 1994.

Tommasini, Anthony. *Virgil Thomson: composer on the aisle.* New York: W.W. Norton, 1997.

Tortelier, Paul. *A self-portrait: in conversation with David Blum.* London: Heinemann, 1984.

Tovey, Donald Francis. *A Companion to Beethoven's Pianoforte Sonatas.* Revised by Barry Cooper. London: The Associated Board, [1931], 1998.

Tovey, Donald Francis. *Beethoven.* London: Oxford University Press, 1944.

Tovey, Donald Francis. *Essays and lectures on music.* London: Oxford University Press, 1949.

Tovey, Donald Francis. *Essays in musical analysis.* London: Oxford University Press, H. Milford, 7 Vols., 1935–41.

Tovey, Donald Francis. *The forms of music: musical articles from The Encyclopaedia Britannica.* London: Oxford University Press, 1944.

Toye, Francis. *Giuseppe Verdi: his life and works.* London: William Heinemann Ltd., 1931.

Truscott, Harold. *Beethoven's late string quartets.* London: Dobson, 1968.

Tyler, William R. *The letters of Franz Liszt to Olga von Meyendorff, 1871–1886, in the Mildred Bliss Collection at Dumbarton Oaks.* Translated by William R. Tyler. Washington: Dumbarton Oaks, Trustees for Harvard University; Cambridge, Massachusetts: distributed by Harvard University Press, 1979.

Tyrrell, John. *Janácek: years of a life. Vol. 1, (1854–1914) The lonely blackbird.* London: Faber and Faber, 2006.

Tyrrell, John, Editor and Translator. *My life with Janácek: the memoirs of Zdenka Janácková.* London: Faber and Faber, 1998.

Tyson, Alan, Editor. *Beethoven studies 2.* Cambridge: Cambridge University Press, 1977.

Tyson, Alan, Editor. *Beethoven studies 3.* Cambridge: Cambridge University Press, 1982.

Tyson, Alan. *Mozart: studies of the autograph scores.* Cambridge, Massachusetts; London: Harvard University Press, 1987.

Tyson, Alan. *The authentic English editions of Beethoven.* London: Faber and Faber, 1963.

Underwood, J. A., Editor. *Gabriel Fauré: his life through his letters.* London: Marion Boyars, 1984.

Vechten, Carl van, Editor. *Nikolay, Rimsky-Korsakov: My musical life.* London: Martin Secker & Warburg Ltd., 1942.

Vinton, John. *Essays after a dictionary: music and culture at the close of Western civilization.* Lewisburg: Bucknell University Press, 1977.

Volkov, Solomon, Editor. *Testimony: the memoirs of Dmitri Shostakovich.* London: Faber and Faber, 1981.

Volta, Ornella, Editor. *A mammal's notebook: collected writings of Erik Satie.* London: Atlas Press, 1996.

Wagner, Richard. Beethoven: *With [a] supplement from the philosophical works of A. Schopenhauer.* Translated by E. Dannreuther. London: Reeves, 1893.

Wagner, Richard. *My life.* London: Constable and Company Ltd., 1911.

Walden, Valerie. *One hundred years of violoncello: a history of technique and performance practice, 1740–1840.* Cambridge: Cambridge University Press, 1998.

Walker, Alan. *Franz Liszt. Volume 1, The virtuoso years: 1811–1847.* New York: Alfred A. Knopf, 1983.

Walker, Alan. *Franz Liszt. Volume 2, The Weimar years: 1848–1861.* London: Faber and Faber, 1989.

Walker, Alan. *Franz Liszt. Volume 3, The final years, 1861–1886.* London: Faber and Faber, 1997.

Walker, Bettina. *My musical experiences.* London: Richard Bentley and Son, 1890.

Walker, Ernest. *Free thought and the musician, and other essays.* London; New York: Oxford University Press, 1946.

Walker, Frank. *Hugo Wolf: a biography.* London: J. M. Dent, 1951.

Walker, Frank. *The man Verdi.* London: Dent, 1962.

Wallace, Grace, *[Lady Wallace]. Beethoven's letters (1790–1826): from the collection of Dr. Ludwig Nohl. Also his letters to the Archduke Rudolph, Cardinal-Archbishop of Olmutz, K. W., from the collection of Dr. Ludwig Ritter Von Koĺchel.* London: Longmans, Green, 2 Vols., 1866.

Wallace, Robin. *Beethoven's critics: aesthetic dilemmas and resolutions during the composer's lifetime.* Cambridge; New York: Cambridge University Press, 1986.

Walter, Bruno. *Theme and variations: an autobiography.* London: H. Hamilton, 1948.

Warrack, John Hamilton. *Writings on music.* Cambridge: Cambridge University Press, 1981.

Wasielewski, Wilhelm Joseph von. *Life of Robert Schumann: with letters, 1833–1852.* London: William Reeves, 1878.

Watkins, Glenn. *Proof through the night: music and the Great War.* Berkeley: University of California Press, 2003.

Watkins, Glenn. *Pyramids at the Louvre: music, culture, and collage from Stravinsky to the postmodernists.* Cambridge, Massachusetts; London: Belknap Press of Harvard University Press, 1994.

Watkins, Glenn. *Soundings: music in the twentieth century.* New York: Schirmer Books London: Collier Macmillan, 1988.

Watson, Derek. *Liszt.* London: J. M. Dent, 1989.

Weaver, William, Editor. *The Verdi-Boito correspondence.* Chicago; London: University of Chicago Press, 1994.

Wegeler, Franz. *Remembering Beethoven: the biographical notes of Franz Wegeler and Ferdinand Ries.* London: Andre Deutsch, 1988.

Weingartner, Felix. *Buffets and rewards: a musician's reminiscences.* London: Hutchinson & Co., 1937.

Weinstock, Herbert. *Rossini: a biography.* New York: Limelight, 1987.

Weiss, Piero and Richard Taruskin. *Music in the Western World: a history in documents.* New York: Schirmer; London: Collier Macmillan, 1984.

Weissweiler, Eva *The complete correspondence of Clara and Robert Schumann.* New York: Peter Lang, 2 Vols., 1994.

Whittaker, William Gillies. *Collected essays.* London: Oxford University Press, 1940.

Whittall, Arnold. *Exploring twentieth-century music: tradition and innovation.* Cambridge; New York: Cambridge University Press, 2003.

Whittall, Arnold. *Music since the First World War.* London: J. M. Dent, 1977.

Whitton, Kenneth S. *Lieder: an introduction to German song.* London: Julia MacRae, 1984.

Wightman, Alistair, Editor. *Szymanowski on music: selected writings of Karol Szymanowski.* London: Toccata Press, 1999.

Wilhelm, Kurt. *Richard Strauss: an intimate portrait.* London: Thames and Hudson, 1999.

Will, Richard James. *The characteristic symphony in the age of Haydn and Beethoven.* Cambridge: Cambridge University Press, 2002.

Willetts, Pamela J. *Beethoven and England: an account of sources in the British Museum.* London: British Museum, 1970.

Williams, Adrian, Editor and Translator. *Liszt, Franz: Selected letters.* Oxford: Clarendon Press, 1998.

Williams, Adrian. *Portrait of Liszt: by himself and his contemporaries.* Oxford: Clarendon Press, 1990.

Williams, Ralph Vaughan. *Heirs and rebels: letters written to each other and occasional writings on music.* London; New York: Oxford University Press, 1959.

Williams, Ralph Vaughan. *Some thoughts on Beethoven's Choral symphony: with writings on other musical subjects.* London; Oxford University Press, 1953.

Williams, Ralph Vaughan. *The making of music.* Ithaca, New York: Cornell University Press, 1955.

Williams, Ursula Vaughan. *R.V.W.: a biography of Ralph Vaughan Williams.* London: Oxford University Press, 1964.

Wilson, Conrad. *Notes on Beethoven: 20 crucial works.* Edinburgh: Saint Andrew Press, 2003.

Wilson, Elizabeth. *Shostakovich: a life remembered.* Princeton, New Jersey: Princeton University Press, 1994.

Winter, Robert, Editor. *Beethoven, performers, and critics: the International Beethoven Congress, Detroit, 1977.* Detroit: Wayne State University Press, 1980.

Winter, Robert. *Compositional origins of Beethoven's opus 131.* Ann Arbor, Michigan: UMI Research Press, 1982.

Winter, Robert and Robert Martin, Editors. *The Beethoven quartet companion*. Berkeley: University of California Press, 1994.

Wolf, Eugene K. and Edward H. Roesner, Editors. *Studies in musical sources and style: essays in honor of Jan LaRue*. Madison, Wisconsin: A-R Editions, 1990.

Wolff, Christoph and Robert Riggs. *The string quartets of Haydn, Mozart and Beethoven: studies of the autograph manuscripts: a conference at Isham Memorial Library, March 15–17, 1979*. Cambridge, Massachusetts: Department of Music, Harvard University, 1980.

Wolff, Konrad. *Masters of the keyboard: individual style elements in the piano music of Bach, Haydn, Mozart, Beethoven, Schubert, Chopin, and Brahms*. Bloomington: Indiana University Press, 1990.

Wörner, Karl Heinrich. *Stockhausen: life and work*. London: Faber, 1973.

Wright, Donald, Editor. *Cardus on music: a centenary collection*. London: Hamish Hamilton, 1988.

Wyndham, Henry Saxe. *August Manns and the Saturday concerts: a memoir and a retrospect*. London and Felling-on-Tyne, New York, The Walter Scott Publishing Co., Ltd., 1909.

Yastrebtsev, V.V. Edited and Translated by Florence Jonas. *Reminiscences of Rimsky-Korsakov*. New York: Columbia University Press, 1985.

Yates, Peter. *Twentieth century music: its evolution from the end of the harmonic era into the present era of sound*. London: Allen & Unwin Ltd., 1968.

Young, Percy M. *Beethoven: a Victorian tribute based on the papers of Sir George Smart*. London: D. Dobson, 1976.

Young, Percy M. *George Grove, 1820–1900: a biography*. London: Macmillan, 1980.

Young, Percy M. *Letters of Edward Elgar and other writings*. London: Geoffrey Bles, 1956.

Young, Percy M., Editor. *Letters to Nimrod: Edward Elgar to August Jaeger, 1897–1908*. London: Dennis Dobson, 1965.

Young, Percy M. *The concert tradition: from the middle ages to the twentieth century*. London: Routledge and Kegan Paul, 1965.

Young, Rob, Editor. *(Brief Description): Undercurrents: the hidden wiring of modern music*. London; New York, N.Y.: Continuum, 2002.

Yourke, Electra Slonimsky, Editor. *Nicolas Slonimsky: writings on music*. New York, N.Y.; London: Routledge, 4 Vols. 2003-2005.

Slonimsky, Nicolas. *The great composers and their works*. Edited by Electra Slonimsky Yourke. New York: Schirmer Books, 2 Vols. 2000.

Ysaÿe, Antoine. *Ysaÿe: his life, work and influence*. London: W. Heinemann, 1947.

Zamoyski, Adam. *Paderewski*. London: Collins, 1982.

Zegers, Mirjam, Editor. *Louis Andriessen: The art of stealing time*. Todmorden: Arc Music, 2002.

Zemanova, Mirka, Editor. *Janácek's uncollected essays on music*. London: Marion Boyars, 1989.

INDEX

The order adopted for the listing of the individual entries in this index is chronological – according to the sequential unfolding of the events under discussion. Thereby, the reader is provided with both a guide to the contents discussed in the main text and a time-line of the principal events bearing on Beethoven's life and work.

CREATION ORIGINS PP. 1-61
BEETHOVEN'S ORCHESTRA
    PP. 3-7
Composition of
Instruments
Sound of
Historic performance-practice

VIENNA: CONCERT VENUES
    MUSIC MAKING PP. 8-11
Tonkünstler-Societät
Burgtheater.

Christus am Ölberge.
Redoutensäle
Gesellschaft der Musikfreunde
Kärntnertortheater
Theater an der Wien
Augarten
Morgenkonzerte
George Polgreen Bridgetower

BEETHOVEN AND CONDUCTING
    PP. 11-16
Role of director of orchestra

Beethoven conducting
Mémoires of Hector Berlioz
Ignaz von Seyfried recollections of
Louis Spohr, recollections of
Wilhelmine Schröder-Devrient,
  recollections of

ACCOUNTS OF BEETHOVEN
  GROWING FAME PP. 16-21
Maynard Solomon
Beethoven and piano instruction
Carl Czerny
Ferdinand Ries
Carl (Kaspar Karl) van Beethoven
Joseph Mähler, Beethoven's
  portrait
Beethoven's residence, Mölker-
  bastei Pasqualati House

HEILIGENSTADT TRIUMPH OVER
  DEAFNESS PP. 21-27
Onset of deafness
Recollections of:
Ferdinand Ries
Franz Gerhard Wegeler
Gerhard von Vering
Johann Schmidt
Heiligenstadt, watercolour
Johann Peter Lyser
Heiligenstadt Testament
Anton Neumayr
Archduke Trio, reference to
Alexander Wheelock Thayer

COMPOSITION ORIGINS
  SKETCH SOURCES PP. 27-32
Sketches, importance of
Gustav Nottebohm
Beethoven's resolve to 'make a new
  start'
  1800
    Sketch origins of Second Sym-
      phony
    Ritterballet, reference to
    Salvatore Viganò, Beethoven's
      collaboration with

Prometheus mythology, significance of

LANDSBERG 7 SKETCHBOOK PP.
  32-34
Ludwig Landsberg
Period of use
Second Symphony, origins of
Related compositions

KESSLER SKETCHBOOK P. 34
Christoph Kessler
Period of use
Second Symphony, development of

SAUER SKETCHBOOK PP. 34-35
Ignaz Sauer
Period of use

NEGOTIATIONS WITH PUBLISHERS
  PP. 35-48
  1802
    Carl (Kaspar Karl) van
      Beethoven, role of
    Gottfried Christoph Härtel
    Akademie concert, plans for
    Baron von Braun: Kärntnertor
      Theater Burgtheater
    Theater an der Wien
    Second Symphony, progress
      with
    Challenge of pirate editions
    Johann Anton André, putative
      negotiations with
  1803
    Breitkopf & Härtel, negotia-
      tions with
    Leipzig Messe - 'Easter Fair'
    Kunst und Industrie-Comptoir,
      Beethoven's collaboration
      with
    Nikolas Simrock, negotiations
      with
    Xavier Kleinheinz
    Second Symphony, progress
      with

Beethoven considers relocating
to Paris
Beethoven's response to criti-
cism
Gottlob Wiedebein
Eroica Symphony, sketch draft

PUBLICATION IN PARTS PP. 48-50
Nineteenth-century publication con-
ventions
Bureau des Arts et d'Industrie, pub-
lication of Second Symphony
in parts
Jonathan del Mar, views of
Title Page
Dedicatee, Prince Karl von
Lichnowsky

TEMPO INDICATIONS METRO-
NOME MARKS PP. 50-52
Wiener Vaterländische Blätter,
Beethoven's views regarding
metronome marks
Bernhard Schotts
Sir Roger Norrington, views on
authentic performance

PUBLICATION IN FULL SCORE PP.
52-56
Precedents for publication in full
score:
Christus am Oelberg
Mass in C
Wellington's Victory Symphony
Choral Symphony
Publication of Beethoven's sympho-
nies in full score
Nikolaus Simrock, negotiations with
Cianchettini & Sperati, English full-
score publication
London, Title Page
Breitkopf & Härtel (Gesamtaus-
gabe) 'complete edition'
Beethoven House, Bonn complete
edition - work in progress

RECEPTION HISTORY PP. 62-149
RECEPTION IN BEETHOVEN'S
LIFETIME: CONCERT PER-
FORMANCES PP. 63-86
1803
Wiener Zeitung
Early performances of Second
Symphony
Theater an der Wien
Beethoven's first public appear-
ance as a dramatic vocal com-
poser
First rehearsal of Second Sym-
phony
Ferdinand Ries, recollections
of
August von Kotzebue,
response to Second Sym-
phony in Journal Der
Freymüthige
Andreas Streicher, response to
Second Symphony in Journal
Allgemeine musikalische
Zeitung
1804
Alexander Wheelock Thayer's
summation of Beethoven's
achievements
Gewandhaus Orchestra, per-
formance of Second Sym-
phony
Allgemeine musikalische Zei-
tung, review of Second Symphony
Augarten concert, Anton
Schindler's remarks concerning
Berlin, reception to Second
Symphony
1805
Allgemeine musikalische Zeitung, review of Second Symphony
Der Freimüthige, Beethoven's
advocates and critics
1806

187

Freidrich Mayer, singer
Ignaz von Seyfried conducts
  Fidelio
Bureau des Arts et d'Industrie,
  Trio arrangement of Second
  Symphony
1808
  Liebhaber-Concerte founded
  Johann von Häring
  Gesellschaft von Musikfreun-
    den
1811
  Giuseppe Cambini, writes arti-
    cles from Paris to Allgemeine
    musikalische
  Munich performance of
    Second Symphony
1817
  George Thomson writes to
    Beethoven from Edinburgh
1819-1820
  Concerts Spirituels established
  Grosser Redoutensaal concerts
  Swiss Music Society, Basel per-
    formance of Second Sym-
    phony
1822
  Friedrich Rochlitz, meeting
    with Beethoven
  Allgemeine musikalische Zei-
    tung, reflections on nature of
    symphony
1824
  Adolf Bernhard Marx, reflects
    on Beethoven's achievements

TRANSCRIPTIONS PP. 86-90
Popularity of
Second Symphony transcribed:
Beethoven-Ries
Nikolaus Simrock
Carl Friedrich Ebers
Johan Anton Andre?
Anton Diabelli
Friedrich Mockwitz
Karl Zulehner

Johann Nepomuk Hummel
Carl Burchard
Hanss Sitt
August Horn
Theodor Kirchner
Albert Lavignacy
Theodore Lack
Ernst Naumann
Piano transcriptions:
Carl Czerny
Franz Liszt

BEETHOVEN'S EARLY RECEPTION
  IN FRANCE: PARIS PP. 90-93
Concerts Français
Exercises Publics
François-Antoine Habeneck
The Quarterly Music Magazine
Kreuzer Kreuzer
Hector Berlioz, writings of

BEETHOVEN'S RECEPTION IN
  ENGLAND: THE PHILHAR-
  MONIC SOCIETY PP. 93-98
Second Symphony performed
Argyll Rooms
Ferdinand Ries
Johann Salomon
Muzio Clementi
George Polgreen Bridgetower
Negotiations with Beethoven
Ignaz Moscheles
King's Theatre
Richard Wagner
Sir Arthur Sullivan

LATER NINETEENTH-CENTURY
  RECEPTION PP. 98-104
  1850
    Changing sound of orchestra
  1857
    Modest Musorgsky, recollec-
      tions of
  1870
    Richard Wagner: Beethoven
      Birth Centenary celebrations

1875
Cosima Wagner
1883
Felix Weingartner
Carl Reinecke
Hans von Bülow
1888-89
Gustav Mahler
1896
Sir George Grove
The Musical Times

RECEPTION IN THE TWENTIETH
CENTURY PP. 104-140
1901
Samuel Coleridge Taylor
1909
Sir Herbert Beerbohm Tree
1916
Ernest Markham Lee
1917
Romain Rolland
1925
Paul Bekker
1927
Beethoven: Death Centenary
celebrations
Sir Herbert Hamilton Harty
1934
Marion Scott, commences
Beethoven Master Musicians
series
1935
Sir Donald Francis Tovey, pio-
neering Beethovenian
1936
Sir John Barbirolli, recollec-
tions of
1942
War-time performance of
Beethoven in America
1954
Gordon Jacob
Donald Nivison Ferguson

1959
Arturo Toscanini, interpreta-
tion of Beethoven
1961
Otto Klemperer, recollections of
1968
Igor Stravinsky
1970
Robert Simpson
Anthony Hopkins
1972
Joseph Braunstein: Musica
Aeterna
1973
Basil Deane
Louise Elvira Cuyler
1977
Maynard Solomon
1979
William Preston Stedman,
Beethoven's orchestration
1985
Denis Matthews
1987
Sir Roger Norrington, histori-
cally informed performance
1988
Donald Jay Grout and Claude
Victor Palisca
1989
Barry Cooper, collaboration
with Jonathan el Mar
Nikolaus Harnoncourt, histori-
cally informed performance
1991
Nicholas Marston
1992
Philip Downs
1994
Elizabeth Csicserry-Ronay,
translations of Hector Berlioz's writings
1995
Richard Osborne

189

1997
David Wyn Jones

RECEPTION NEARER OUR OWN
TIME PP. 140-154
2000, Scott Burnham and
Michael Steinberg

2002, Alfred Peter Brown
2003, Conrad Wilson
2005, BBC Radio 3, Beethoven
celebrations

ABOUT THE
AUTHOR

Terence M. Russell graduated with first class honours in architecture and was a nominee for the coveted Silver Medal of the Royal Institute of British Architects. He is a Fellow of the Royal Incorporation of Architects in Scotland (retired), was formerly Reader in the School of Arts, Culture and Environment at the University of Edinburgh, a Fellow of the British Higher Education Academy, and Senior Assessor to the Scottish Higher Education Funding Council. Alongside his professional work in the field of architecture — embracing practice, teaching and research — he has maintained a lifetime's interest in the music and musicology of Beethoven. He has an equal admiration for the work of Franz Schubert and was for many years an active member of the Schubert Institute, UK. His book writings in the field of architecture include the following:

The Built Environment: A Subject Index, Gregg Publishing (1989):
- Vol. 1: Town planning and urbanism, architecture, gardens and landscape design
- Vol. 2: Environmental technology, constructional engineering, building and materials
- Vol. 3: Decorative art and industrial design, international exhibitions and collections, recreational and performing arts
- Vol. 4: Public health, municipal services, community welfare

Architecture in the Encyclopédie of Diderot and D'Alemebert: The Letterpress Articles and Selected Engravings, Scolar Press (1993)

The Encyclopaedic Dictionary in the Eighteenth Century: Architecture, Arts and Crafts, Scolar Press (1997):
- Vol. 1: John Harris, Lexicon Technicum
- Vol. 2: Ephraim Chambers, Cyclopaedia
- Vol. 3: The Builder's Dictionary
- Vol. 4: Samuel Johnson, A Dictionary of the English Language
- Vol. 5: A Society of Gentlemen, Encyclopaedia Britannica

Gardens and Landscapes in the Encyclopédie of Diderot and D'Alemebert: The Letterpress Articles and Selected Engravings, 2 Vols., Ashgate (1999)

The Napoleonic Survey of Egypt: The Monuments and Customs of Egypt, 2 Vols., Ashgate (2001)

The Discovery of Egypt: Vivant Denon's Travels with Napoleon's Army, History Press (2005)